KENNEDY CAMPAIGNING

⊠ KENNEDY CAMPAIGNING

⊠ *The System and the Style as Practiced by Senator Edward Kennedy*

⊠ By MURRAY B. LEVIN

 BEACON PRESS, *Boston*

THE AUTHOR gratefully acknowledges permission to reprint parts of James Reston's May 11, 1966, column in *The New York Times,* © 1966 by The New York Times Company, reprinted by permission; the Eagle Publishing Company for permission to reprint material by A. A. Michelson, © 1962 by Eagle Publishing Company; and Atheneum Publishers for permission to reprint material from *The Image or What Happened to the American Dream* by Daniel J. Boorstin, © 1961 by Daniel J. Boorstin.

To Betty Lee and Stan

Acknowledgments

I was originally encouraged to undertake this study by Professor V. O. Key, Jr., of Harvard University, who has encouraged and inspired so many students of party politics. His long illness and untimely death prevented me from expressing my gratitude to him in person. I owe him a considerable debt.

Several graduate students aided me materially, particularly during my investigation of campaign contributions and expenditures. They spent months copying, adding, substantiating, cataloging, and investigating the reported contributions and expenditures of Kennedy's and McCormack's campaign treasurers. It was a difficult, tedious, and very long undertaking for Mrs. Valerie Bennett, Mrs. Selby Joffee, Mrs. Susan Bove, and Miss Marilyn Dexheimer; I greatly appreciate their efforts.

Mr. Bernard Borman, who was instrumental in the movement to revise the Massachusetts law which regulates the reporting of campaign contributions and expenditures, helped me greatly.

My colleagues, Professors Andrew Milnor, Howard Zinn, Betty Zisk, and George Blackwood were kind enough to read parts of the manuscript and their comments are most helpful. Mrs. Gladys Topkis's suggestions, both as to content and style, are reflected in many passages of this book. Professor Robert Wolfe of Columbia called my attention to the relevance of the concept of the deference vote in American politics. Mr. Tom Cole of the Massachusetts Institute of Technology discussed many of the issues raised in this book — much to my benefit.

I must also thank Senator Edward Kennedy, former Attorney General Edward McCormack, Professor H. Stuart Hughes, and Mr. George Lodge who permitted me to interview many of the men who managed their campaigns. Gerard Doherty, a major Kennedy aide, now Chairman of the Massachusetts Democratic State Committee, and former State Representative Sumner Kaplan, who served Edward McCormack as campaign manager, helped me a great deal. Mr. Douglas Bailey, Mr. David Goldberg, and Mr. Paul Grindle, aides of George Lodge, were most helpful as were Mr. Chester Hartman and Mr. Jerome Grossman of the Hughes organization. Secretary of State Kevin White made the 1962 records of campaign contributions and expenditures conveniently available to me. Mr. James Cain and Mr. and Mrs. Leo Flaherty of Secretary White's office greatly eased my work in the archives of the Massachusetts statehouse.

My analysis of how Edward Kennedy wrested from Edward McCormack, the nephew of the Speaker of the House, the senatorial endorsement of the 1962 Democratic state convention and a victory in the Democratic primary is based upon fifty-five tape-recorded interviews with delegates, replies to hundreds of questionnaires mailed to delegates, and dozens of tape-recorded interviews with candidates, campaign managers, public relations men, fund raisers, academic brain trusters, speech writers, area-coordinators, and ward leaders. The men interviewed on tape granted permission to quote from the interviews after the 1962 election had taken place. I have decided, where possible, to let the participants themselves describe the convention and the primary election. The credibility of the interviews is, of course, a problem. Some campaign aides had reason to be less than candid when discussing sensitive subjects, campaign finance for example. In a few instances the remarks of one aide contradict those of a colleague. Occasionally, respondents stated, immediately after an interview was completed or months later, that they had withheld information. In the overwhelming majority of cases, however, the remarks of campaign advisors are consistent with those made by colleagues. This book would not have been possible without their help.

In addition, I want to thank Miss Aurelie Dyer, Mrs. Katherine Burnett, and Miss Concepta O'Connor, who typed parts of the manuscript, and Mrs. Davela Birnbaum who proofread sections of it. Mrs. Helena Lothrop labored for months deciphering my handwriting and typing the five revisions of this book. My debt to her and her spelling is considerable.

The Boston University Graduate Research Fund and the Aaron E. Norman Fund, Inc., provided me with financial assistance. Mr. Charles Collingwood of the Columbia Broadcasting System was most kind in helping me secure funds for research.

I wish to thank four publishers in this country who were — for a variety of reasons — unwilling to publish this book. They gave me the opportunity, through Mrs. Adeline Naiman, to work with the staff of the Beacon Press — a most pleasant and rewarding experience.

Murray B. Levin

May 19, 1966

Contents

Introduction | xv

CHAPTER 1   *Right Out of Univac* | 3

CHAPTER 2   *The Lament of Knocko McCormack* | 61

CHAPTER 3   *He Can Do More for Massachusetts* | 98

CHAPTER 4   *If His Name Was Edward Moore* | 182

CHAPTER 5   *Serious Money* | 233

CHAPTER 6   *The Political Campaign as Pseudo Event* | 285

Index | 305

Illustrations

Convention signs and hoop-la

McCormack's father, "Knocko," at the convention

Balloting begins in convention hall

Kennedy magnetism

McCormack campaigning

Kennedy campaigning

McCormack meets a voter

"If his name was Edward Moore . . ."

Kennedy and McCormack at the second debate

The McCormacks vote

Senator-elect Edward Kennedy and his wife

BETWEEN PAGES 108 AND 109

Introduction

EDWARD M. KENNEDY, the junior Senator from Massachusetts, is a prominent figure now in American public life. In the future he may become even more prominent. He is among the most sought-after speakers in the Senate. He receives honorary degrees. He is asked to give commencement addresses. He holds press conferences. He is photographed with the great and the near-great. He is a trustee of a large university. He is president of a foundation. He is a dispenser of patronage. People listen to his opinions.

This book is about the Kennedy system of campaigning, the Kennedy style, and how it was used in 1962 with Edward Kennedy. In some ways, the 1962 campaign of Edward Kennedy provided the acid test of the Kennedy campaign system because the Kennedys attempted what many knowledgeable politicians thought was impossible, i.e., to "convert" a twenty-nine-year-old novice who had never been elected to public office into a Senator of the United States. In retrospect, it was an impressive feat.

How the Kennedys seek and achieve power reveals much about American life and politics. How do they approach delegates and mobilize their forces at a convention? How do they allocate their time, their money, and their manpower? How do they set up a campaign organization? How do they prepare for television debates, and what principles do they follow while debating? How do they utilize public opinion data to plan strategic moves and how do they succeed so brilliantly in manufacturing pseudo events — events which are frequently contrived, but always newsworthy? How many millions of dollars does it cost and how do they report their campaign expenditures and contributions?

These are the relevant questions concerning the Kennedy campaign system. It is a system and it is the envy of aspiring American politicians.

A study of the Kennedy system is particularly relevant now since it is widely assumed that Robert Kennedy is running for the Presidency. Occasionally one even hears speculation that

Edward Kennedy will follow suit. The Kennedys are leading presidential prospects for many reasons.

Edward and Robert Kennedy are two of perhaps three or four men now in American public life who can legitimately be called prestigious national celebrities, a rare and powerful political asset. For millions of Americans, the Kennedy brothers have "class" and evoke excitement. They associate and are seen with poets, scholars, church leaders, socialites, beautiful women, and statesmen. Yet they can take off their white tie and tails, compel the presidents of steel companies to rescind price increases, invade Cuba, force Ross Barnett's hand, relentlessly pursue Jimmy Hoffa, deftly criticize President Johnson, and campaign day and night. They like "the good things in life" yet they can rough it — climb mountains and trek through jungles. They are elegant yet willing to get their hands dirty. They are rich but work hard. They can drink imported wines or Coca Cola. They travel in society yet can be friendly with the man in the street.

The patrician sons of an enormously wealthy father, Edward and Robert Kennedy attended "proper" Eastern prep schools and Ivy League colleges, married socially prominent debutantes, belong to the liberal wing of their party, live in the best part of town, summer in the "right" places, speak with a broad *a*, and ski. Their wives wear clothes designed by "in" couturiers, and their homes are photographed as examples of gracious but informal living. They are what *Vogue* calls "beautiful people." They are not quite "us" yet they are us. They symbolize, in other words, two opposing but fundamental American ideals — aristocracy and equality — and therefore they can be most things to most Americans.

Henry Cabot Lodge, Claiborne Pell, Joseph Clark, Richardson Dilworth, Adlai Stevenson, Leverett Saltonstall, Nelson Rockefeller, William Scranton, Stuart Symington, and John Lindsay are more or less in this tradition.

These men frequently win elections, in part, because they are socially prominent and have the funds necessary to play big-time politics. Some also win because they are bright, reasonable, energetic, and good looking. The secret of their appeal, however, has much to do with the fact that since they have breeding and an aristocratic demeanor, voters tend to see them as dedicated public servants, as non-politicians. By many, they are seen as honest — not politicians on the make — because they have so much money. What is too frequently forgotten in a world which equates honesty with a failure to steal money is that candidates with unlimited financial resources may spend their money to create the kinds of events which appear spontaneous, but are in fact contrived — pseudo events as it were. This is a subject to which we will return.

The ultimate appeal of the rich politician-celebrity, particularly the younger and more glamorous among them, is perhaps that they serve as models for millions of American mothers and fathers who would like their sons to be dedicated, good looking, public spirited, athletic, unneurotic, glamorous, honest, exciting, well educated, and very rich. Who would not want their boy to have the advantages that Edward Kennedy or John Lindsay enjoyed? Their political appeal, in other words, is ultimately based on the fact that they provide one of the most satisfactory ego ideals for Americans who live in an affluent and bourgeois society. Mayor Lindsay is frequently mentioned as a potential Presidential aspirant precisely because he is a miniature Protestant version of the Kennedy brothers. Indeed, it is not surprising that a different kind of celebrity — the movie star, the astronaut, and the famous football coach — contemplates running for high office.

*   *   *

While clearly the Kennedy brothers fit the pattern of the politician-celebrity, it is at least possible that they share a unique and dreadful advantage. Chief Justice Warren commented after the assassination of President Kennedy that all Americans are "responsible" for John Kennedy's death. If millions feel some guilt for "their part" in creating a culture that produced the assassin, or if they disliked or criticized the President during his lifetime and, therefore, feel some guilt or contrition for so doing, they might expiate these feelings, symbolically, by returning another Kennedy to the White House. Those who experience deep grief wish not to relinquish the warm feelings and excitement the deceased once evoked. Death often transforms admiration into reverence. And those who grieve frequently displace the deceased with a living person — a symbolic substitute who may look like the deceased, may be related to the deceased, or may continue the ideals of the deceased.

The memory of assassinated presidents who were deeply loved, and the legends that surround them, may or may not, in the course of decades or centuries, wither away and be relegated to the dust bin of vague recollection. Their effect, in the short run, however, probably is very great.

All these advantages might count for little if the Kennedys had minimal skill in the arts of campaign management. The money, the style, the social status must be merchandized with some artistry if these assets are to be converted into votes. Meticulous and intelligent campaigning often makes the difference between victory and defeat. The Kennedys, however, are consummate masters of the art of political campaigning and the pseudo science of public relations, as we hope to illustrate.

* * *

While the focus of *Kennedy Campaigning* is on a Massachusetts Democratic convention and primary, Edward Kennedy, as we will see, began his preparations for the nomination well before 1962. Those who wish to observe the Kennedy campaign system as it is geared for a convention should follow the career of Robert Kennedy in the next few years. As James Reston noted in the *New York Times* on May 11, 1966:

> The public relations aspects of this exercise are very similar to the techniques established, with his help, during the period when John F. Kennedy was mounting his campaign for the Presidency after the 1956 election. Once the areas of political opportunity are identified, the scholars are mobilized. The evening seminars continue at his country house in Virginia. The writers are brought in and the speech is finally launched with all the care of a major advertising campaign.

His speech to the Senate on Latin America was first sent out for review to Latin-American experts in the universities, in the State Department (Assistant Secretary Lincoln Gordon) and even in the White House (Walt W. Rostow).

It was then split into two parts, one for delivery on Monday and the other on Tuesday. It ran to 54 pages of single-spaced typewritten copy on long legal folio sheets, complete with six other pages summarizing the document for indolent scribblers. "The speech," said the instructions to reporters, "is in seven (7) numbered sections with an introduction and a conclusion . . . and . . . not for release before delivery, 6 P.M. on the actual day the speech is concluded. . . ."

Nothing was overlooked. The whole packet was delivered to reporters days in advance, the networks advised, and video tapes cut on the key passages, all in time for the national news shows on each day of delivery. . . .

In short, he is working hard and working with zeal and purpose, and this is clearly only the beginning of a long campaign.

KENNEDY CAMPAIGNING

CHAPTER 1 ☒ *Right Out of Univac*

Smith's appointment was the tip-off that something funny was about to occur here in Massachusetts.

—A LIBERAL DEMOCRAT

ON DECEMBER 28, 1960, just three days before the end of his term, Governor Foster Furcolo of Massachusetts, a Democrat, appointed Benjamin Smith II to fill the vacancy in the United States Senate created by the resignation of President-elect John Fitzgerald Kennedy. Although Furcolo announced that the appointment was "in the interest of promoting party unity," many believed that John Kennedy had insisted on the appointment of a man without political ambition, who would be content to return to private life in 1962, when another Kennedy would be eligible for the post. The President-elect could certainly count on Smith's loyalty since he had been Kennedy's roommate at Harvard, was a close friend, and had been an usher at the Kennedy-Bouvier wedding.

The Governor, apparently almost unaware of Mr. Smith's existence prior to Kennedy's "suggestion," was not in a position to refuse because Kennedy could have remained in the Senate until after January 1, 1961, when Governor Furcolo was to be succeeded by a Republican, John Volpe. Although some Furcolo aides believed that the President would never permit a Republican to name his successor, *Time* reported the rumor that "Kennedy put it on the line to Furcolo: make the appointment or we'll get Republican Governor-elect John Volpe to do it once he takes office."[1]

The new senator, appropriately named Mr. Smith, was a mystery even to the cognoscenti of Massachusetts politics. His record of public service included one term as city councilman of Gloucester and one term as mayor. He had also acted as a Kennedy aide in some of the former senator's primary campaigns, but his appointment offended both party regulars and liberal activ-

[1] *Time,* January 12, 1961, p. 15.

ists. As one of the leaders of the rather small but articulate liberal wing of the party said:

> The appointment was a slap in the face to every single Massachusetts Democrat, because there are many, many, many more people that could have been chosen for the job. . . . I still think that the President should have used his power to appoint somebody who would have done something for the Democratic party in some constructive fashion, instead of picking out one of his wedding-party members.

Shortly after his brother's inauguration as President, twenty-nine-year-old Edward Moore (Ted) Kennedy went on a "fact-finding" trip to Africa, and on his return rented an apartment in Boston and was appointed a dollar-a-year assistant district attorney in Suffolk County — the overwhelming Irish and Democratic stronghold in which Boston is located. Mrs. Edward Kennedy later said that her husband wanted to move to New Mexico, Wyoming, or California, to avoid living in his brother's shadow, but that "eventually . . . we both decided you can't run away from being the President's brother no matter where you go, and we came back to Massachusetts."[2] Many politicians in the Bay State, however, began to suspect that "Teddy" was planning to capitalize on this relationship by becoming a candidate for the Senate in 1962, when he would be thirty, the minimum age required by the Constitution for a United States senator.

Their suspicions — or perhaps their fears — were intensified late in 1961, when Edward Kennedy began an extensive series of "non-political" appearances and speaking engagements throughout the Commonwealth. Exhibiting the phenomenal energy and determination that his brother had demonstrated during the presidential campaign, this engaging young man, whom the President called "the best politician in the family," toured every corner of the state, exposing Massachusetts voters once again to the famous Kennedy voice, smile, and gesture. *Time* described a typical "nonpolitical" Kennedy day:

2 *New Bedford Standard-Times,* May 26, 1962.

On a recent Sunday, he drove from Hyannisport to Natick to deliver a breakfast speech to a men's group at Temple Israel. After 11:30 Mass, he hurried to a Framingham neighborhood coffee meeting, followed it up with a luncheon speech in Framingham, an appearance at a "silver get-acquainted tea" given by the Medford St. James Church Women's Guild, a talk to a parents' group at the Wrentham State School for retarded children. That night he attended the General Casimir Pulasky Skyway Committee banquet, held in Dorchester, quoted part of Poland's national anthem in Polish, enthusiastically danced the polka with a score of girls.[3]

While her son made speeches to groups of Irish Americans, Italian Americans, and Jews, customarily talking about his recent trips to Ireland, Italy, and Israel, Mrs. Rose Kennedy, a veteran campaigner in her own right, spoke to Catholic Holy Name Societies, whose traditions and rules forbid political speechmaking.

During these months, a close friend of the Kennedy family, Boston Municipal Court Judge Francis Xavier Morrissey, whose nomination to the federal bench by President Johnson in 1965 caused such an uproar, began to introduce Edward Kennedy to influential members of the state Democratic party. Although some party leaders were at first incredulous and then dismayed by Kennedy's apparent plan to run for the United States Senate at his youthful age, and despite the fact that he had never held elective office, no one dared to underestimate the attraction of the Kennedy name in Massachusetts, the patronage power of the White House, and the Kennedy penchant for remembering friends and punishing enemies. The President's brother received enough encouragement from key party leaders to proceed with his plans.

Before the voters in Massachusetts were to have the opportunity to vote for Edward Kennedy, however, he had to present himself to the professional politicians of the state Democratic party, who meet in convention every two years to endorse candidates for the United States Senate and other state-wide offices. The outcome of the state convention is heavily influenced by

3 *Time,* October 27, 1961, p. 25.

the decisions of a relatively small number of party leaders who for reasons that we will discuss later, are able to select and control a substantial number of the delegates. The candidate endorsed by the state convention must also run in a primary and may be opposed by any candidate who can secure 2,500 nomination signatures (which is quite easy to do). Nevertheless, the convention endorsee in Massachusetts almost invariably wins the primary. Endorsees have been opposed in recent years, but only a few challengers have been successful, and three times it took one with the magic name of John F. (Francis) Kennedy to defeat the endorsee for state treasurer. The endorsee enjoys an advantage in the primary not mainly because he has the support of what is euphemistically called the party organization in Massachusetts — it is more or less a shadow organization — but because his name is placed first on the ballot. Scholars estimate that this position is probably worth at least a bonus of 5 per cent of the vote.[4] The endorsee does receive some minimal financial support from the State Committee.

* * *

The activities of Edward Kennedy were now of national interest and he appeared on "Meet the Press" on March 11, 1962. Many of the issues that were to become salient in the campaign were touched upon during the program. Lawrence Spivak, for example, raised the issue of Kennedy's youth and political inexperience. "The question of age," Kennedy said, ". . . is something again which is relative. As far as Congress and Executive mansions of this country — many of them are represented by people in their thirties. In my travels to the developing countries of Africa and to Latin America . . . many of the leaders I met . . . were in their thirties." To queries about a possible Kennedy dynasty, he quipped, "If you are talking about too many Ken-

[4] See, for example, Leon Kamin, "Ethnic and Party Affiliation of Candidates as Determinants of Voting," *Canadian Journal of Psychology*, Vol. 12 (1958), reprinted in S. Sidney Ulmer, ed., *Introductory Readings in Political Behavior* (Chicago: Rand McNally and Co., 1961), p. 69. See also Angus Campbell, Philip E. Converse, Warren E. Miller, and Donald Stokes, *The American Voter* (New York: John Wiley and Sons, 1960), p. 276.

nedys, you should have talked to my mother and father at the time they were getting started. . . . All I am asking is not to be the Kennedy candidate, but the candidate for the Democratic party."

When asked about his position on federal aid to private schools, a delicate problem in Massachusetts, with its Catholic majority, Kennedy said, in a way that was fairly typical of his spontaneous remarks:

> I think that it is quite evident from the legislation which is enacted presently that there is an opportunity to provide aid to private and public schools which would be considered constitutional. Under the National Defense Act this is evident. Under the present legislation, which provides for school lunch programs, legislation which provides to assist the child himself in the form of textbooks, the assistance which would be provided in the question of national interest are all areas in which we can find — be considered, at least, constitutional, and I think I would certainly support these areas and possible other areas which might be considered constitutional.

Richard Clurman, of *Time*, who asked the question, suggested that Kennedy's position differed from that of the President. Kennedy replied, "That is your interpretation and your conclusion. . . . I am delighted to answer in any way any question as to what my position is." Asked whether he believed that his candidacy might be embarrassing to the President, Kennedy answered:

> I think . . . one of the responsibilities of the President is building a majority for his program in the Congress and the Senate. And I think if I were to be successful that this would certainly contribute a voice of support in the Congress and Senate. And I feel that this might be of sufficient support for his program — I think it might be helpful.

Four days later, in Massachusetts, on March 14, 1962, Kennedy formally announced his candidacy for the United States Senate. "I make this decision in full knowledge of the obstacles I will face, the charges that will be made, and the heavy responsibilities of the office to which I aspire." As for the "charges," he declared, "I am aware that my brother is the President and my other brother Attorney General. I am convinced, however, the people will choose the candidate they consider most effective." He also pointed out emphatically that neither the President nor the Attorney General would campaign for him in Massachusetts, but that his sisters would "come for a visit and we won't keep them in a closet all the time."[5]

A former Massachusetts office holder who had campaigned for John Fitzgerald Kennedy in West Virginia later said:

> Nobody wants to be against the President of the United States. I don't think any of these working, good Democrats in Massachusetts want to embarrass the President by having his brother defeated. I think they'd like the kid not to be in it, not to be running. . . . I've heard many of them say, "Jesus, how can I be against the President's brother? How can he be defeated? It'll look terrible. . . ." The name Kennedy is a great thing in Massachusetts. Much greater than McCormack is. It's an image. . . . Running against a Kennedy is almost like running against the Church.

Although running against a Kennedy in Massachusetts may be like "running against the Church," the Attorney General of Massachusetts, Edward J. McCormack, nephew of Speaker of the United States House of Representatives John McCormack, decided to take the risk. On April 8, 1962, before a national television audience on "Meet the Press," the younger McCormack said that his decision to run for the United States Senate had been taken in 1960. "I took a calculated risk," he stated, "that the then United States Senator would be elected President and this opportunity would present itself to run for the Senate in 1962. So this is a decision of long standing with me."

During the half-hour program McCormack was asked several questions on the relative power of the Kennedy and McCormack clans in Massachusetts and also about his stand on federal aid to education. The panelists, however, concentrated on corruption in Massachusetts and McCormack's position as the Com-

5 *Boston Globe,* March 15, 1962.

monwealth's chief law enforcement officer — an issue of great concern to McCormack and his advisers. For them a major question was whether Massachusetts voters would see McCormack as a typical Boston politician and an ineffectual Attorney General.

In reply to the panelists' questions McCormack said that he "broke up" a million-dollar gambling syndicate and prosecuted some men involved in a state-wide fraud that had to do with unemployment compensation. He asked his audience to note that he was chairman of a special commission that had proposed a model code of ethics bill, that he had tried cases involving conflict of interest in the Metropolitan District Commission and other state agencies, and that he had exposed corrupt activities in the Massachusetts Parking Authority. These were the answers he was to use throughout his campaign.

In response to a question about alleged bookmaking in Boston, McCormack said:

> As Attorney General I represent the entire state. . . . We have seven district attorneys who represent districts of the state. Boston happens to be in the Suffolk County District. It is not a district attorney's function, I feel, to be a super-police officer, but if it is, if someone could have moved in on this case, it was the District Attorney . . . and perhaps an assistant district attorney Kennedy who happens to be running for this job.

On federal aid to private schools McCormack said on "Meet the Press," "I favor aid to education for public and non-public schools. I have said that if a bill came before me as a United States Senator that included aid only to the public schools, I would vote for it." When asked whether he supported the Kennedy legislative program in every aspect, he replied, "I support basically the President's foreign policy. I support most of the domestic issues that I feel the Kennedys sponsor. I differ on some." McCormack then spelled out his differences with the administration:

> I differ, for instance, with the Attorney General, Bob Kennedy, on two bills which he has either sponsored or endorsed,

one a bill on wiretapping. He has sponsored a bill which in effect says that anyone in the state who wants to invade someone's right to privacy shall get a court order, but he as Attorney General can make his own determination. I sponsored a bill on wiretapping in Massachusetts to restrict my own power. . . . I feel we are a government of laws and not a government of men and that the Attorney General, along with any local official, should have to go to court and bring the invasion of the right of privacy within the purview of the Fourth Amendment.

I also differ on his habeas corpus, which in effect makes it more difficult to appeal a state court conviction to the federal court system, because I feel that in some sections of this country some of our citizens, notably the Negro in the South, cannot in some cases get a fair trial in the state court system. I don't want to make it more difficult for him to get into the federal court system. I want to make it easy.

Since both candidates were and are members of the liberal wing of the Democratic party in Massachusetts and both of them supported President Kennedy's program in large measure, it was going to be difficult for convention delegates or primary voters to choose between Kennedy and McCormack on ideological grounds. The choice would be made, as so often happens in American politics, on the basis of personality, family, background, political record, or political expediency. The delegates, whose judgment on the contenders precedes that of the voters, are probably little concerned with ideology, and their decisions rest chiefly on an estimate of which candidate is most likely to win, which candidate is most likely to respond to their future needs. Most of them are interested in "the issues" only insofar as "the issues" will affect the voters. Felt needs, future advantage, and past political debts were the criteria most delegates utilized when evaluating the candidacy of the Speaker's nephew and the President's brother.

Edward Kennedy's candidacy for the United States Senate was essentially based on three facts: He was the attractive, energetic brother of the President of the United States; he was a Kennedy; and he was able to raise the funds necessary to wage a major state-wide campaign.

Edward Kennedy, after attending Milton Academy, went to Harvard where his education was interrupted by two years of service in the United States Army in Europe as a private first class. Returning to Harvard, he was graduated in 1956 and then went to the Law School of the University of Virginia. He was admitted to the Massachusetts bar in 1959 and then was appointed assistant district attorney of Suffolk County.

A candidate for major public office in the United States usually campaigns on the basis of his record. The record may be genuine or imaginary, significant or trifling, but the candidate must be able to cite some past political administrative experience or professional accomplishment when asked what it is that entitles him to run. Since Kennedy, who had never held elective office, could cite neither, he and his staff of advisers were forced to construct a public portrait of him based on what they called "Edward M. Kennedy's Community Service." His campaign brochure cited this record:

NAMED as one of the ten outstanding men of the year by the Boston Junior Chamber of Commerce.

ORDER OF MERIT — REPUBLIC OF ITALY — for interest and achievements in behalf of Italian culture and progress, both in Italy and the U.S.

CITATION OF SERVICE for work as chairman of the most successful American Cancer Society campaign in Mass. history.

YOUTH SERVICE for outstanding service and contributions to the Progress of Youth Program of the Nation as chairman of the United Fund Health and Fitness Fair.

CHAIRMAN of the United Fund Health and Fitness Fair.

TRUSTEE and member of the Executive Board, Massachusetts Chapter, Arthritis and Rheumatism Foundation.

MEMBER of the Board of Trustees of Boston University.

CHAIRMAN of the American Cancer Crusade, Massachusetts Division, in 1961, which recruited 101,000 volunteers and raised a record $1,328,000.

JUDGE ADVOCATE of the Polish American Veterans Post of Boston.

DIRECTOR of the Massachusetts Division of the American Cancer Society, Inc.

MEMBER of the Massachusetts Bar and Boston Bar Associations.

CHAIRMAN of the Massachusetts Delegation to Italy in commemoration of the First Centennial of Italian Unification, May, 1961.

MEMBER of the Advisory Board, Emmanuel College.

PRESIDENT of the Joseph P. Kennedy Jr. Foundation.

MEMBER of the General Casimir Pulaski Memorial Committee of Mass.

McCormack was to imply, during the campaign, that Kennedy's "record" was contrived or synthetic, that he had been appointed a chairman, a director, a member, a trustee, etc. only because he was a Kennedy and had received citations and an order of merit for the same reason. The image of Kennedy presented to the electorate — that is, his visible printed public profile — did not include the essential facts around which the image was built: his relationship to the President of the United States and his membership in the Kennedy family.

Obviously Kennedy would have to find a way to handle the issue of his political inexperience. He would have to deal with the fact that he was barely thirty years old. He would have to face the charge that he was exploiting his political influence and family name. And he would have to deal with the charge of dynastic ambition and nepotism. Some of these problems he simply ignored and in some instances he turned what his antagonists hoped were liabilities into assets. As his brochure put in, "He is personally known by every major figure in government — when he speaks, they listen." His campaign slogan, "He Can Do More for Massachusetts," strongly implied that he could do more because he was the President's brother.

There was, however, one delicate problem that the Kennedy entourage felt it had to meet squarely. Shortly after the announcement of his candidacy, stories began to circulate in Massachusetts that Kennedy had been forced to withdraw from Harvard College for cheating. Newspapermen asked the college to confirm or deny the report and received only a terse "no comment." Hundreds of delegates who were to go to the convention had heard the rumor. The Kennedy camp was concerned that a massive whispering campaign would seriously damage Kennedy's reputation with some delegates and a significant number of voters. It was decided, therefore, to acknowledge the affair before the convention and the primary. Carefully worded, this public declaration would permit the Kennedy family to tell the story as they wanted it told at a time of their choosing. It was hoped that a public statement would also make Kennedy look forthright and would more or less remove the issue from the campaign.

On March 30, 1962, just two weeks after Kennedy had announced his candidacy and approximately ten weeks before the convention, a release to the press was carried on the front page of many newspapers throughout the country and was widely discussed.

I entered Harvard in 1950 at the age of 18. During the second semester of my freshman year I made a mistake. I was having difficulty in one course, a foreign language. I became so apprehensive about it that I arranged for a fellow freshman friend of mine to take the examination for me in that course.

The Dean learned of this, and my friend and I were asked to withdraw with the understanding that we might reapply for admission after a period of absence, provided that during that time we could demonstrate a record of constructive and responsible citizenship.

[After serving for two years in Europe as an infantryman, Kennedy returned to the United States.]

Upon my return, I made my application to Harvard and was accepted for readmission. My friend who was also readmitted, and I later represented Harvard in intercollegiate athletics. I worked hard, passed all my courses — some with honors — and was graduated in good standing in 1956.

[Kennedy then went to the University of Virginia Law School.]

The authorities at that institution were fully aware of all the facts surrounding the Harvard incident. They have an honor system at the Law School of the University of Virginia. I was accepted at that institution and graduated in good standing three years later.

What I did was wrong. I have regretted it ever since. The unhappiness I caused my family and friends, even though eleven years ago, has been a bitter experience for me, but it has also been a very valuable lesson. That is the story.

Only a few Kennedy delegates whom we interviewed were disturbed by his announcement. "I could see a poor man doing that," one of them said, "but I could never see a Kennedy with a million dollars who could get all the tutoring . . . that he needed. Really, that hurt me. I didn't believe that one. I don't go for that stuff." Most of the Kennedy delegates, however, found an excuse for the incident.

A Kennedy delegate who was a school teacher remarked, "I see this all the time. I punish children by flunking them for the term, but I believe that for the next term . . . if a person proves that they're learning by a mistake, have improved by a mistake, I'd never hold it against them. . . . You don't kick a man when he's down."

Said another supporter:

At that particular time, it was more or less a boy's prank . . . and he was just unfortunate enough to be caught. It's happened before and it will happen again in many colleges. . . . We have many occasions here of young fellows getting into trouble at one time or another — certainly you can't hold it against them forever. I really didn't call it cheating. It's just something that maybe he wanted to go somewhere that day or week. . . .

Some Kennedy delegates even interpreted their candidate's experience so as to increase their admiration for him:

A lot of others have made the same mistake and became much better men because they did make the mistake probably. I honestly believe that the man that never made a mistake was buried the day he was born. And if you have made a mistake, and I don't know a man who hasn't made a mistake some place in his life, and when they start digging skeletons like that out of his closet — pretty cheap politics.

Another Kennedy delegate reported his method of handling co-workers who badgered him about the college experience:

> Well, they were saying . . . they wouldn't vote for a man that — "Well," I says, "did you ever cheat in an exam?" They say, "Yeah, but I'm not a Kennedy." I says, "Well, that just proves one thing — there is a human being in the Kennedy family." . . . I says, "What would you do if you had a million bucks?" They says, "I'd go out and I'd have a ball." I says, "That's right." I says, "Would you go to college and get an education and try to be smart, and try to be President?" They says, "In a pig's ass I would." He went to college, he got a million — now he's got ten million — he's got a family, probably a little bit of a playboy — he went down, he got in a jam, but now he's man enough to admit it — he went back there and graduated from Harvard. . . .

Kennedy apparently managed the potentially dangerous cheating issue with such skill that even McCormack never mentioned it during the campaign.

*   *   *

Edward McCormack was born and raised in South Boston, the solid Irish enclave which spawned most of the legendary figures of *The Last Hurrah.* In the days when Yankees dominated the professions, controlled the banks and insurance companies, and excluded the Irish, Italians, and Jews from the universities, an ambitious Irish boy from "Southie" could pursue a career in the Church, professional athletics, crime, or politics — areas of endeavor that place little emphasis on birth or academic training. "Politics," John McCormack once remarked, "was the natural thing for anyone born in South Boston." Appointed to the United States Naval Academy by Congressman McCormack, Edward was graduated in the middle of the class. He then attended the Boston University Law School, where he served as editor-in-chief of the *Law Review,* and was graduated first in his class.

Like most of the Irish politicians who ultimately came to dominate politics in the Bay State, McCormack worked his way up through the party hierarchy, carefully making friends by helping people who sought jobs or favors or who needed a contact at City Hall. He was elected to the Boston City Council in 1952 and again in 1954 and 1956 and during his last term served as president of the Council. In 1958 the Massachusetts legislature appointed McCormack interim attorney general of the Commonwealth when the incumbent died. He was elected to the office a few months later with a plurality of 82,000 votes and re-elected in 1960 with a plurality of 430,000 votes.

As the Commonwealth's chief law enforcement officer, he established a Division of Civil Rights and a Consumers' Council in the office of the Attorney General, both of which have become models for other state governments. He also sponsored or supported legislation designed to curb wiretapping, eliminate discrimination in housing, establish a code of ethics for public employees, and abolish capital punishment. Further, the Attorney General published a pamphlet dealing with the rights of arrested persons which received national attention, and he proposed a bill designed to establish a Public Defenders Committee which was enacted.

Although McCormack's concern for civil rights and civil liberties in a community where Senator McCarthy had strong support among the Boston Irish[6] was regarded as "bad politics" by many party workers, his efforts in this area and his distinguished record in law school undoubtedly were attractive to delegates concerned with such matters — the more affluent and better-educated delegates from suburbia and the college towns — a group, however, with a very small voting bloc at the convention.

McCormack's problem with the delegates was three-fold. He had to convince them that he had a reasonable chance of defeating the Republican candidate in November. He had to convince them that he had a better chance than Edward Kennedy, the brother of a President. And he had to convince them that, if elected, he could satisfy their demands more readily than Kennedy could. In retrospect, the statement of his problems implies

[6] Lawrence Fuchs, "Presidential Politics in Boston, the Irish Response to Stevenson," *New England Quarterly*, December, 1957, p. 439.

obvious and negative answers on all three counts. The Kennedys are the most popular and appealing political family in Massachusetts; the delegates knew this. The Kennedys have far greater financial resources than the McCormacks; the delegates knew this. The Kennedys have far more patronage at their disposal than the McCormacks; the delegates also knew this.

McCormack's chances, therefore, did not look very good since he was, in addition, the chief law enforcement officer of the state during a period when it was engulfed in what the *Boston Herald* called "a tidal wave of corruption." Although several minor state and local office holders were convicted of larceny and fraud, involving hundreds of thousands of dollars prior to and during McCormack's tenure as Attorney General, a substantial bloc of the voting public continued to believe that the Commonwealth was infested with corruption, and that politicians, particularly Boston politicians, were crooks.[7] In other words, McCormack's advisors were worried that he would be seen as a Boston "pol" — or, what is worse, a South Boston "pol."

Most key delegates are not disturbed by being seen as politicians since they are politicians, but they have to consider what *voters* think of politicians. Many assumed that McCormack could not overcome this stereotype and so could defeat neither Kennedy nor the Republican candidate. One of the Attorney General's more influential advisers put McCormack's problem succinctly:

> I think another disadvantage that McCormack is going to have . . . is that he has been Attorney General . . . in this especially chaotic period, where there have been endless investigations . . . at all levels of state, county, and local governments, which ultimately kicked up to McCormack in one way or another for bringing in grand jury proceedings and so forth . . . I think that there inevitably will be some people in the community who will feel, even apart from politics, that perhaps he has not moved as aggressively or as forcefully in some areas as they would seem to have liked him to move,

[7] Murray B. Levin, *The Alienated Voter: Politics in Boston* (New York: Holt, Rinehart and Winston, 1960), Chap. 2.

and this of course will lend itself to the charge that to some extent he's been attempting to cover up perhaps for Democrats who may have gone astray. . . .

McCormack's "answer" to the problem was to state, and conscientiously so, that he had vigorously prosecuted wrongdoing as Attorney General, that he had inherited and not created the problem, and that it would take some time to cleanse the state. But McCormack could not solve his problem by making a public announcement, as Kennedy did with the cheating issue, because McCormack was confronted with deep-seated stereotypes and convictions that cannot be destroyed, or even significantly altered, during a four-month campaign. The candidate who pleads innocence or denies complicity assumes a defensive posture — probably not a good thing from a strategic point of view.

The likelihood that McCormack would be stereotyped as a South Boston "pol" was further enhanced, in the opinions of some of his advisers, by the fact that

> McCormack has this unfortunate mannerism of talking, or appearing to talk, somewhat out of the side of his mouth, and while this is a very small thing, it's the kind of thing which, I think, instinctively causes people to be a little distrustful and suspicious in terms of television appearances. I think McCormack tends unfortunately not to project as favorable an image as Ted Kennedy. . . .

It may well be a "very small thing" but it was another factor which led some to conclude that McCormack was a "pol" and a loser.

Other personality factors, according to a number of delegates, would damage McCormack's chances. "McCormack tends to be a little less easy to perhaps warm up to," an aide suggested. "Put it this way . . . if you have Kennedy and McCormack come into a room to meet somebody who has never met either of them . . . I think on a superficial basis . . . within a matter of the first few minutes, I think the initial Kennedy reaction would be more favorable than the initial McCormack reaction." A politician friendly to the McCormacks said that the Attorney General gives the impression of being "a bit of a snob. He can't seem to unbend and become one of the boys. He can't transmit a magnetism to the people. McCormack tends not to project as favorable an image as Ted Kennedy, who's young, dynamic, and good-looking." A member of the Kennedy brain trust — a distinguished professor—described the candidates' images in slightly different terms:

> I think his [Kennedy's] great strength is this phenomenal energy which is not just energy, it's force, a natural sense of command, decision, execution, activity. . . . McCormack's more judicial. He's a very intelligent person and he's a compassionate man. He has a judicious and judicial temperament. I think he would make a very fine judge. But he doesn't have this energy or force. He doesn't excite people. He doesn't bowl over anybody. Or, as one fellow said, "I am underwhelmed by him." But it depends on the role you put him in. I think he would make a really great judge whereas Kennedy is the executive, or certain kind of legislative, type.

*　　*　　*

The convention delegates' estimate of the two candidates led most of them before the convention to conclude that Kennedy best suited their needs. Many of them, however, came to this conclusion reluctantly and with some trepidation because, they felt, a choice between Edward Kennedy and Edward McCormack involved, in a broader sense, a choice between John Kennedy and John McCormack.

A struggle between two Kennedys and two McCormacks is national news. Washington columnists were quick to point out that the President needed the active and wholehearted support of the Speaker because Kennedy's margin of victory over Nixon was extremely narrow and because support for much of his program on the Hill was, at best, hesitant and tenuous. The question at issue, they thought, was whether John McCormack would attempt to scuttle the President's program if his nephew was defeated by a Kennedy.

Despite public disclaimers to the contrary and occasional alliances of convenience, relations between the Kennedys and the McCormacks had never been overly cordial. In 1956 John Kennedy wrested control of the Massachusetts Democratic State Committee from John McCormack. Although control of the State Committee does not automatically mean control of the party, particularly in Massachusetts where the Democratic party is dominated by feudatories who refuse to be united under any monarch, it does involve control over some delegates to the national convention. The loss of these plums seriously weakened McCormack's ability to serve the faithful. When John Kennedy won the presidency, John McCormack suffered the further indignity of losing control of federal patronage in Massachusetts, a privilege that had been extended to him by Presidents Roosevelt and Truman.

The Speaker, according to some of his followers, has neither forgotten nor forgiven John Kennedy's "take-over." One Massachusetts party functionary remarked, "It's a most amazing fight, and I think that anyone who survives this one with his head above water, he can survive almost anything." Many convention delegates felt the same way.

Washington columnists did not discount the possibility that the Speaker might engage in a personal vendetta against the President if his nephew should be defeated by Edward Kennedy. Marquis Childs, for example, wrote:

> Here in Washington the prospect has produced something close to dismay among Democrats on Capitol Hill. They fear it will complicate an already complex relationship and make the course of the President's program through Congress more difficult than before.
>
> That relationship is, of course, between the President and the Speaker of the House, and it goes down to the fact that the House has become a kind of great barrier reef for proposed legislation. Both gentlemen on the surface refute any intimation of animosity. But their differences, tangled with the intricate rivalries of Massachusetts politics, cannot be smoothed over. And if they are embittered by the coming campaign the Speaker will hardly be encouraged to give his all in trying to put over pieces of the presidential program, with which, in any event, his sympathy is slight.[8]

[8] Marquis Childs, "Ted-Eddie Fight Causing Dismay on Capitol Hill," *Berkshire Eagle*, March 19, 1962.

Even if John McCormack refused to permit his personal felings to interfere with his obligations as a party leader, other congressmen, already chafing under the pressures of the White House lobby, might regard the election of Edward Kennedy as an affront to their folkways — another reason for being less than enthusiastic about the President's program. As Childs noted:

> Sitting members of Congress, regardless of party, have their own trade union and most of them have gained admission by a long apprenticeship. This applies with special force to the Senate, a number of Senators having moved from the House to the other chamber. Now along comes a young man, who, as viewed by the trade union, proposes at a single bound by reason of money and family to move into first place.[9]

The elevation of the President's brother to the Senate might not only strain the President's relationship with the Speaker and some indignant members of Congress but also alienate elements of the liberal community, sensitive to the charges of nepotism that had already been leveled against the Chief Executive. The McCormack forces were delighted when Professor Mark DeWolfe Howe of the Harvard Law School, a vigorous supporter of John Kennedy and of Edward McCormack, suggested that the younger Kennedy's candidacy was bound to embarrass the President:

> Surely the youngest of these brothers is not ignorant of the fact that the President's admirers and supporters have not always found it easy to justify the inclination toward nepotism which has been suggested by a number of his appointments. By the decision to seek an office which would now be manifestly beyond his reach were he not the President's brother, Teddy Kennedy has shown a reckless desire for self-advancement — an ambition so childishly irresponsible that it pays no regard to the damage which it does to the good name of the President. Perhaps the candidate has taken these issues into account and is willing to let the public assume that he has received a fraternal blessing. To foster this assumption is in itself an outrage, for it makes it virtually impossible for the President's admirers to extinguish the hostile suspicion of his

[9] *Ibid.*

critics. Perhaps Teddy Kennedy is gambling on the hope that those who support the President will not aid and comfort his enemies by voting against his brother. To engage in such a game of chance is to corrupt the political process. It is not surprising, I think, that Teddy's conduct has brought chuckles of malicious delight from the President's critics and words of indignation from his supporters.[10]

Max Lerner wrote:

> I shall have to speak plainly about what I regard as a massive error in judgment on the part of the whole Kennedy family and of the President himself. The error lay in allowing the youngest Kennedy to make a race from which there can be no retreat with grace and in which a final victory will carry heavy elements of defeat.[11]

The ominous warnings of the press, of course, proved to be without foundation. The Speaker worked tirelessly for the President's program despite the fact that his "favorite nephew" was opposed by the Kennedys. John McCormack may have been deeply angered and outraged, but his public position — Washington correspondents make the Speaker's position very public — and his role as a prominent party leader really made it impossible for him to sabotage the President's program.

The likelihood of sabotage was enormously exaggerated by the press because it made superb and dramatic copy: the President and the Speaker locked in a bitter struggle involving their relatives. The story was, however, essentially contrived by the press, basically without fact, a manufactured event.

Political columnists who like to speculate on the deeper and more permanent issues of American life and politics utilized the 1962 senatorial campaign in Massachusetts to analyze popular attitudes toward the concentration of political power in one family — the so-called issue of dynastic politics. According to popular folklore, Americans disapprove of patrician rule and dynastic politics. Until quite recently, politics in this country, particularly

---

10 *The Reporter*, July 19, 1962, p. 8.
11 Max Lerner, *New York Post*, June, 1962.

state and local politics, was not a status-conferring profession although in the eighteenth and early nineteenth centuries numerous patricians and members of the intellectual elite (the two were frequently synonymous) played a major role in our national life. They were soon displaced, however, by "the people." The Age of Jackson symbolizes the triumphs of populist attitudes and marks the demise of "the aristocracy" in politics. Since that time remarkably few distinguished American families have trained their young for political careers. To mention the Adams family, the Lodges, the McCormacks, and the Kennedys of Massachusetts, the Roosevelts and Wagners of New York, the Tafts of Ohio, the Longs of Louisiana, and the Byrds of Virginia is virtually to exhaust the catalogue of so-called dynastic political families. In almost every case their family public service does not even extend for more than two generations, and to call them dynastic is not very descriptive. The dynastic issue was more of a press creation that a real thing; the press gave it life primarily because of its attention-getting value.

Edward Kennedy's candidacy would have been a much more significant and reliable test of the issue if the Kennedys had been the only "dynastic" family seeking a seat in the Senate in 1962. The charge of dynastic ambition, however, was also leveled against the McCormacks.

Edward McCormack's rise to prominence and his opportunity to run for the Senate at a relatively early age were undoubtedly related to his being a McCormack and a nephew of the Speaker of the House. Much of the financial support and national press coverage received by the Attorney General during the campaign resulted from this relationship and from the fact that he was running against a Kennedy.

The issue of dynasty became more salient and interesting when George Cabot Lodge, former Under Secretary of Labor in the Eisenhower administration, son of former United States Senator, United Nations Ambassador, and vice-presidential candidate Henry Cabot Lodge, and great grandson of the Senator Henry Cabot Lodge who was Woodrow Wilson's nemesis, announced his candidacy for the Republican senatorial nomination. The situation assumed comic proportions when Kennedy, Lodge, and McCormack were joined by still another "dynastic" candidate — Professor H. Stuart Hughes, Chairman of the Department of History and Literature at Harvard University and grandson of former Chief Justice and unsuccessful Republican presidential candidate Charles Evans Hughes. Professor Hughes announced his intention to run in the general election as an Independent, a "peace" candidate, and an advocate of unilateral disarmament. The only "commoner" to counter this aristocratic field was Laurence Curtis, sixty-six-year-old veteran Republican congressman, who campaigned on the slogan that a seat in the Senate of the United States "should be merited, not inherited."

Despite the proliferation of well-connected competitors for the same Senate seat, newspapermen friendly to the McCormacks suggested that the issue of dynastic ambition could be seriously leveled only against Edward Kennedy. They raised the question of how many voters believed there were already "too many Kennedys" in government and they expressed the hope that a substantial number would be infuriated by Edward Kennedy's attempt to "ride into office on his brother's coattails."

A veteran politician whom we interviewed suggested, however, that resentment against the Kennedys in Massachusetts was restricted to a very narrow segment of the Democratic electorate, "the intelligentsia, a certain educated group, a certain thinking group"—a group that customarily fails to vote in Democratic primaries. His comment was quite accurate. Some observers even proposed that Edward Kennedy's membership in the first family and the dynastic and aristocratic character of his candidacy were enormous assets for him among the hundreds of thousands of Irish Catholics who comprise the dominant faction of the state Democratic party. Although the Irish have won political control of the Bay State, they never have been quite accepted — never have quite accepted themselves — as the social equals of the Yankees they supplanted. The Boston Irish politician has been stereotyped as a crook by many Irish and non-Irish. Americans of Irish extraction have been excluded from the "right" clubs and, until recent years, forced to play a secondary role in the state's economic and cultural life. The Kennedys, however, "proved" that Irish Americans can be statesmen as well as politicians, social and cultural leaders as well as cigar-chomping ward bosses. The Kennedys have power, money, glamour, and — what is more important to the Irish — class and respectability. By identifying with them, the Irish of Massachusetts can fulfill in fantasy the American dream of economic, social, and political success.

This yearning for class and respectability among Irish Americans was noted by several politicians. One state legislator, for example, said:

> The Irish voter wants to be dignified . . . he wants to be identified with clean candidates, and Kennedy projects that image. . . . The "lace curtain Irish" who have achieved some financial success and social success are particularly anxious to be respectable, and I think that they and the active church-going women members of Sodality and men members of the Holy Name Societies are particularly prone to be affected by the charges of corruption against the Democratic party, and those are the people who in my opinion are a great source of strength for Ted Kennedy. . . .

A university professor who was a prominent member of the Kennedy brain trust commented:

> It impressed me deeply, the extent to which the Irish identify with him [John F. Kennedy]. To some people this is like a son, you know. Just this enormous ethnic identification. Kennedy means Teddy as well as the President. Then there is the fact that he is the leader of the party. Whether it's reasoning or not, it's association. . . . "We're for Kennedy because he is the leader of our party and so we are for his brother. . . ." People in Massachusetts judge on the family basis very strongly. . . . That way of making associations is very strong . . . the family reasoning. . . . These people — I don't pretend to know how many of them, but it seems lots of them — think this man, a Kennedy, makes a tremendous candidate for the party in Massachusetts. He is like his brother, he talks like his brother, he looks like his brother. He's got all the advantages of the image. He makes a good candidate for that reason.

An old-time Irish ward politician who was close to McCormack said:

> I honestly believe the Americans of Irish extraction look up to the Kennedys as royal blood. . . . They like John Kennedy because he's Irish and Catholic and has taken them up a few steps socially. . . . Everybody realizes and recognizes the Kennedys are all wealthy. Now, a lot of people say, if I had a lot of money I'd be enjoying myself, I'd be over in the Riviera, I'd be cutting out coupons, but these people want to serve the public. And this is the great thing they have going for them. They are not ones to sit back and enjoy the money that they've inherited or compiled over the years; they want to do something useful. And this in the Irish makes them proud. I'm sure this is the basic thing among the Irish, to know the Kennedys is a social step upward. Everyone will tell you they've pictures of the President in their homes, these Irish people, Americans of Irish extraction. And they'll tell you, oh yes, I knew Rose Fitzgerald when she lived up in Wells Avenue. Or I knew Honey Fitz when he came out to speak at a communion breakfast fifteen years ago.

A. A. Michelson, of the *Berkshire Eagle*, adroitly stated the issue: "There is a sort of 'princely' effect in the Ted Kennedy campaign. In any dynasty the king is respected and obeyed, but everyone loves the prince, and Ted Kennedy seems to have that attraction, wherever he goes."[12]

*   *   *

Delegates to the state convention, the first voters in the Kennedy-McCormack contest, are elected by ward and town committees from among their own membership. The law establishing the committees was drafted so that only those who are most interested in state and local politics are likely to participate in the election of committee members. Members are elected in April of every fourth year, during the presidential preferential primary. The turnout in these elections rarely exceeds 10 per cent of the people eligible to vote, and the overwhelming majority of those

12 *Berkshire Eagle*, April 7, 1962.

who do vote are professional politicians, elected officials, state and municipal employees, their families and friends, and others taken to the polls by the "pros" who wish to control the ward committee in order to control the selection of delegates.

A small number of professionals therefore play a decisive role in the election of ward and city committee members and ultimately, therefore, in the election of delegates. Although the power structure within many ward and city committees is such that delegates cannot be dictated to, thousands of committee members are elected only because local influentials recruit them, have their names placed on committee slates, and use their influence to elect them. Hundreds of delegates vote as they are requested to by the local mayor, state representative, or city chairman in return for favors tendered them by him in the past. Those who seek the convention endorsement must ally themselves, then, with local political notables.

The chairman of a ward committee in Boston described the process by which he kept his status as a political notable and got out the vote:

> You got to get people who you can drag out. . . . Most people aren't aware there's elections going on, so what you do is you carry on a campaign three ways: First is you get your people who you're friendly with in the entire ward and you have to nail them down and tell them we're going to pick you up by automobile. . . . Secondly, you concentrate on areas — large apartments or projects where you can go to the doors, you have an automobile downstairs, you take the housewives out and you bring them down to the polls and you bring them back. And the third is around four or five o'clock if you go down to Egleston Square with about ten or fifteen automobiles . . . with a loudspeaker, and you ask who wants rides, we'll take you to the polls before you get a ride home. Usually in rush hours a lot of people will do it. Fourth is your contact with every union member in the area . . . for example, the ILGWU alone has five hundred-odd members in Ward 14. We make sure they're registered, the Hebrew Bakers' Union, the Hebrew Butchers' Union, they must have about three hundred, and hat shop and millinery workers, the

Amalgamated, a lot of needle-trades workers there. . . . It's a question of work. Very few people will go out to vote by themselves. . . .

The apathy of the electorate is extremely important to the professionals; a very small turnout symbolizes to them the absence of any significant opposition. It is customary in many Massachusetts towns and cities for state representatives and senators, mayors, selectmen, county commissioners, city councilmen, and other local officials to propose slates of committee members composed of old friends and relatives, for whom they have done favors in the past, and those who are likely to need succor in the future. To insure election in an average Boston ward it is necessary to receive perhaps three or four hundred votes.

One state representative, who has controlled his ward committee for many years, said:

When we decide to put up a ward committee to choose delegates there has to be a leader. . . . I want to control those ten delegates. I am the leader. I put on my slate people who are friends of mine . . . people who I know, trust, love, and respect me and my judgment. I don't pick guys from all over the ward who think they are generals too. There's only room for one general on a team. . . . Less than 5 per cent of the people vote in the presidential primary. So therefore all it is is a case of you and your fifteen-man committee . . . getting their friends out to vote for this particular slate, and that's what we do. And you have to win. It doesn't enhance my reputation if I lose a ward-committee fight when four or five months later I have to run for "rep." They say, "Hey, you know who beat him? A nobody in the ward committee fight." . . . I made two hundred phone calls, and I got two hundred and fifty people, or about 15 per cent of the vote in my ward. . . . And I tried to get my people to do the same thing in each of their precincts, which, of course, they don't. They don't have the same ability to get people out because they're not office holders. They're just everyday good people who are not politicians but who will go on the ballot as ward committeemen. So you elect fifteen ward committeemen, and of those fifteen, that group sits down and they choose the ten who will be delegates. And that's why you have to control eight of the fifteen votes.

The process by which this state representative recruited his slate and campaigned for its election is typical of what occurs in a substantial majority of towns and cities in Massachusetts.

In many wards the task of the leader is simplified if he happens to have, in addition to friends and political dependents, some relative who is willing to run for the ward committee. One staunch Kennedy supporter described the basis of his control in terms that would be appropriate if he were discussing the power structure that makes politics a closed family corporation in so many Southern towns:

> My mother is the secretary, my closest friend is treasurer, another individual is the vice chairman; the other delegate, a county worker, and his mother are members of the committee, and one other relative of mine, and three other close friends. There is only one other individual on the committee that I'm sure I couldn't count on ten times out of ten. Only one out of ten. . . .

The local political leader invests considerable effort in ward and town committee campaigns because his control of the committee and the delegates will ultimately enhance his position in the community power structure and perhaps even increase the likelihood that he will be able to fulfill more grandiose political ambitions. He runs slates for ward committees, urges friends and neighbors to vote in presidential preferential primaries, and supervises the election of delegates because he wishes to place in his debt those candidates for state-wide and national office who seek the convention endorsement and who, if elected, will be in a position to grant or expedite the favors and patronage he needs to secure his power in the local community. Candidates need the support of state representatives and senators, mayors, county commissioners, city councilmen, and sheriffs who can influence delegates; these officials, in turn, need the good will and political indebtedness of state and national office holders and their colleagues. A bond of mutual dependence thus exists between the controller of votes at the convention and the seeker of the endorsement. A state representative supporting Kennedy made this quite explicit:

> I am the elected representative in my district, right? So when we decide to put up a ward committee to choose delegates, there has to be a leader. There's a leader in every group, maybe two leaders in some groups; the smaller the group, the more sure you are of having one leader that controls four or five votes. This I believe in strongly. When I put up a ward committee slate and I have ten delegates on it, I want to control those ten delegates. I'm the leader. If they want something — they have to go through me. I want to control those ten votes. I don't want to put my neck out, run for ward committee, run as a delegate, have ten votes and have nine different ideas on who they should vote for. If they have to go to Ted Kennedy, Chub Peabody, John Volpe — whoever the candidate may be, for a favor or for some consideration or some legislative interest they may have, who do they go through as delegates? They go through the leader: me. So in order to be closer to the candidates who are running for office, I want that candidate to know — you come out to Ward _____, you see me. I'm the votes there. And that's how it works.

That *is* how it works in most wards because the majority of those who are active in the precincts and wards are unskilled and semiskilled laborers, owners of small businesses, lawyers whose practice depends primarily on political connections, town, city, and state employees, elected petty officials, politicians who prefer not to hold public office, state legislators, and their relatives and friends. Their stake in politics is often material. Their livelihood frequently depends in part upon their political contacts. Their position in the political pecking order, one state representative suggested, depends on their reputation as "go through, do favor, type guys." The loyalties of thousands of committeemen, the decisions of hundreds of delegates, and the alliances of scores of influential politicians depend upon a myriad of calculations, most of which are made in terms of their felt needs and their immediate or future political advantage. Convention in-fighting and political wheeling and dealing are dominated by a relatively small number of professonals who can influence the votes of four, six, or in a few cases, ten or fifteen delegates.

Some political scientists deny that significant numbers of delegates can be influenced. The old-style ward bosses, they argue, have disappeared now that the federal government has assumed their former role as social worker and economic benefactor. The fact remains, however, that hundreds of ward committee members in Massachusetts from depressed areas and low-income city wards need help and are willing to follow the lead of local politicians who provide it. The favor requested is often petty — the provision of a temporary summer job on a state highway, admittance to a state hospital or a state school, the expediting of a state income tax refund, the return of a suspended motor vehicle license; nevertheless, local leaders who have political contacts and who can satisfy these demands create a backlog of political debts and gratitude which they can convert into votes, loyal ward committeemen, obliging delegates, and political power.

Ward chairmen, particularly from low-income areas, entrench themselves in the local political elite because they attend the needy (who vote) and assiduously develop skills as errand boys and political brokers. One city chairman, who managed to bring about the election of several McCormack delegates, described in graphic terms his primary function in the political system and the source of his influence in the city committee:

> People would come here . . . with all types of problems, like a license — they lost their license. They want advice on some problem that they're having. It's all imaginary but you see what's happened now, government's gotten to be so complicated and the average guy is lost; it's more — it's so remote from him, all these forms you have to fill out, all these regulations. Well, people come here every day. They could do it themselves. You just tell them to go to — but they want you. They feel — they created the impression that they have to have somebody intercede for them. They don't. But they got that in their minds. You see, they want you to pick up the phone — will you call and tell them I'm coming. You see,

you don't even have to do it. . . . But it's been created in the public's mind that the government's so vast and that it's impersonal — that you've got to have somebody pass the word for ya. It isn't so, but that's what's working for the political leader. The political leader isn't dead — the boss isn't dead. The bosses are going to be stronger if they keep making more of these laws. I can see this every day. The more laws they make, the more the voter, as you would say, feels alienated. He feels remote from the government. It's too big, too complicated. He can't cope with it.

His counterpart in the Kennedy camp, a favor-doer of long standing, reported that he "cashes in" on his reputation as a "good guy" by appealing to delegates on a personal basis. "Some of them owe me their life. I put it on a personal basis. . . . Well, fellow, you asked me to do many things for you and I've always done 'em for you. Do you owe McCormack anything? No, I don't owe McCormack anything. Well, you owe me something, don't you? Will you pay back by voting for Kennedy? It's that type of routine." This "type of routine" is standard in many ward and city committees. Delegates customarily have closer ties to the ward chairman than to the candidates. Their decision to vote for a particular candidate has little, if anything, to do with the candidate. But by supporting the chairman's choice they not only repay their "debts" but also ingratiate themselves with the chairman, whose services may be necessary in the future. Quid pro quo between delegates and the local leaders is the basis upon which hundreds of votes at the convention are cast.

To engage in quid pro quo with his committee members and delegates, however, the local leader must support an endorsee who ultimately is elected and therefore able to "pay him back" for his support at the convention. He must be with a winner. He may therefore be forced to support a likely winner who promises him less than a likely loser who promises him more. In either case, his decision is almost totally unrelated to the candidate's stand on issues and very strongly related to his own felt and pragmatic political needs.

Perhaps the classic example of this process was reported by a ward committeeman — a Kennedy man — who described how and why a particular state representative is able to control thirty-one votes and how he operates on the floor of the convention:

> We are talking now about an individual who represents a ward in Boston. His best friend represents the next-door ward in Boston. The brother-in-law of the second man is a ward chairman of another ward in Boston. You have three wards now. Each ward has approximately, well — one has ten, one has ten, and one has eleven or twelve delegates. By ruling of the city-committee chairman in Boston, no ward delegation may have more than fifteen members. This sets a maximum limit. This means that as a practical political problem, anyone with eight votes controls that ward committee. That's all you need, eight votes. When you have a representative from a ward, he has his brothers, his wife, his sister-in-law, his cousins, and three or four fellows that he's done favors for. In this particular case I would say they don't need eight, they have fourteen or fifteen in each one of those wards. And they have this through friendship because they are state leaders, because he is a state representative, or because they have some direct practical influence over his economic way of life or something the individual did in the past. All these things combine, this one individual . . . his best friend controls the ward beside him, and his best friend's brother-in-law, who is also friendly with this representative, controls another ward not too far away in Boston. So therefore this one man has these three wards, and he does what he wants with them.

Apparently there were other delegates who were interested in making the best deal. According to an office holder who has attended several conventions, many delegates and committee chairmen do not care who receives the endorsement. Like small nations, they profess neutrality in order to strike the best possible bargain with the major powers.

I'll give you two specific examples of this, . . . the delegates from _____ and _____. . . . Of course both sides have been trying to move in and win them over, and these fellows have said, "Look, we don't care for Mc-

Cormack, we don't care for Kennedy. Basically it doesn't make any difference to us who the nominee is in the party. We are sitting tight. We're uncommitted" — the feeling being that if they can sit tight and remain uncommitted, and this is a tight fight, then they are going to be in a position to bargain with either side and make the best possible bargain for themselves. When I say bargain, I'm thinking largely in terms of patronage jobs. . . .

The delegates described above are obviously extreme examples of what Edward McCormack termed "soup kitchen politics." Both are nevertheless representative of the majority of ward chairmen. However, many delegates are not concerned with making "the best deal." A sizable minority of the delegates to Democratic conventions in Massachusetts — perhaps one-fifth — are, in fact, middle-class professionals, businessmen, academics, and housewives who are not interested in the loaves and fishes of party patronage. Very few aspire to public office or seek political jobs or favors. Their participation in Democratic precinct and ward politics stems from their commitment to the principles of the New Deal and the New Frontier. They are antagonistic to the current leadership of the state party, and they hope that their efforts at the grass roots will ultimately lead to party and governmental reform. They are not beholden to local political leaders and they cannot be told for whom to vote at a state convention. Many seek election as delegates in order to endorse candidates who advocate their economic and social ideas or their concept of party reform.

One of the most affluent and better-educated delegates, a Kennedy supporter, who belongs to the "reform" wing of the party, estimated that

probably a third of the delegates are making their selection on an ideological base . . . but I think that for many people, the impetus for their enthusiasm for a candidate stems from the fact that either they expect something eventually in the way of a job for friends or, believe it or not, many of them just like the idea of being able to call a candidate by his first name. It gives them a certain amount of status.

A young politician who supported Edward Kennedy because he said it was "politically wise" to do so suggested:

> Delegates in general are self-seeking, non-educated, very pro-
> vincial, uncomplicated, simple individuals. . . . The cities
> are the worst offenders, the major Democratic wards of cities
> are usually slum or semi-slum areas. Individuals who are
> delegates are usually a, let's say, . . . a medium-to-poor law-
> yer who has been active in the party; his wife, who perhaps
> does not know a Republican from a Democrat, except that
> she votes the way her husband does; the policeman on the cor-
> ner; a fireman or two; a house-painter — very low social and
> economic level in general. . . . As you move out to the other
> wards in the cities, and by that I mean close to the suburban
> areas, where they have seven or eight thousand average in-
> come . . . , you'll find . . . quite a few more lawyers, a few
> executives, a better class of people in the sense of higher eco-
> nomic class, higher social class, higher literacy rate . . . and
> yet not the type of people that you sometimes feel should be
> making these decisions. In other words, they are not the most
> aware people in terms of politics. . . . In the downtown area,
> you have barbers, and you have a lot of city workers and you
> have a few union leaders, and in general not a very outstand-
> ing group. Now there are exceptions. In areas you'll find a
> rising, young capable lawyer. Or a young fellow that's in the
> insurance business, that happens to take an interest in the
> party. There are exceptions, but not many. In the towns,
> it's a little bit better. . . . A leading candidate for the office
> of governor said to me . . . once every two years these fel-
> lows are big men and they try to make the most, and that's
> very true. They drink more than any group of people I've
> ever seen in my life. They eat more . . . they make more
> noise and they, in general, are not very pleasant company.
> There are many exceptions but in general they are not the
> type of people that one would hope they would be. . . .

A very different interpretation was offered by a university
professor who served on the Kennedy brain trust:

> I thought the reporters from out of town, in a way, missed the
> real character of the convention. They came in there with a

lot of stereotypes from *The Last Hurrah* and what they saw was Sonny McDonough and Knocko McCormack and Mucker McGrath — and that's all they wanted to see. But if you went down to the floor and walked around you saw an awful lot of staid, sober, middle-class people. . . . I thought that when they had this long delay before they started the senatorial nomination . . . I said, O Lord, there are going to be more guys down there rolling around. Give those guys three hours and any number of them are going to go out and get plastered. I didn't see a single drunken person at that convention at any time. . . . This just is not old-time politics. . . . I thought there were a lot of straightforward middle-class people there, business, professional, and so on.

Many "straightforward middle-class people" were delegates to the convention, but they were heavily outnumbered by professional politicians, office-holders, and the delegates whom they latter recruited and could therefore strongly influence. If our analysis of the power structure of the convention makes sense — if the "pros" vote in terms of felt needs and political expediency, in terms of quid pro quo, in terms of which candidate is likely to win — and if it is true that several hundred delegates are handpicked by professionals because of their loyalty and indebtedness to local political notables, then it is obvious, *at least in retrospect,* that McCormack could not possibly have won the endorsement because the patronage power available to the Kennedys, real and potential, far outweighed that available to the McCormacks. A state representative or senator who asked himself whether support for Kennedy or McCormack at the convention would be more likely to enhance his political career would have had to answer in favor of the President's brother.

Regardless of how well-organized or disorganized, how active or passive, how rich or poor, were Kennedy and McCormack, the dynamics of the 1962 convention were ultimately determined by the fact that the President of the United States and his Attorney General were infinitely more powerful than the Speaker of the United States House of Representatives. The manner in which Edward Kennedy and Edward McCormack campaigned for delegate support, the arguments they presented, and the offers they made were based on the relative power and influence of their office-holding relatives. The arithmetic of presidential power, more than any other factor, structured the situation. Again, we emphasize that this is obvious in retrospect. It was not so obvious in January of 1962, five months prior to the convention.

* * *

Although the McCormack forces appreciated the position of strength from which Edward Kennedy launched his campaign for delegates, they had, in the months preceding the convention, some reasons to be optimistic. John and Edward McCormack had made themselves "available" to "needy" and "'deserving" Democrats during their forty-four years in elective office. They had cultivated the friendship and gratitude of state legislators, mayors, aldermen, city and town clerks, county commissioners, sheriffs, and public employees, by maintaining a policy of "the open door." They were masters of the game of personalized politics as it is practiced in Massachusetts, and they assumed that the "regulars" would reciprocate at Springfield.

Many months before the convention, and for these reasons, advisers even suggested that Kennedy bypass the convention, claim that he did not believe in party bosses and "politicians," and take his case directly to the people. This tactic, in their opinion, might not only avoid a major defeat but also reinforce Kennedy's image as a non-politician. It would have been difficult and embarrassing, however, for a brother of the President to ignore a party convention and oppose an endorsee.

Assuming that most of the influential delegates were party regulars who felt a deep attachment to Edward and John McCormack, McCormack's campaign manager analyzed what he thought were the Attorney General's assets:

> I think his advantage lies in the fact that delegates feel some sort of affinity with guys that go through the party wars; and he's been through 'em. He's been on the ballot fifteen times; he's known as a party man, a guy that's held up the party banner. He's known as a guy with a democratic policy, insofar

as having people come in and see him. . . . This guy can talk in terms of union men, working men, laborers. He's a non-Brahmin and this, delegate-wise, I think means a great deal.

Before it was suggested to delegates what a vote for or against the brother of the President might mean for their future, McCormack co-ordinators, in many parts of the Commonwealth, did find that the Attorney General's reputation as a party regular made it easy for them to garner support among the faithful. A McCormack aide in the western part of the state reported that the Attorney General had "a great reservoir of strength" among members of city and town committees.

Most party people have a great deal of respect for the McCormacks. They're very well known in party circles. They are loyal party people. . . . Everybody knows Eddie's reputation. . . . They know how he's conducted office, and so there's no problem. As a matter of fact it was the easiest thing in the world to elect McCormack delegates. They didn't have to work too hard, because the natural inclination of the party people is for McCormack. That's why I think he's going to win, I mean he's just a natural, he's so well known in party circles. He doesn't have to fight hard.

The McCormack campaign for delegates was waged primarily by the candidate himself — contacting delegates on the telephone — and several assistant attorneys general and old cronies who might have been transformed into a disciplined and effective organization if provided with a modicum of intelligent direction and a little inspiration from the candidate. The attorney general of Massachusetts is empowered by law to appoint twenty-four assistant attorneys general at his pleasure. Twenty-two members or former members of McCormack's staff were delegates to the convention, and most of them were influential members of local political elites. Several assistant attorneys general and other employees in McCormack's office spent much time working on the campaign while on the state payroll, standard operating procedure for many years in Massachusetts. One delegate predicted that this hard core of assistants would be most effective in wooing delegates because McCormack

> made sure that these assistants got themselves elected as delegates or got their friends elected delegates or got their cousins elected delegates. So he's got a pretty good organization of maybe forty people himself . . . who are political people, every one of them. He made a few appointments because he needed a few legal minds. But he was able to find good legal people who were also, in many instances, good Democratic politicians, from various geographic parts of the state.

In addition to his personal staff, McCormack received aid from some adept and highly practical party professionals, who supported him out of a deep sense of personal loyalty. He also received the support of many liberals, academics, and civil libertarians who had supported John Kennedy in 1960. This group included approximately fifteen members of the Harvard, Brandeis, Boston University, and Boston College faculties who formed the McCormack brain trust; the president of Americans for Democratic Action; the former head of the Boston branch of the NAACP; and several members of COD, a Democratic party reform group. The aphorism that "politics makes strange bedfellows" was applicable to the McCormack organization. Party hacks and patronage-hungry ward heelers, little concerned with ideology, joined hands with liberal intellectuals who were impressed by McCormack's stand on civil liberties, civil rights, and the death penalty.

A member of the McCormack entourage described this strange and seemingly incompatible melange as

> . . . a very unusual combination. He's got all the liberals, he's got most of the Jews. . . . The ADA people or the COD people are with him because of the fact that Eddie McCormack has been a great champion of civil rights, civil liberties, against capital punishment, against wiretapping. He's been for the things that they're for, and against the things that they're against, and they have stood by him. And this is not easy for some of these people, because they also like the Administration. . . . They're always with Jack Kennedy and

he's also a great liberal. . . . The Kennedy people are very upset that all these liberals are against them. . . .

Then he's got another group . . . the professional politicians. . . . They're more at home with a guy like Eddie McCormack than they are with the Kennedys. They've never been friendly with Kennedy. . . . A lot of hardened, real tough, real professional pols . . . are with Eddie McCormack because he's John McCormack's nephew, and they know John, they've done favors for him, they've worked for him. They love John McCormack and they want to be with him. . . . Now, John McCormack is also making phone calls . . . doing a lot of work. He's feeling very bitter about this, very upset that there's any possibility that this kid can beat his nephew. . . . And don't forget that during the whole Truman-Roosevelt administration, John McCormack was the chief dispenser of federal patronage here in Massachusetts. . . . These are the old-time guys that really have a feeling of loyalty and are doing it for what's been done in the past and for the associations of the past and because they like Eddie and they like John, and they feel that this is right, and they've stuck by it.

The strategy McCormack utilized in his drive for delegates was based primarily on an appeal to his record and to his uncle's reputation as a favor doer. To the party-oriented he stressed his role as a loyal party man; to the patronage-oriented he stressed the fact that he had cleared all appointments through local city and ward committees; to the liberals he emphasized his support of civil liberties, his opposition to the death penalty and to wiretapping, and his stand on behalf of anti-discrimination legislation in housing. To counter the charge that he was a dynastic candidate, McCormack recalled that he had started at the bottom and served a long apprenticeship, despite the power and influence of his uncle.

In mid-April the Attorney General gave a luncheon for Democratic members of the state legislature at which he appealed for their support. According to a former legislator, a major speechwriter for McCormack, the Attorney General spoke more or less as follows:

First of all, I appreciate the fact that you are attending here. Many times in the past — certainly every time I have run in the past — I have attempted to get the members of the legislature together as a body to ask them for their support. I am doing the same thing now. I realize that there are tremendous pressures which are going to be brought to bear and have been brought to bear upon you in this fight. All I say to you is this . . . I deeply appreciate the support you have given to me in the past in my campaigns. Without that kind of support I never could have won, because I know of the great influence legislators can be in the carrying on of political campaigns. And I know that many legislators have opened doors for me in communities at the local level which I could not have opened in my campaigns in the past without their help and assistance. I want your help and assistance in this fight. I am not going to embarrass any member of the legislature by putting you on the spot and asking you directly, Are you going to be with me or are you not? . . . These are decisions you must make for yourself. You have your problems, you have your own situations to consider, but I want your help. . . . If you can't be with me in this fight all I ask of you is this: If anybody in your district says to you, What kind of a fellow is Eddie McCormack, what kind of an attorney general has Eddie McCormack been, then, whether you're with me or you're against me, I ask you to be honest and to point out to them that . . . my door has always been open to members of the legislature who have come to me with problems involving constituents or problems affecting their district. Tell them about what I've done for you as a legislator even if you're not with me. Don't distort or don't attempt to malign me because of the fact that you're with my opponent. All I ask of you if you're not with me at least be honest in telling them how I have tried to do a job as attorney general. . . .

The McCormack "approach," which one aide called "the soft sell," was also followed by several aides, who made thousands of telephone calls to delegates prior to the convention. For example:

Well, it depends on whom I was talking to. When I'm talking to a liberal, I put it up to him quite flatly that they cannot afford to let McCormack down after what he has done for liberals in this state. . . . There is still the question of whether a Boston Irish politician really feels these things in his heart or is he doing it for political expediency, and my only answer to that . . . is that you can't psychoanalyze these political candidates. . . . If the Democratic party is going to be built into something that . . . has some meaning, . . . when it gets a candidate who does a good job in public office, . . . we should reward him. . . . It is important to those who come after the McCormacks and the Kennedys — people who are going to be candidates for office in the future — that they be able to look back and say, "Well, the Democratic party will not let you down if you do a good job," whereas on the other hand, if they look back and see that McCormack had a brilliant career as Attorney General and then was booted out for young Ted Kennedy when he came along, I argue that it would demoralize the whole party and we'd be right back where we started from, . . . [with] personal factions. . . . If he says he's for Kennedy, . . . I ask him why. . . . I try to shame him if he's got no particular reason. . . . Now we need a new look to the Democratic party and look at all the corruption in Massachusetts and we got to have a winner and then you rationalize it. But basically you'll find many people for Kennedy because their political enemies are for McCormack and I suppose this works vice versa too.

In the tradition of the old-style Massachusetts politician, McCormack contacted delegates primarily through lieutenants in the field, in contrast to Kennedy, who personally visited perhaps thirteen hundred of them. The Attorney General telephoned almost every delegate but his campaign for delegate support, in contrast to the Kennedy campaign, was amateurish and apathetic. His aides rationalize this fact by pointing out that, unlike Kennedy, the Attorney General could not campaign full time because he was forced to attend to the duties of his office. Be that as it may, McCormack does not enjoy the rigors of campaigning as much as Kennedy does; he does not meet people easily, as Kennedy does; and he is not as facile as Kennedy with the handshake, the smile, and the quick hello.

A member of the Kennedy brain trust characterized the difference:

> . . . actually it was expressed to me by one of the McCor-
> mack workers, and he said, "While Eddie is working on dele-
> gations . . . Teddy is working on delegates." And he illus-
> trated, McCormack would telephone [a city committee chair-
> man] and say, "Well, how's the delegation?" And [the man]
> would say, "Great, solid, you have nothing to worry about.
> Practically solid." All the time, Kennedy was in there, not
> using the buckshot approach but using the rifle-shot ap-
> proach, working on individuals. And there's no question
> that [the committee chairman] was very astounded when he
> saw the results of that vote [in his area]. . . . In a way,
> Eddie used more of an old-style approach. He worked with
> the people of influence . . . instead of working with indi-
> viduals. . . . The Kennedy approach was just what they
> used in Los Angeles, but on a smaller scale. Now, I don't
> pretend to know what that was altogether. But it was, you
> know, the names of all the delegates. And when you know as
> much as you can about each one, then you approach them
> . . . individually. And the candidate sees them. . . . Ken-
> nedy saw 85 per cent of the delegates. A heroic effort, physi-
> cally. And then, of course, he had other people who pre-
> sumably had influence see them, who knew them or were
> friends.

Although McCormack and his aides utilized the "soft sell" on most occasions, their approach apparently changed a few days before the convention, when it became obvious to them that Kennedy had a substantial lead. At this time McCormack enlisted the support of John Thompson, Speaker of the Massachusetts House of Representatives, and William Callahan, Chairman of the Massachusetts Turnpike Authority and former Commissioner of the Department of Public Works. Many liberals in Massachu-setts place much of the responsibility for the political condition of the Bay State on these two men. Callahan, now dead, was often referred to by his detractors — and not without cause — as "the most powerful man in Massachusetts." One prominent Republi-can legislator frequently called him "The Maharaja of the Macadam." Because of his power to grant contracts worth hundreds of millions of dollars and thousands of jobs, Callahan was in a position to apply considerable pressure on delegates, particularly those delegates who were state legislators with needy constituents.

Thompson, also now dead, was known in the House as "The Iron Duke" and "The Czar" because of his arbitrary tactics, joined Callahan in a frantic effort to convert delegates to the McCormack cause. Newspapers reported that a steady stream of legislators committed to Kennedy were seen entering and leaving the Speaker's office during the few days prior to the convention. Their efforts failed.

*　　*　　*

Edward Kennedy's campaign for delegate support, like John Kennedy's pre-convention campaign for the presidential nomination, was a "heroic" effort in terms of the candidate's seemingly inexhaustible capacity to contact, cajole, and charm delegates. It was meticulously planned, well staffed and financed, and executed to the last detail. The Kennedy approach varied from delegate to delegate; in some cases ideological commitment was the bait, in others more conventional fare.

Both Kennedy pre-convention situations were analogous in several ways. At first the Kennedys were conceded relatively little chance of winning their party's endorsement. Edward Kennedy's chances, of course, were considerably better than John Kennedy's — for obvious reasons. Nevertheless, Edward was considered to be the underdog, perhaps an advantage. Five months before the convention it would have been difficult to find many Democratic politicians in Massachusetts who believed that Kennedy would soundly defeat McCormack for the party's endorsement. Most of those active in ward and city politics throughout the state, as we have noted, were old friends of the McCormacks who had committed themselves to support the Attorney General during the early spring. Several had already begun to use their influence among ward and city committee members to insure the election of pro-McCormack delegates.

Although Edward Kennedy had been warmly received by groups of voters throughout the state for several months before he announced his candidacy, neither he nor the President had deep roots within the state party organization. John Kennedy was viewed with some suspicion by many Irish politicians from South Boston, who did not feel very comfortable with a Harvard-educated Irish Brahmin, in part because John Kennedy had largely bypassed them during his 1952 and 1958 campaigns for the Senate by creating his own personal organization of "Kennedy Secretaries." While in the Senate, too, he remained more or less aloof from the problems of the state Democratic party. The "Balkanization" of state Democratic politics — the internecine warfare among feudatories and their ethnic retainers — and the corruption continued, perhaps even expanded, during the 1950's while John Kennedy concentrated his efforts on national and international politics in preparation for his bid for the presidency. State party reform was not among his primary concerns.

Edward Kennedy's campaign manager, familiar with this situation, pointed out that the Kennedy forces were at a serious disadvantage during the early stages of the campaign because

> . . . many of the Kennedy people . . . had never really been involved in delegate situations, in delegate problems; involved in the knockdown, dragout, primary fight situation. Many of them are excellent workers, but they have never been involved in a real close fight. We found ourselves in a great deal of difficulty with the Attorney General because he had a built-in core of people, mainly his attorney generals and his special assistant attorney generals . . . and these people have the know-how. They've moved in delegate fights before . . . at least our opponents know the names and numbers of all those people. Initially we lacked people with know-how that could go into some of these areas and do the job for us early.

Fortunately for his candidate, many of the "Kennedy Secretaries" who had worked for John Kennedy in 1952 and 1958 still lived in Massachusetts and remained loyal to the Kennedys. "What you've got to remember," one former Kennedy Secretary remarked, "Kennedy did not begin from scratch."

It may look as though he started from scratch, but he inherited his brother's campaign committee. Of course, he had

to go around and ask them to work for him. . . . He called
me up one day and I said, "What, where, and when?" and
went to work. . . . He had places or spheres of influence where
he could go . . . we went to these various cities and towns all
over Massachusetts, and I don't think there was a city or town
we didn't go into. What we did then is we picked up what we
call cleancut young men . . . people that were unspoiled in
the art of politics . . . key men in every section of Massachusetts. At that time I had quite a discussion with the President as to what to call them, and there was talk about calling
them chairmen, and I said, "Call them chairmen, you're in
trouble." We called them secretaries, to give the impression
that ultimately we're going to have a chairman in every section, and that was what created the original secretaries of
Kennedy. Now from that spawned this other tremendous
campaign committee. . . . So this young Ted, he has inherited as they say *that* organization, plus all the other
friends that Jack had made over the years.

The Kennedys did not really lack "know-how." They had
developed several very sophisticated techniques for dealing with
delegates and delegations in 1959 and they had numerous and
loyal lieutenants and members of the family who were familiar
with that special brand of politicking appropriate to conventions.
One of the family even moved to Massachusetts during the
late spring of 1962 to manage Edward Kennedy's campaign. The
President's brother-in-law, Stephen Smith, established himself in
Boston at the Ritz-Carlton Hotel and took over control of the
Kennedy operation. Although he was not the "official" campaign
manager, he did, in fact, direct the quest for delegates. Smith
and Edward Kennedy made the critical decisions, often after con-
sultation with Washington.

Stephen Smith had played an active role in John Kennedy's
presidential campaign and was thoroughly familiar with the techniques utilized by the Kennedys prior to and during the Los
Angeles convention. He applied them to the Massachusetts situation, but always behind the scenes. He granted no interviews.
He made no public statements. He remained in Kennedy's Boston headquarters where he carefully worked on the first two

problems of the pre-convention campaign: the determination
of who "controls" Democratic state conventions and the gathering of a complete case history for every delegate.

The Kennedys, like the McCormacks, assumed that ultimately a small group of men and women "control" a relatively
large number of delegates to the convention. One ward chairman, a staunch Kennedy supporter, spelled out this assumption:

> As you know, the convention is really controlled by . . . a
> hundred people, each of whom may control an average of six
> or seven delegates. . . . The key people are state representa-
> tives, or state senators, or state committeemen, constitutional
> officers, and one or two congressmen. . . . They control more
> delegates than anybody else . . . and that's the way conven-
> tions work. . . . There may be ten or fifteen people that can
> control a substantial number of delegates and these ten or
> fifteen people agree on what to do. They swing the conven-
> tion whatever way they want to.

Months before the Springfield conclave Edward Kennedy
and his colleagues attempted to identify these men and assess the
number of delegates that each was reputed to control. Through
an extensive series of conferences with the leaders of both
branches of the state legislature — mostly arranged by Judge Morrissey — and innumerable telephone calls to former delegates and
personal visits with ward committee members, the candidate and
his agents gradually came to know who could govern the selection
of delegates, who was amenable to persuasion, and who was committed to the opposition. A state representative described the
earliest phase of the Kennedy pre-convention operation:

> They have a sixth sense. They apparently seek out, as quickly
> as possible, who the key people are. Early in the campaign
> they didn't go around seeing all the sixteen hundred dele-
> gates, because they were smart enough to find out through a
> beautiful operation — they had checks and cross-checks and
> cross-checks on the cross-checks — they would make phone
> calls, they would talk to the delegates: "Who was the key per-
> son?" Then they'd have another person call them . . . and

they'd keep doing this . . . and they'd know what votes you
did or did not control.

To compete seriously with McCormack, Kennedy had to
convince the more powerful state representatives, state senators,
and others who might influence committee members that their
future interest, or that of the party, would be best served by entering into an alliance with him. Given the arithmetic of presidential power it is not surprising that some of the potentates of the
party quickly saw the point. The President of the state Senate,
one of the state's most powerful Democrats, joined the Kennedy
camp along with the majority floor leader and six or seven state
senators.

Although Kennedy did not ignore the older, more seasoned
professional politicians, he made a special effort to attract the
younger state representatives, senators, mayors, and city councilmen, many of whom were disturbed by the current image of the
party and therefore amenable to the argument that only a Kennedy, with the power of the White House behind him, would be
willing and able to "reform" the party. Said one young representative:

> I'm interested in party reform and I hope and feel that Ted
> Kennedy could do more in this field than his opponent. . . .
> I think it's obvious to him that his brother, the President, did
> nothing to help the state of Massachusetts . . . partly in a
> very selfish vein, because he didn't need state organization to
> win in Massachusetts. Ted Kennedy now needs state or-
> ganization, needs party organization, needs the politician
> where his brother didn't, and I think this is something that
> should be brought back to the President, and I think the situa-
> tion is so far afield party-wise in Massachusetts that unless we
> get some direct impetus from the White House possibly a
> real proper organization of the Democratic party would not
> be possible.

But one politician who refused to become a delegate to the
convention suspected that "Many of these young people that
you might think are young idealists that want to be with Kennedy . . . because they're going to clean up the party, that's bal-

oney. I don't believe that. I believe they're with him because it's best for them."

Some state representatives believed that the party could be reformed only by a candidate who was above suspicion of corruption and free of political entanglements. Although McCormack cleared appointments through town and city committees, he suffered, in their opinion, from his long association with Boston politicians. His opponent, they felt, was untainted. Kennedy attempted to take advantage of this situation by arguing that, if elected, he would try to rejuvenate the state committee, replace its chairman, and restore the city and ward committees to their "proper" place. A Kennedy delegate who is a state legislator described how Kennedy presented his ideas on party reform to a group of delegates:

> They asked him about how he would recognize Democratic committees and they were griping about the fact that no one ever paid any attention to the Democratic delegates except when they want their vote. . . . Ted said he viewed this campaign as one that will reinstitute, if he's elected, the power and stature of the Democratic town committee. That he is there tonight because he recognizes the great importance of the Democratic town committees. . . . He could go up the street . . . and say, I'd like to have Joe Blow run my campaign, rather than down to the Democratic chairman's house and say, I want your support. . . . And he wants to work through the regular party organization, and if he is elected he wants to make it stronger. . . . I think he is interested in political network of and structure of the Democratic party.

His arguments may well have affected their decision. Nevertheless, they undoubtedly believed that an early alliance with the Kennedys could do them no harm and might do them much good. Regardless of their motives, approximately thirty young state representatives joined the Kennedy camp. Almost all of them had carefully selected ward and town committee slates in 1960 and supervised the election of delegates in 1962. Their combined efforts, coupled with those of the President of the state Senate, the majority leader, and a handful of older and unquestionably professional state representatives and senators, assured Kennedy the support of at least 650 delegates out of 1,719. Since most of them were not only well respected in their local communities but also experienced in the particular art of convention politics, many of them served as Kennedy campaign co-ordinators. They introduced the candidate to committee chairmen and delegates outside their immediate bailiwick, arranged dinner parties, contacted headquarters with bits of information about delegates and local political circumstances that permitted the Kennedy forces to ingratiate themselves with the uncommitted. Their efforts, according to Kennedy's campaign manager, were "a very key element in the cities. When I say fifty state representatives and senators together—it's been a key element in the older cities— it's kept us from going right down the drain in places like Lynn, in places like Salem, Beverly, Peabody, in places like New Bedford . . . Worcester . . . Lowell. They've gone in and really done a job." When asked whether Kennedy could have won the endorsement without the support of these legislators, his manager replied, "I believe we'd have lost it."

After Kennedy gained the support of the younger legislators, his staff created an organization modeled after that used by the President during his quest for the party's nomination in 1960. They first assigned a co-ordinator to each of the Commonwealth's forty senatorial districts. Each co-ordinator acted as a liaison officer between the main campaign headquarters in Boston and Kennedy men who wielded some influence in the ward and city committees located in the district. The co-ordinators gathered vital statistics on the delegates from workers in the field and transmitted them to headquarters, where a card containing this information was prepared for every delegate. Stephen Smith maintained the delegates' dossiers, constantly revising them as new data were received. Gradually the Kennedy organization collected thousands of bits of information which were verified, recorded, and then put to good use.

Kennedy's campaign manager described how this information was used:

We take . . . _____, the co-ordinator in that area.

It is his responsibility to know each one of these . . . delegates. He reports weekly to us on the ones that are off, the ones that are on, the ones that are wavering. He reports to us . . . any personal problems that any of these delegates might have . . . any great honors that any one has ever won, pertaining to anything we can do to be of help or service to any of them. Sometimes it's a letter of endorsement to somebody; it's a recommendation to someone else. . . . Before, things were done on a hit-or-miss basis; someone comes in and says, "Oh, this guy is from Quincy, you got to write a letter," and the letter was never written. But Smith always had these worksheets — a letter to Joe Jones, and in another week he'd check it. Has Joe Jones's letter gone out? There was constant control. . . . If a guy went to a church social — a guy who had been with us and said something that might not have been too complimentary to our candidate, we would know that almost the next day. . . . We know where every single vote is. We know who's been talked to. You can give me anybody's name and I can tell you when they've been talked to, who talked to them, and what Teddy has to do — some personal contact, telephone calls — so that we have left nothing to chance, and we've tried to see these people with local people, not a lot of outsiders. . . . [McCormack's people] had an initial advantage which they've thrown out the window. If they had only moved forward with this disciplined corps of assistant attorney generals starting, say, the first of April, we'd be in serious trouble. But they just let them all sit on their hands and now they are all running around like chickens without a head. One of them is rushing from Fall River to West Bridgewater and from West Bridgewater over to Stoughton. You just can't do it that way.

Initially, when we started our control system, the man who was handling West Bridgewater, sure, he got a polite and deferential hello, but after a week or two weeks or three weeks they got to know this guy, to trust him, to like him. So they're going to tell him things and he's not going to rush in all out of breath, "How you going to vote, how you going to vote?" It's just done slowly, deliberately. . . . I think it's very discernible and very perceptible, the last ten days we've picked up and gone right by, and we'll get even stronger.

Although these data were not punched on IBM cards or processed by a computer, Stephen Smith was apparently so familiar with them that he could match an undecided or pro-McCormack delegate with the Kennedy agent who would be most likely to have something in common with him. Said Kennedy's campaign manager:

> We find out, for example, that Joe Jones, from Quincy, is very active in Little League, and we find . . . two or three people very close to Quincy . . . who are with Kennedy. We send one of these people down. They start out at a mutual level of Little League and they talk and they become friends. . . .
>
> There's a fellow in one of the southern towns who . . . thought that he had played baseball with one of Ted Kennedy's rommates. A contact was made. So is there any friendship and he says ya, fine. . . . You find . . . a delegate from, say, Marlboro undecided, but he's always taking a cue from . . . some fellow in Framingham. . . . So when this is noted on a card, you talk to the guy from Framingham, . . . tell him that Ted Kennedy's good for the party, . . . then find out if he belongs to a labor union and what type of work he does. So Ted does see him and talks with him and they talk baseball and they talk football and they talk. . . . It's really a selling problem. . . .

One co-ordinator described the efficiency of the Kennedy operation.

> I see the same general efficiency that I saw in the Los Angeles convention here in Boston. . . . They got a very meticulous organization, as you know, and they got a very beautiful G-4 on everybody and everything. . . . That organization is too mechanical, too precise for a fellow like McCormack to beat it. . . . They have their staff meetings, they have areas assigned all the way down with the regular echelon of command. . . . If you're in a certain district, you call up for a certain man; if you got a certain problem bothering you, you call up somebody else. That man has the last word on the particular phase of the campaign to which he's assigned, and if you ask him about the other fellow's phase of the cam-

paign he couldn't tell you. Now that is something that . . .
I have never seen in any other political campaign, and I've
been involved in a few in the last twenty-five or thirty years.
. . . It's a machine in the true sense of the word. . . . Everybody has got a job to do and every little part of that machine
fits in for a reason.

A state representative who was a little part of that machine,
for example, informed Kennedy that one of his delegates was
unable to attend a Kennedy rally because she had to take her
son to a physician. That evening she received a telephone call
from Kennedy, who said he was sorry that she had been unable to
attend the rally and inquired about her son's health. In her response to a post-election questionnaire she wrote, "You don't find
men like that in today's politics." This attention to detail characterized the Kennedy campaign.

After the organization was firmly established and data on all
the delegates were collected and collated, the Kennedy campaign for delegates moved into what the campaign manager called
a "comprehensive exposure phase." From March 18 to May 7 a
series of parties was arranged for the purpose of introducing the
candidate to as many delegates as possible. At one of these parties, reported an aide, Kennedy made a very effective speech.
"I'm sorry I didn't take a tape of it," he said. "He had these
things right at his fingertips, extemporaneous, no notes. . . . And
if you turned your back on him, you'd swear to God it was the
President half the time." These parties, said Kennedy's campaign manager,

> . . . did make a good impression. The delegates . . . many
> of them, came forward that night and gave a commitment.
> . . . Some held back and waited a little while. . . . And
> then, by process of accretion or accumulation, everybody sud-
> denly became aware of the fact that we had been all over
> the state and we had pretty good exposure. And one group
> started comparing notes with another group. . . . In the
> delegate parties, we were able to make appraisals as to where
> we were strong, weak, who had to be seen, where we could
> get clusters of delegates together. . . .

The "comprehensive exposure phase" included Kennedy's wife. Mrs. Joan Kennedy appeared not only at delegate parties but also at meetings of women's groups and she displayed her talent and experience as a fashion model at the Cardinal Cushing Benefit showing clothing designed by Oleg Cassini. The *Boston Globe* featured a large front-page photograph of her in a white evening gown. "Among all the lovely Boston models," the newspaper reported, "the blond, slender Mrs. Edward Kennedy won first prize with the women."

The final phase of the Kennedy campaign began on May 7, when the candidate intensified his efforts to reach personally all delegates who were not yet pledged to him. In an almost incredible display of energy, he visited approximately thirteen hundred delegates. A McCormack man commented on this activity:

> I don't say he's been in every town, but I guarantee that he's been in 75 to 80 per cent of the towns and cities of Massachusetts. He's been in places like . . . Gill, who ever goes to Gill? This guy went to Gill to see one delegate they've got there. Most people wouldn't know where Gill was, including Eddie McCormack, including Foster Furcolo, including John Kennedy, or you. You know where Gill is? Okay. Anybody in this room know where Gill is? Well, Ted Kennedy has been to Gill. Ted Kennedy has been up and down. He's spent full time and has personally either telephoned or personally seen every one of these delegates. I think that when he started, he was on his back. I think since then he has picked up many, many delegates because he's also a very personable guy, not a bad fella, personable, attractive, decent-looking guy who looks exactly like his brother, talks like his brother, and the Kennedy image that everybody in Massachusetts would love to be on their coattails.

Although Edward Kennedy's political appeal has obviously been enhanced and will continue to be enhanced by the fact that he is a Kennedy, there is no doubt that he is a superbly effective, and energetic, campaigner in his own right. Said Kennedy's campaign manager:

> The greatest thing in the world he likes is for you to say, "There's seven delegates all against you and they want to sit

down and talk to you." "Beautiful," he'd say. "Beautiful!"
He'd go into that room and take his coat off, and the thing always happens — halfway through two of them jump up and
say, "I'm with you!" . . . Go into a hall, one guy will boo
him, and he's the guy, the one guy he seeks out.

Although Kennedy had a substantial majority of the delegates by mid-May, the Kennedy forces were disturbed by the
fact that most of the suburban, affluent, and liberal delegates —
relatively few in number — were pledged to McCormack. They
were also not cheered by the fact that almost every well-known
member of the academic community who publicly declared himself for a senatorial candidate supported McCormack or Hughes.
Kennedy, through his pledge to reform the Democratic party,
however, did win the support of five prominent liberal political
scientists who could and did serve their candidate as a showcase
and brain trust. Kennedy received endorsements from Professor
Robert Wood, of the Massachusetts Institute of Technology, an
expert on urban affairs; Professor Samuel Beer, of Harvard University, former President of Americans for Democratic Action and
an authority on British politics; Professor James McGregor Burns,
of Williams College, a biographer of Presidents Roosevelt and
Kennedy; Professor John Plank, of the Fletcher School of Law
and Diplomacy, a Latin-American specialist; and Professor Norman Greenwald of Brandeis University, an expert on Massachusetts politics and the politics of the Middle East. Professor Wood,
who was later appointed Under Secretary of the Department of
Housing and Urban Affairs by President Johnson, had originally
agreed to help prepare position papers for McCormack.

Prior to the convention, three of these professors announced
in a letter to delegates that their support for Kennedy was based
not on "questions of personality, ability, or views on public policy" but rather on their belief that Kennedy would bring about
a "thorough-going reform of the organization and processes of
the Democratic party in Massachusetts." Although these men are
well known in university circles, they had little or no luck in
converting the academic community to the Kennedy cause.

One Kennedy brain truster explained his choice in the following terms:

> I would like to give you the view of the academic group in regard to Ted Kennedy's candidacy, because it takes a certain amount of thought on our part to support a very young man. Our major consideration is that here is a candidate who can serve as an excellent technician in Washington. We are especially impressed by the need in Washington today of people who have the capacity and the technical skill to make our system of government work. It is no longer a matter of formulating new programs and presenting them to the nation. It is primarily a question in Washington today of implementing programs that have been well debated, well thought out, and seem very desirable to the nation. And we feel that Teddy, in spite of his youth, in spite of his political inexperience, can do much more in Washington for the nation in making the machinery of government work. . . . People talk about Kennedy power. But certainly the defeat of the Kennedy administration on the major proposals is indicative that perhaps the President does not have enough power. And in terms of capacity and political savvy, we feel that Ted would make the best contribution to the nation at this time. That is, someone who can work with a new system, someone who has a sense of direction and, more important, has the personal capacity, as we have been able to judge it. We may well be wrong, but this is our view of Ted among the other candidates, that he has the capacity to push through much-needed programs, more capacity than the others. We think, for example, that the great failing of McCormack is that he is not forceful, that he is probably a reasonably liberal person, a person who would make a good senator for Massachusetts. We're convinced . . . that he could not possibly win because of . . . the fact that he has been Attorney General at a critical time, the fact that he has not done much on the issue of corruption. . . . We think not only that Ted can win against a strong Republican candidate such as Lodge, but that he has the capacity in Washington to make a significant contribution to the advancement of the administration's program.

McCormack's advisers believed Kennedy's promise to reform

the party was opportunistic and insincere. Four years after Edward Kennedy assumed his seat in the Senate and took charge of state party affairs, the Democratic party was in no less disrepair. In 1966 a Republican was Governor, a Republican was Lieutenant Governor, a Republican was Attorney General. Democratic notables continued to oppose convention endorsees, destroy each other in primary elections, vote for Republicans in general elections, and pave the way for Republican victories — despite the fact that a substantial majority of the enrolled voters in Massachusetts are Democrats.

The Kennedy pre-convention operation was impressive and efficient. So was Edward Kennedy's performance. One may, however, ask whether the organization ever would have been set up and how successful it would have been if the candidate had not been the brother of the President and the brother of the United States Attorney General. Although John Kennedy made no speeches in his brother's behalf, although his name did not appear on the list of those who contributed to Edward Kennedy's campaign, and although he advanced no arguments in public in favor of his brother, the President of the United States was the dominant figure during the pre-convention campaign and at the Democratic state convention. His name, power, and prestige were invoked by Edward Kennedy and some of his aides throughout the campaign.

When contacting delegates, Kennedy and his people implied that the candidate could do more for them as well as for Massachusetts. "Win or lose," the *New Republic* stated, "Ted Kennedy from now on will be in charge of patronage for the Kennedy administration in Massachusetts. That word is being quietly spread among the delegates to the state Democratic convention. . . ."[13] Kennedy, according to the same periodical, approached a local politician in the following manner:

"I want you to go along with me," he said in effect. "I want you to travel with me and be seen with me. You're a big man here and I need your help."

The politician, not quite overwhelmed with this flattery, declined on grounds that he had business of his own to attend to. Kennedy called him back for one last word. "All right,"

Kennedy said. "But remember: win or lose, I'm handling the patronage in Massachusetts. . . ."

Ted, who insists he is "running on my own," nevertheless refers to his oldest brother constantly in both public and private talks. He is fond of telling humorous anecdotes about "my brother Jack" and seldom lets them forget whose brother he is. He has charmed many a delegate by saying, abruptly and earnestly, "You know, Jack was asking about you just the other day." The notion of the President of the United States worrying about an obscure politician from Dedham or Watertown is one they do not quite accept, but they like to hear about it just the same.

To a woman legislator, previously cold to him, Ted remarked: "You know, Mary, down in Washington they all say: when you want to know something about southeastern Massachusetts, just ask Mary." She left with stars in her eyes.

One legislator, returning from a conference with Ted, gave this summary: "Teddy's been an Assistant District Attorney for a year or so. He's completely unqualified and inexperienced. He's an arrogant member of an arrogant family." The legislator grinned. "And I'm going to be with him." [14]

In various ways, Kennedy campaign aides implied that a vote for McCormack was a vote against the President or that a vote for McCormack was a vote against federal aid for Massachusetts. In the words of one delegate:

Some of the Kennedy people . . . who were on some of the ward committees [said] . . . that if we don't support Kennedy, . . . we'll lose favor at the White House. How can we go to the White House and ask for favors and get anything for our area unless we support Ted Kennedy?"

Another McCormack delegate reported

. . . telephone calls — telephone calls from dear friends and neighbors who you've known a long time — people calling

13 *New Republic*, June 4, 1962, p. 8.
14 *Ibid.*

you and telling you they're ashamed of you because you're not voting for the Kennedys. Are you mad at the President? I didn't know it was sacrilegious not to vote for a Kennedy. I thought we had a right to vote for whomever we thought was a better man.

An elderly female delegate who supported McCormack told of yet another attempt to win a vote for Kennedy:

Mr. _____ came to my house and he wanted me to vote for Kennedy, and I told him I was sorry. . . . I thought that McCormack was the man. . . . And he said, "Well, now, I'm going to ask you something. Suppose I get the President —I can get him right now on the line. If he comes and asks you would you vote for his brother, what would you say?" I said, "I won't, I won't change."

These delegates, like several others who were interviewed, ex-pressed a deep love for the Kennedys and strong positive feelings for the Democratic party. The lady quoted above remarked, "I love all the Kennedys . . . they're a wonderful family. They're very, very wonderful people." When asked what she liked about the party she responded, "Oh, I love 'em all. I love 'em all. No matter who 'tis, that's the first thing I look to, who's a Demo-crat. I never think of the Republicans." This woman was not interested in patronage and could not be appealed to on that basis. The Kennedy aide, however, knew that she wanted a copy of a photograph of herself and Edward Kennedy that had been taken a few weeks before. She recounted with some pathos, anger, and much regret her final conversation with Kennedy's agent.

When he said that he could get the President right on the line, I said I had always voted for the Kennedys. . . . Then he said, "If you love them, why don't you vote for them?" I said, "I told you the reason." So then I said to him, "What became of the pictures that were taken at the hotel that Sun-day morning?" . . . And I says I'd like to have one. I said, "My picture is among them." And he said, "Well, you wouldn't want a picture when you don't want to vote for him." So I haven't got a picture, although I understood, in fact I talked with . . . [the] state committee woman, and I asked her if she got any of the pictures. She said, "Yes, I've got quite a few of them, but your picture isn't amongst them." So you see, he didn't send my picture.

CHAPTER 2 ☒ *The Lament of Knocko McCormack*

*They're cold, they're cold . . . I got here at 12:30 last night, and I
got in the elevator with an old friend from Northampton. He's
been in the American Legion with me for years, and I say, "Hello,
Commander." And he hangs his head, and he says, "I can't be
with you Knocko." "What do you mean?" says I. "I've been offered a good federal job if I go with Kennedy," says he.*

— EDWARD MC CORMACK'S FATHER, KNOCKO, as quoted in *Time*

THE DEMOCRATIC CONVENTION, the first official test of strength
between the Montagues and the Capulets of Massachusetts politics, took place in Springfield on June 8, 1962. More than two
hundred newspapermen, including reporters from *Time, Life,*
and *Look,* representatives of the major wire services, syndicated
Washington columnists, and television commentators, sat on the
stage behind the chairman's podium. On the floor and in the
balcony of the steaming convention hall over seventeen hundred
delegates — bumpkins from small towns, hard-nosed, big-city politicians mouthing cigars and sweating profusely, a few prominent
attorneys, businessmen, some members of Americans for Democratic Action, a few elderly ladies in wheelchairs, a couple of
drunks, and an occasional Brahmin — mixed with photographers
and television cameramen. Aides of the candidates, eager to report the latest switch or rumor, wandered among the delegates
and communicated with headquarters via walkie-talkie: "Black
Seven, this is Green Four. Do you hear me?" "It's a little Los
Angeles," observed a Kennedy aide who had worked for the President at the national convention. As if to remind the delegates of
the stakes involved, a large photograph of President Kennedy
and a drawing of Speaker McCormack hung high above the stage.

*   *   *

The weeks preceding the convention had been hectic for both
candidates. McCormack, when he realized that he would be
soundly defeated, reminded the delegates (and, through them,
the electorate) that "Any man or woman pledged to McCormack
has nothing to fear." On May 15 he announced that he would

disclose documentary evidence of mounting pressure against his candidacy emanating from the White House.

In support of this charge, McCormack said: "Ask the delegates wearing McCormack badges what pressure was put on them," he told the press. When reporters asked him to be specific, McCormack instructed them to contact William C. Hartigan, a former assistant postmaster general, who had resigned his federal post in May to campaign for the President's brother. "Ask him," McCormack said, "what department head he talked to in room 1008 of the Parker House Hotel in Boston on April 29 and 30." Hartigan promptly replied to the press that such meetings did take place but that they were called solely for the purpose of discussing matters of concern to the postal service.

On May 28 the Attorney General claimed that agents of Edward Kennedy offered postmasterships to delegates in North Adams and Williamstown in return for votes. He also stated that the Newburyport delegation switched to his opponent because a Kennedy worker promised that a minor traffic violation would not stand in the way of a delegate who sought employment in the post office. Further, he went on, he had a report that the Auburn delegation switched to Kennedy because a prominent Democrat who was apparently in difficulty with the law had been promised absolution in return for a Kennedy vote at the convention.

Following McCormack's accusations, an official of the Post Office Department announced to the press that the number of vacant postmasterships in Massachusetts was below the national average.

On June 7 when he had failed to document his charges, the Attorney General announced, to the surprise of many, that he did not wish to win the endorsement and "lose the presidency for the Democratic party in 1964." This tactic led one Washington columnist to remark that McCormack "has suddenly become protective of the President, a fellow Bay Stater who has gotten along very well so far without the help of either Eddie or his uncle, the Speaker of the House." [1]

1 Mary McGrory, *Boston Globe*, June 8, 1962.

McCormack suggested that he was "doing the President a favor" by attempting to defeat Edward Kennedy. "I happen to believe," he remarked, "the President would be more hurt if Teddy is elected. There is a lot of talk about the national dynasty issue now. The Republicans would have the greatest domestic issue if Ted is elected, but if Ted is defeated, the dynasty issue is dead."[2]

On the eve of the convention McCormack did document one charge that might have been damaging to Kennedy. When announcing his candidacy, the latter had stated publicly that he had voted regularly since he was old enough to vote. Waving photostatic copies of voting records, the Attorney General asked:

> Why did he make this statement when, in fact, the official records of the election department of the City of Boston prove he voted in only one primary and two final elections — in 1958 when his brother ran for the U.S. Senate, and in 1960, by absentee ballot, when his brother was elected President . . . ? What interest did he have when in 1953, 1955, and 1959 he did not vote for city officials to guard the destiny of his city — for which he now claims he can do more . . . ? Must he or a member of his family be a candidate for office for him to participate in the democratic process of voting? If Mr. Kennedy wants people to vote for him, for the highest legislative office in the world, I feel he owes an explanation to the people of Massachusetts and to the city of Boston as to why he did not vote for anyone other than a Kennedy in the period between 1953 and 1960.

Stating that he did not believe in "last-minute charges," the Attorney General released Kennedy's voting record to the press two days prior to the convention "in order that ample opportunity would be provided for a reply."

Although Kennedy failed to "reply," his campaign manager did say, for the benfit of the press, that McCormack's remarks

[2] A nationally known pollster, who had been interviewing voters throughout the country, reported to the author that the great majority of Republicans believed Kennedy's candidacy was a disgrace while most Democrats thought there were not enough Kennedys in office.

represented "yet another, and I sincerely hope the final, chapter of his by-now pathetic efforts to mislead the people of this state. . . . This type of statement certainly makes it questionable to me in respect to his pledge to conduct this campaign solely on the basis of the issues." Despite the formulaic rhetoric of his campaign manager, Edward Kennedy never denied McCormack's charge. He denied, however, that the White House exerted pressure on his behalf. "I have been asked," the President's brother remarked, "whether any pressure has been or is being exerted on Democratic delegates in my behalf in the White House or Justice Department. The answer is an unqualified no." At a press conference, the President repeated the disclaimer. "I am very sympathetic. I would like to comfort my brother, but I am not involving myself in the campaign. No member of the White House staff is planning to go to the convention, nor will be to the best of my knowledge in Massachusetts between now and the convention."

During three weeks of charges and countercharges McCormack succeeded in publicly documenting only the fact that Kennedy failed to vote in several elections. Since the Attorney General knew that an overwhelming majority of the delegates were firmly pledged to his opponent, his allegations were really intended for the consumption of the primary constituency rather than the delegates. His failure to document all but one of the charges, however, made it possible for voters who were disillusioned with the rhetoric of Massachusetts politics and skeptical of politicians to see McCormack as just another politician crying wolf.

McCormack's unsupported allegations even disturbed members of his own brain trust. A close adviser remarked that

> . . . one of the greatest mistakes of strategy was the candidate's public declaration that he had material on pressure from Washington. I was surprised to read that. We do have materials; if you just collected that which is in the printed record, they're impressive, and you could kind of tick them off. But I thought that something was going to be forthcoming. If I had known that the declaration would be made with-

out any attempt to substantiate it . . . I'm sure that the brain trust would have acted as a political board of strategy to veto any such public statement. I don't know how this happened to slip in.

* * *

While McCormack repeated his charges and Kennedy denied or ignored them, Kennedy agents worked slowly and efficiently behind the scenes during the few days prior to the convention to make certain that the key committees — rules and credentials — were controlled by Kennedy delegates. The chairman of the Democratic state committee, John M. "Pat" Lynch, appointed a Kennedy delegate as temporary chairman of every committee. Although Lynch maintained that he had such power "by custom," McCormack described his behavior as "dictatorial." "Obviously," remarked the Attorney General, "Mr. Lynch is bending every effort to swing the convention to Teddy Kennedy." Lynch, McCormack asserted, "is manipulating the committee appointments in order to provide the necessary complement of puppets who will do his bidding in committee and on the convention floor."

On Thursday, June 5, when agents in the field reported heavy Kennedy majorities in almost every delegation and the credentials committee seated sixteen pro-Kennedy delegates and one pro-McCormack delegate, several of the Attorney General's advisers suggested that he withdraw from the convention and take his case to the voters. The Attorney General refused and ensconced himself in a suite in the Sheraton-Kimball Hotel, where aides ushered in dozens of delegates, many of whom told the candidate that they preferred him but could not vote against the President's brother.

On the day before the convention a brass band heralded Kennedy's arrival in Springfield and a wild demonstration occurred when the huge Kennedy motorcade entered the city. Several newspapers previously reluctant to predict the outcome ran banner headlines forecasting a Kennedy victory. The President's brother tersely announced to the press that "I don't feel it will be close." One of his aides correctly predicted an easy first-ballot victory and stated that Kennedy had the support of 1,196 of the convention's 1,719 delegates. While McCormack sound trucks boomed, "Don't be pressured. Stay with Eddie McCormack and we'll win," the Attorney General told the press that "all we have to do is hold what we have."

McCormack men, not fully aware of the impending disaster, continued to buttonhole Kennedy delegates in a last-minute and desperate effort to convert the opposition. Ineffectually, almost pathetically, they reminded Kennedy men that Edward McCormack was the deserving candidate, who had labored long and hard in the vineyards of the party, while Kennedy was an interloper — a presumptuous upstart. They appealed to whatever sense of party loyalty Kennedy men might have. They suggested that Kennedy would simply be a rubber stamp for the President. And they argued that the President would suffer in future campaigns because of Edward Kennedy's candidacy.

After hours of frantic politicking on the steps of the convention hall, in hotels, motels, and the "Y," the candidates, who were prohibited by the rules from being present on the floor, retired to their hotel rooms to observe the convention on television.

Congressman Edward M. Boland of Springfield placed the name of Edward Moore Kennedy in nomination. In a speech extolling the virtues of the candidate and the dedicated public service of his family, Boland declared:

> This man does not have to run on his name or on the accomplishments of his family, brilliant and illustrious as they may be. He can stand on his own two feet, on his proven record of service to his country and the Commonwealth. . . . I have the greatest respect for the other candidate for this nomination, and for what he has done. But the nomination for the office of senator from Massachusetts should not be given as a reward for service rendered. It should be given to the man who will best perform the work that must be done. The senator's office is the center of activity on behalf of our state, and the man who sits there must speak with a voice that will be heard.

The Attorney General's name was placed in nomination by Salvatore Camelio, Vice-President of the Massachusetts State

Labor Council, AFL-CIO. In his speech Camilio paid homage to the American credo of working your way to the top and the fact that McCormack had played "the political game."

> Nobody starts at the top. If you want leadership, responsibility, you start at the bottom and work your way through the chairs, so to speak. . . . No one can say of his appointment policies that he has slighted or neglected any of those groups whose political aid and assistance he sought. . . . And no one can say that he has embarrassed or forgotten those whose support made his political victories possible.

With McCormack aides still desperately talking to delegates in a final effort to swing the convention, the clerk began the roll call. Hoping to establish an early trend both candidates had campaigned with great vigor to win the support of the first two delegations on the roll — Berkshire and Bristol. Berkshire, as expected, went for McCormack, thirty-one to twenty-seven. A Kennedy delegate demanded a roll-call vote but the count stood as it was originally announced. The roll-call vote, however, gave one McCormack delegate the opportunity to exclaim, "Being too old for a post office job, I'm for McCormack."

The clerk then intoned: First Bristol, and the chairman reported forty-three votes for Kennedy, nine for McCormack. The tally was challenged and found accurate. After the Second and Third Bristol delegations gave clear majorities to Kennedy, Knocko McCormack urged his son to withdraw. "You could see," Knocko was reported to have said, "they had this thing sewed up so I advised my boy not to put his people on the spot because they will be needed when we go to the primary."[3] The Attorney General took his father's advice only after 24 districts had given his opponent a lead of 691 votes to 360.

McCormack, with a broad smile, entered the auditorium amidst thunderous cheers and began his concession speech with a query: "With all this enthusiasm, how did I lose?" After thanking the delegates who supported him, the Attorney General announced his intention to contest the primary. "I respectfully

[3] *Haverhill Journal*, June 14, 1962.

request," he said, "my name be withdrawn from further consideration at this convention and I will now take my case to the people." Kennedy then thanked his supporters and told the delegates that "the voice of the Democrats this evening has been a free voice. It has been a clear voice and a true voice." McCormack men then filled the hall with hisses.

When McCormack aides described the Kennedy organization as raw political power they were mistaken. The power was there, but it was highly refined and tailored after the machine developed by John F. Kennedy at the Los Angeles convention. Kennedy command headquarters, under the control of the candidate's brother-in-law Stephen Smith, was set up in a suite of rooms at the Sheraton-Kimball Hotel. Two hundred and forty floor workers, six for every delegation, met frequently with Smith during the forty-eight hours prior to balloting, checking and rechecking Kennedy's strength in each delegation. Six Kennedy aides equipped with walkie-talkies reported switches and rumors from the floor while Smith communicated with Kennedy workers through a multi-circuit switchboard at the Sheraton-Kimball.[4]

A second Kennedy headquarters was set up in the room allotted the candidate backstage. In addition to a twelve-circuit switchboard, this communications center contained a diagram of the auditorium seating plan and the position of delegations, and the names of Kennedy walkie-talkie aides who covered the floor and the delegations they were responsible for. Communications between headquarters and the field were evidently so good that one Kennedy co-ordinator remarked, "I felt as though I were back in the army. They want to know where you are all time."

According to John Phillips, who covered the convention for *Commentary,*

. . . it was a lesson to watch the Kennedy corps shepherding

[4] *Time* emphasized the amateurish character of McCormack's organization in contrast to Kennedy's when it pointed out that "while he [McCormack] was struggling to get telephone calls placed through the hotel's harried switchboard operators, Teddy's people set up a separate twelve-circuit switchboard. At the convention auditorium, where McCormack and Kennedy had been allotted a single room backstage, Kennedy had another twelve-circuit switchboard while McCormack had a single line." *Time,* June 16, 1962, p. 14.

their faithful right up to the microphones. When a delegation was polled each member was required to declare himself before television cameras. "Ted will be looking at you," men were told, "and you know who else will be." As if they didn't know, a few old timers succumbed to inebriation and would have missed the polling entirely except for the efficiency of Kennedy workers patrolling the hotels and saloons. "Get those guys back here. Make them vote." The order was from a man in a shiny blue suit. In a few minutes the old guys were back in the auditorium like sheepish children and encouraged all the way to the microphone. "Awrighty Billy, let's giver the go!" "I cast my vote for Ted Kennedy!" "That'sa boy Billy. Gawd bless ya. . . ."[5]

The Attorney General's father, Knocko McCormack, described the plight of his son:

> They're cold, they're cold . . . I got here at 12:30 last night, and I got in the elevator with an old friend from Northampton. He's been in the American Legion with me for years, and I say, "Hello, Commander," and he hangs his head, and he says, "I can't be with you, Knocko." "What do you mean?" says I. "I've been offered a good federal job if I go with Kennedy," says he.
>
> And over in Worcester there's another guy. He's like a first cousin to me for 50 years. . . . He says they promised him the postmastership in Worcester. . . . It's pressure, pressure, pressure, post office, post office, post office.[6]

*   *   *

It may be smart politics to insist that the opposition is applying substantial pressure to delegates. Nevertheless, veteran politicians in the Bay State and an occasional newspaperman noted that several delegates to past conventions — perennials, as it were — refused to attend the 1962 conclave because of the pressure applied to them by Kennedy and by McCormack or because of the pressure they imagined would be exerted if they did attend. Com-

[5] John Phillips, "Up in Massachusetts," *Commentary*, November, 1962, p. 432.

[6] *Time*, June 16, 1962, p. 14.

menting on the turnover of delegates in 1962, a former delegate observed, "These guys, especially the cute ones, don't want to get caught in the squeeze. No matter who wins, somebody's going to dump them."

Although politics in Massachusetts, as elsewhere, is for many the process of getting people to behave as one wants them to behave through the application of penalties or rewards, the contest between Kennedy and McCormack was extraordinary because the principals were, or were thought to be, in a position to invoke sanctions and grant rewards far beyond those available to the average senatorial candidate.

According to one prominent academic who was a member of the Kennedy brain trust, the kind of political pressure "that would raise eyebrows" was utilized but utilized infrequently by his candidate.

> I think . . . kinds of pressure shade on into many varieties. . . . Where a certain privilege would really illicitly be withdrawn from you that's one. . . . Suppose you get a job by political means because you supported somebody and then somebody with that political control comes along and says, "I'm going to take it away from you." Well, you lose it the way you get it. I mean, is that pressure? . . . I would say the kind of pressure that would raise eyebrows I think would account for a tiny fraction . . . 5 per cent maybe.

Several members of the McCormack entourage did not accept this interpretation. They charged that Kennedy or his aides had intimated hundreds of delegates with threats of presidential retribution or won them with promises of federal patronage.

Of the sixty-five delegates interviewed prior to the convention, however, only one claimed that his job security had been seriously "threatened." He reported that a Kennedy aide who was an executive in his firm told him

> . . . that everybody in the company is with Kennedy, and I should join the group and if I don't he's going to put us all down on a card and he's going to "take it right down the line. . . ." See, this job I'm on as supervisor, I'm on a tem-

porary basis, and I guess he feels that if I don't fall in line he'll put pressure on me to have me sent back as a worker again. . . . He called me up over the phone and said I'm with him or against him, [he said] . . . the Scripture says you're either with a guy or against a guy. . . . [On another visit] he forgets himself, and he's got that blustery way, and he's shouting and hollering. That's when he mentioned that he's going to put it all down on the card that I'm for Mc-Cormack and he's going to "take it right down the line."

This delegate voted for McCormack at the convention and was not demoted by his employer. Many delegates whom we interviewed reported second- and third-hand instances of threats and promises by Kennedy or his agents to other delegates, but not one stated that Kennedy or McCormack or any of their agents had offered him a bribe, promised him a job, or threatened him with the loss of a job, with an investigation of his income tax returns, or with physical violence.

Douglas Cater of *The Reporter* found that

A great many delegates and others were prepared to relate second-hand episodes that proved impossible to verify. Two politicians favoring McCormack reportedly found their income-tax returns being reviewed. But they were unwilling to make their cases public, and considering present exposures of Massachusetts corruption there could be ample cause for such reviews. A delegate who was a lawyer reportedly got the offer of a job if he would vote for Kennedy. Reached after the convention by telephone, he would not discuss the matter "at the present time." Another lawyer-delegate was reportedly told that "unless he supported Kennedy" he would get no assistance for an immigrant client from Senator Ben Smith, who now occupies the seat for which Kennedy and McCormack are fighting. Smith's assistant now claims that the Senator never even talked with the lawyer about this client. And the lawyer, in patently guarded language, now says he has never been personally refused anything by Senator Smith.[7]

Many delegates clearly thought that, win or lose, Kennedy

[7] Douglas Cater, *The Reporter,* July 5, 1962, p. 18.

would control federal patronage in Massachusetts. A McCormack delegate reported that a Kennedy man had telephoned him several times and said: "Be on the right side and you can get more from the Kennedys than you get from the McCormacks." The delegate labeled this argument the "Christmas tree approach. They'll give you something if you'll give them something."

According to one McCormack delegate:

There have been reports in many areas that the Kennedy people, in sitting down with delegates or with politicians, legislators, or others from the area, have used a variety of techniques. For one, there has been the kind of subtle, implied — well, to some extent, veiled threat of disfavor with the President himself. . . . You know that Jack is going to be the President certainly for eight years, Bobby is the Attorney General, if you support anyone other than Teddy in this fight you can be sure — and this is done, I think, to some extent very diplomatically, but the threat nevertheless is there. You're going to incur the displeasure and favor of both the Attorney General and the President who is going to be on the political scene for a good many years. Sometimes this becomes more direct and blunt, and there have been some people who have been told, well, you know, there aren't too many practical politicians, if anybody has anything to hide at all, you're certainly not going to want the Attorney General prying into income-tax returns, this kind of thing, so the boys better pretty well be in line. This is the kind of pattern of veiled intimidation, coercion, and threats, sometimes less veiled and more blunt and direct, which I have personally heard reported to me by some members of the legislature who have had occasion to sit down and talk with some of Kennedy's forces.

Now there's a reverse side of that coin, perhaps a more positive side of the coin. . . . It's an obvious fact that . . . Kennedy's star is on the political ascendancy and that to a large extent the McCormack star is on the decline, John McCormack certainly being considerably older and his years on the national scene being limited and the area of his influence being limited, also by the existence of Kennedy as president. Some people have been told, well, if you identify yourself and ally yourself with the Kennedys, you know we're not going to forget you, this is to your political advantage in the future, and we're not going to forget those people who have helped us when we needed help and assistance here.

Some delegates who are not interested in patronage for themselves, however, are influenced by offers to their friends or colleagues. A Kennedy delegate from one of the larger industrial cities in the Commonwealth said:

Well, we have one fellow that we hope to land down with the national parks, and we thought we'd be much better off voting for Kennedy at the convention for the simple reason . . . if we go with Kennedy we'll be able to get that favor, we believe in fact, we've been promised to some degree. . . . We have other fellows in the . . . post office that will be taken care of, such as the fellow who tops the list for . . . head supervisor in the postal annex. That hasn't been appointed and we think — I personally think — they're holding it up until after the election to see if _____ goes with Kennedy.

The feeling of the young Democrats in this city is that the Kennedys will be in power a long time, and we need favors to keep our organization going, like any other political organization. We can receive them from the Kennedys and we won't receive them from the McCormacks.

McCormack hoped to neutralize the political value of the post office by publicizing his charge that Kennedy was using postmasterships as bait and by suggesting that delegates insist on their appointments being made prior to the convention. His campaign manager commented on the latter strategy:

Just today somebody called me on the phone and said, one of our people, there's a problem out in Gardner because the postmastership is going to be given to one person, and three delegates said if that's done they'll vote for Kennedy. I contacted our man, and I said you better go back and tell those delegates — as I understand it, this guy who's supposed to get the postmastership said that if he doesn't get it before the convention, that he isn't going to go for Kennedy. And my man will probably be visiting those people this afternoon and give 'em the pitch I just gave him. . . .

By publicizing these charges McCormack and his aides believed the Attorney General was

. . . going to effectively kill the appointments for these guys that might be thinking they're going to get them. . . . The postmastership situation and the talk of it makes the situation fluid insofar as a delegate is concerned. I say to a delegate, "I'm going to get a postmastership . . . if you'll vote for a certain candidate." The guy says, "Sure, if you're going to get it, I'll do it." Two days later an opposing candidate comes back and says, "Look, that guy is never going to get that postmastership because it's public knowledge now, and nobody'll dare appoint him." So the candidate says, "Well, the hell with it, I won't vote for [his candidate]."

Since McCormack failed to document these charges, the advice of his aides was almost certainly unsound.

The charges of extraordinary pressure, however, did not emanate solely from the McCormack camp. Kennedy aides frequently alleged that McCormack and his aides resorted to threats and promises. According to the *Boston Herald,* which strongly favored Kennedy, "a clerk in the Middlesex Registry of Deeds yesterday charged that he had been fired by his boss for voting for Ted Kennedy in the Democratic Senatorial hassle Friday. . . . Registrar Edmund Buckley of Cambridge denied the charge and labelled McDermott's story an attempt to gain publicity and smear me in the eyes of the public." [8] McDermott was not discharged.

From all these reports Cater concluded:

. . . two facts are fairly evident: a number of lesser politicians, whether authorized or not, did speak in terms of rewards and punishments; and a number of others listened to them with anxieties that may or may not have been justified. Such actions were undoubtedly taken on behalf of both candi-

8 *Boston Herald,* June 10, 1962.

dates. But the punitive powers that may be feared from a state attorney general leaving office in a few months are fairly limited, while those which conceivably might be feared from a Presidential administration in office for at least two and possibly six more years are unlimited.[9]

Whether or not either candidate actually used threats and promises, the Attorney General was obviously unable to counter the major weapons in Edward Kennedy's arsenal: the enormous power, to punish or reward, wielded by the President (and the Attorney General) of the United States. An office holder who worked for Kennedy remarked:

I would say that the position of the candidate, brother of the President, certainly weighs upon the mind of every delegate, and of the opposition. Whether in reality or not any action could be taken or is contemplated . . . against delegates, they certainly feel the possibility of its happening. I have had many people say to me, "Well, what can Kennedy do for me?" and then they'll add, "What can he do against me?" To me, when they say, "What can he do to hurt me?" they're immediately recognizing a fact. . . . Every one of these delegates, be they for McCormack or Kennedy, knows . . . what the presidency means and what its potential power is; this obviously entered into their mind as soon as they knew that Ted was an official candidate. . . . There are . . . in _____ County approximately a dozen or fifteen individuals who have been elected delegates for the first time strictly through the influence of a close friend of theirs who is a controller of votes or a controller of a ward. These individuals have been elected on a pro-McCormack slate and yet are just beginning to comprehend now what a McCormack vote would at least mean in their minds, what it could potentially mean for their future.

A delegate who was interviewed by the *Boston Globe* said that he would probably vote for Kennedy. "After all, the guy [President Kennedy] broke the steel companies. Think of what he could do to us!"

[9] Cater, *op. cit.*, p. 18.

One Kennedy aide said his candidate had "more points to work from."

> In other words, if you're influencing a delegate from the Attorney General's office, well, there you are in the Attorney General's office or a friend's, while the Kennedy organization can influence from many areas: a friend who got a federal appointment asked you to vote for Kennedy . . . because his brother was good to him. Or you have a sister-in-law who happens to work for the federal government. . . . She will come home and say, "Well, I think it would be in the best interests of myself if you vote for the President's brother." There has been many appointments given out both in the postal system, in terms of postmasterships, in terms of regional directors, assistants, in terms of appointments to small business administrations, of local men from Massachusetts who now will come to say to their friends, delegates, "As a personal favor to me, would you support Ted Kennedy for the Senate?" I think this is very effective, and I think that this and other reasons will bring about a majority for Kennedy.

The overwhelming power on the Kennedy side made it unnecessary for Kennedy aides to use crude forms of political persuasion. Innuendo and subtle suggestion rather than open threats and direct promises could suffice. Commenting on the approach used by senatorial and gubernatorial candidates, a veteran politician remarked:

> On the whole, I would say . . . that there isn't . . . much . . . difference from the recent previous contests . . . in the sense that there was more fear . . . of the potential power of the different candidates than . . . actual pressuring. I think it's done in a much more sophisticated way, because of the circumstances, than it has been done in the past. I don't believe there's any of this "either you vote for us, or your brother will lose his job working for the state when I am elected." . . . But I believe that the same thing is perhaps being said in a much nicer way. And it's much easier to get across in this election, because the candidates are two such prominent individuals. . . . I mean, for example, that candidate A knows that delegate B has a brother who is up for parole. . . . He

will not go and say, "I will get your brother a parole if you
throw your seven delegates to me. . . ." [He'll say,] "I'm interested in your brother's upcoming parole, and of course no
definite steps will be taken for some time now, probably until
after the convention. We'd appreciate it if you'd just evaluate
the candidates and feel which would be the most beneficial to
yourself, your future, and your family." I think this is a much
nicer way of doing it, and I think it's being done more and
more in Massachusetts today.

One Kennedy aide believed that:

A lot of people in municipal elections or state elections,
they're afraid of what the City Hall or the State House is
gonna do. . . . They don't realize that many times to those
guys who are seasoned in politics, after the fight is over they
forget — they go right on to new business, and the individual
cases . . . which are important to the lowly delegate are
comparatively insignificant to the City Hall, State House, or
White House. But I do concede that there is fear in a lot of
minds. . . . It's a fear that the force is there and will be directed towards them. It's like the people afraid of a lightning
storm. The force is there, they know the force is there, and
they think that the lightning may not strike within miles of
them. But I don't think, outside of what I would call ordinary political pressures which are put in every political campaign, I don't think there's anything extraordinary here.

Nevertheless, one McCormack lieutenant observed:

There's a general feeling about the Kennedy family in Massachusetts. You know, all this business of the people being
threatened with their tax returns, I know of nobody who has
had that, actually, but it's interesting that this has become
common form. There is a feeling about the Kennedys, frequently expressed by a lot of people with whom I talked,
that their power lies not in the fact that they reward their
friends, but that they punish their enemies. There's a kind
of vindictiveness that goes with this kingly image that people
have about the Kennedys, or at least consider that the Kennedys associate with themselves.

Another McCormack aide advanced the view that the most significant "pressure" at the convention — if one may call it pressure — was reverence for and attachment to the President, not fear of retribution. He reported an incident that, in his opinion, explained why Kennedy had been endorsed by the Democratic party:

> I went out to [see] . . . a delegate I had known very well; as a matter of fact, I did him a few favors. I went out to see him because . . . he was originally McCormack, and he had since changed to Kennedy. . . . The first thing he said to me, "How can I vote against the President's brother, because," he said, "look, he was out here to see me the other night himself, personally, and sat right in that chair." He says, "And he talked with me. Nobody else has been here to visit me. . . . This man came to my house and rang my bell and spent an hour with me and talked with me on every phase of politics. . . : He just made me feel good. Here's the President's brother coming to my home, talking to me personally, asking me my ideas and what he could do to help Massachusetts. And this was quite a compliment to pay to me. After all, he is the President's brother, and we all voted for the President, and I can't vote against Ted Kennedy because of this." . . . As long as he lives he'll point to that chair and say: "You know who sat in that chair? The President's brother!"

*   *   *

"Every convention," Theodore White has written, "is a universe in itself, with its own strange centers of gravity, its own fresh heroes and fools, its own resolutions of pressures and forces, and its own irrecapturable mood of stage and place."[10] Although the 1962 Democratic State Convention was ostensibly concerned with Massachusetts politics, the center of gravity and the source of pressure for many influential delegates was, in fact or fantasy, Washington rather than Beacon Hill. The convention, however, was a conclave of Massachusetts Democrats, some of them deeply concerned with the public image of the party during a period

10 Theodore H. White, *The Making of the President, 1960* (New York: Atheneum Publishers, 1961), p. 150.

when several Democrats and officials appointed by Democrats had
been convicted of corrupt practices. Hundreds of delegates believed, and correctly, that a significantly large segment of the
Massachusetts electorate was suspicious of professional politicians, distrustful of incumbents, and therefore receptive only to
candidates who were seen as clean, dedicated, and non-political.
We hope to recapture the particular sense of this convention —
the "mood of stage and place" — by analyzing the attitudes of
delegates who responded to a post-convention questionnaire.

Two days after Edward Kennedy received the endorsement,
a questionnaire and covering letter was mailed to each person on the official roster of delegates of the Democratic State Committee. The letter, written on Boston University stationery, identified the sender as a political scientist who was collecting data on
the convention for the purpose of writing a book on the senatorial campaign. Delegates were assured that their questionnaire was
not coded so as to reveal their identity. In addition to questions relating to age, income, sex, religious affiliation, country of
national origin, occupation, and education each delegate was
asked:

Did you vote for Kennedy or McCormack?
If you did not vote because McCormack conceded before your
 delegation was polled, whom would you have voted for?
What are the most important reasons you voted for (or would
 have voted for) your choice for senator?
What do you like best about Kennedy? What do you like least
 about Kennedy?
What do you like best about McCormack? What do you like least
 about McCormack?
There's been a lot of talk in the newspapers recently about pressures put on delegates by the senatorial candidates or their
 workers. Has any pressure been placed on you? (Yes __or
 No __). If yes, what kind of pressure was put on you and in
 whose behalf?

Four hundred and forty delegates (25.5 per cent of the total
delegate population) completed and returned the questionnaire.
Six returned their questionnaires torn into shreds. Three wrote

letters to the author, two charging that he was a paid employee of Edward Kennedy and the other that he was on McCormack's staff. One delegate telephoned the author and suggested that the Massachusetts Democratic party would be irreparably damaged if the results of the survey were published prior to the general election. McCormack's campaign manager reported, after the general election, that several McCormack delegates had asked him whether and how they should answer the questionnaire. He told them to answer honestly "as long as you don't hurt Eddie."

The data collected through this mailed questionnaire must be interpreted with much caution. The reader must regard it as impressionistic and nothing more. Although approximately one-fourth of the delegates responded — a rather high proportion of returns for a mailed questionnaire of this kind — we really cannot be certain that the group responding was in fact a representative sample of the delegate population. No one, in fact, knows the true characteristics of this population. The McCormack delegates who consulted with McCormack's campaign manager were instructed to report nothing that might hurt McCormack. This may well have caused them to distort their answers. Furthermore, we assume that some delegates may have believed that the questionnaire was coded so that we could determine their identity or may have thought that we were conducting the survey for one of the candidates. If they held either or both of these beliefs we assume that they may have given false answers to some questions. It would also be naïve to assume that all those who did return the questionnaire answered with complete candor the question about pressure. McCormack delegates, who strongly disliked Kennedy, may have seized this opportunity to defame him or vice versa. We do not know. Nevertheless, a careful study of the questionnaire suggests to us that the results are worth reporting.

Kennedy was preferred by 58 per cent of the respondents, McCormack by 42 per cent. Since Kennedy probably would have received approximately twelve hundred votes (70 per cent) at the convention if the balloting had been completed, the sample over-represents McCormack's strength. Approximately four out of every ten delegates who did or would have voted for McCormack responded to the questionnaire whereas only two out of every ten Kennedy delegates responded. With rare exception Kennedy was preferred by a majority of those in every subgroup regardless of whether the subgroup is defined in terms of age, income, sex, occupation, religious affiliation, education, or country of national origin.

A majority (59 per cent) of the 396 males who responded and a majority (55 per cent) of the 44 female respondents preferred Kennedy. He was favored also by a majority of those in every occupational grouping except attorneys and clerical workers, 55 per cent of whom preferred McCormack. Kennedy was also the choice of a majority of those in every income group with the exception of people who reported annual earnings in excess of $25,000. This group gave Kennedy and McCormack each nine votes. Kennedy was the preference of a majority of those in every educational subgroup except among delegates (twelve) who had not completed grammar school. McCormack was preferred by 35 per cent of those who completed high school, 45 per cent of those with some college, 32 per cent of the college graduates, and 49 per cent of those with postgraduate training. The latter group is composed primarily of attorneys. Kennedy was preferred by 62 per cent of the 348 Roman Catholic respondents and 61 per cent of the 46 Protestant respondents. McCormack was preferred by 74 per cent of the 27 Jewish respondents.[11]

The decision to support a particular candidate is frequently made not only in terms of what individuals like about him but also in terms of what they dislike about his opponent. Although relatively little information on this two-dimensional aspect of voting behavior exists,[12] it is not unreasonable to assume that, in an effort to relieve their doubts and anxieties, voters come to prefer

[11] An analysis of public opinion data collected during the ten days preceding the primary election indicates that upper-income Jewish females were the only subgroup in a sample of registered Democrats that preferred the Attorney General. Low-income Jews preferred Kennedy in approximately the same proportions as low-income voters of Irish and Italian ancestry.

[12] See Murray B. Levin and Murray Eden, "Political Strategy for the Alienated Voter," *Public Opinion Quarterly*, Spring, 1962.

their candidate more and dislike his opponent more as election day appproaches.

In response to the question, "What do you like best about Kennedy?" the overwhelming majority of Kennedy delegates (72 per cent) cited what we will call a personality characteristic. Of this group the largest proportion (35 per cent) referred to the candidate's energy and drive. His personal visits to hundreds of delegates, numerous telephone calls, and follow-up letters created the impression among his supporters of a diligent and aggressive campaigner who was willing to fight for the endorsement. One Kennedy delegate mentioned "his fire and fight," another his "enthusiasm and his ability to conduct a vigorous campaign." Several delegates referred to Kennedy's "drive," his "capacity for hard work," his "willingness to go out and work for votes," and "his tireless efforts to win a Senate seat." "He's dedicated," one delegate responded, citing "the fact that he has visited and inspected every village and town and hamlet of the Commonwealth but also most troubled spots of the world with a resulting first-hand knowledge." Another delegate was impressed that "He called me personally on the phone, paid a visit to my home, and I was a delegate from a one-vote town. I felt that anyone who wanted anything that badly would tend to work for the job."

Of those delegates who referred to Kennedy's personality, 29 per cent liked best the candidate's warmth or his willingness and ability to mingle with the common man. Several delegates remarked that as the millionaire son of a distinguished family Kennedy could easily have become a wastrel or a playboy but nevertheless was willing to meet with the average man and able to put him at ease. One delegate liked best Kennedy's "down-to-earth feeling that he is on the same level as the common person. His sincerity and honesty is part of his vote-getting power." Another referred to "his sincerity and his desire to be a public servant although his family's financial position enables him to follow a far easier course." "He is an everyday person," read one response, "not high-hat and very easy to know and like." This theme was repeated with many variations: "His ability as an orator and his love of the common man — to understand their problems, how he can mingle and associate with this segment on their level." "His approach to politics. Nobody is too small or unimportant to meet and talk to. His down-to-earth approach when questioned." "His youth and his ability to make you feel comfortable, be you a wealthy person, or a poor man, or a middle class. I believe he treats everybody alike." "'He's a regular fellow, will mingle with the little fellow." "A young man who is wealthy and could live off the fat of the land and yet is willing to enter the arduous task of politics."

These responses are interesting because they suggest that many Kennedy supporters were casting — in part — what the English call "a deference vote," that is, a vote cast by a person for one perceived as his "better" or superior. English workingmen for years have expressed a marked deference toward and tendency to vote for candidates of aristocratic background and to vote against candidates of their own class. America, of course, has neither a feudal past, a genuine aristocracy based on birth, nor a tradition of noblesse oblige. This does not mean, however, that Americans do not pay homage to or admire people of high social status. More than a century ago, de Tocqueville noted that Americans, although deeply committed to egalitarian values, yearn to break out of "this drab equality" and therefore not only admire but envy those who do so.

Nevertheless, if we interpret these responses correctly, Kennedy supporters like Kennedy because he is aristocratic and wealthy, yet regular, earthy, not "high-hat," and democratic. He symbolized, in other words, two of the dominant values of American life: equality and achievement. He is everyman, but he is also better than everyman and therefore what everyman would like to be. Everyman — if he can simultaneously suppress his envy — can therefore identify with him. His earthiness and lack of snobbishness counteract the envy while his wealth and status exert a strong attraction. One may wonder whether the deference vote did not play some part in the election of John Kennedy, Robert Kennedy, Nelson Rockefeller, Richardson Dilworth, Joseph Clark, Endicott Peabody, Claiborne Pell, Leverett Saltonstall, Henry Cabot Lodge, William Scranton, and Franklin Roosevelt.

The appeal of very wealthy men of high status to the electorate may also be based to some extent on the widespread belief that lower-middle-class and lower-class politicians probably are self-seeking and corrupt.[13] Voters may believe, conversely, that men of high status and great wealth who seek office are motivated by a sense of public service rather than a desire for personal enrichment — in other words, that the rich do not need to steal. One Kennedy delegate remarked that "Kennedy is not in it for a buck. He doesn't need it."

Cynicism toward politics and politicians is, of course, widespread in Massachusetts.[14] A large segment of the population believes that corruption in government is one of the most significant problems confronting the Commonwealth.[15] People who make this assumption frequently abstain from voting or vote for the candidate they believe to be the lesser of two evils — that is, for the candidate who is perceived as less corrupt. Individuals who wish to evaluate the relative dishonesty of candidates seek information pertaining to the character of the candidate rather than his platform or program because they have come to believe that campaign promises are no more reliable than the source from which they stem. They appraise the candidate's character in terms of "gut reactions," intuitive responses to the candidate's smile, eyes, posture, speech, bearing, dress, and family background. We are reminded of the Boston lady who explained why she voted against a particular candidate: "I looked in his eyes," she remarked, "and I knew he was a crook." Many Massachusetts voters, like Diogenes, are looking for an honest man.

[13] The National Opinion Research Center reports that 48 per cent of those interviewed in a national sample of American voters believed it literally impossible for a man to stay honest in politics. *The Public Looks at Politics and Politicians,* Report No. 20, March, 1964.

[14] See Murray B. Levin, *The Alienated Voter: Politics in Boston* (New York: Holt, Rinehart and Winston, 1960), and Murray B. Levin with George Blackwood, *The Compleat Politician: Political Strategy in Massachusetts* (Indianapolis: The Bobbs-Merrill Company, 1962).

[15] See Massachusetts Federation of Taxpayers Associations, *Massachusetts Voters Talk,* October, 1962. Seventeen per cent of those interviewed stated that corruption in government was "one of the most important" problems in Massachusetts, and 80 per cent believed that corruption was a "very important" problem.

It is not surprising, therefore, that the overwhelming majority of pro-Kennedy respondents referred to the candidate's personality and that approximately one out of every five specifically selected "honesty" as Kennedy's most salient character trait. "He is young, honest, and sincere, and he cannot be reached or bribed," one Kennedy delegate commented. Many delegates repeated this theme: "He has clean hands, he's intelligent and a gentleman at all times." "He cannot be accused of corruption." "He cannot be bought." "He's honest. A man dedicated to serving the people — not for wealth and power but with a sense of serving his government and his country." "New face and perhaps a clean one." "I feel that there will be no reason for corruption with Ted Kennedy." He has little personal gains to enjoy by political success." "There is no taint of graft and corruption to him or any member of his family." "He has money so I don't think he will be looking for ways to make extra money for himself." [16]

These perceptions, in our opinion, are linked to other ideas about Kennedy. Eleven per cent of respondents favoring him liked best the "fact" that he was neither a professional politician nor associated with professional politicians: "No stigma of South Boston politics." "He will not have to go to contractors for donations to run his campaign. So far, he is clean." "He is not involved with the present and past of Massachusetts politics." "He is not a political hack." "Ed McCormack is the personification of Democrat in Massachusetts. He has adopted all the clichés of the 'pol.' Ted Kennedy, although young and inexperienced, is not a typical politician of Massachusetts." "He doesn't have power politics behind him — Suffolk County [Boston] Democrats who try to run the show." He "has not held political office and therefore is not open to any possible criticism. Yet, he is mature enough and certainly as intelligent as many other of our present Senators." "He is not subject to charges of association with those suspected of corrupt practices."

[16] Some Kennedy delegates cited other personality traits; Kennedy was perceived as "intelligent" by 16 per cent of those giving a reason of personality; 13 per cent referred to his "voter appeal" and 11 per cent to his "youth"; 7 per cent perceived him as "nice looking," and 7 per cent believed that he was "well educated."

We will note that some of Kennedy's advisers were concerned that delegates and voters would react unfavorably to the fact that the candidate had never been elected to office. The foregoing remarks however, suggest that his inexperience and lack of involvement in Massachusetts politics were assets in the opinion of many supporters and that McCormack's participation in party affairs and his position in office were liabilities. Individuals who have not held office cannot be stereotyped as "politicians," i.e., corrupt office holders who bleed the public. Although the Kennedys are masterful politicians, true professionals who have reduced the art of winning elections to a science, as much as that may be possible, and although Edward Kennedy was backed at the convention by most of the so-called "pols," his supporters preferred to believe that he was a "non-politician," a man above politics, a statesman dedicated to the commonweal. His membership in the Kennedy family, his wealth, his travels abroad, his youth, his education, and the fact that he had not held office were taken by Kennedy respondents as "proof" that he was not a Massachusetts politician, supported by other Massachusetts politicians.

As an aristocratic, wealthy, well-educated non-politician, Kennedy was obviously, according to this image, incorruptible, aggressive, and an appealing candidate. Although the youngest Kennedy has rare political talents in his own right, there is no doubt that his personal charm, the belief that he is qualified, that he can win, that he can do more for Massachusetts, and that he is honest, stem largely from his being part of a family possessing these traits. One out of every ten Kennedy delegates who answered the question "What do you like best about Kennedy?" made some positive reference to the family. "I believe," one delegate responded, "Kennedy is better qualified because all his efforts are in the field of national and international affairs. He was brought up in a family in which, I understand, politics was the topic of conversation morning, noon, and night rather than baseball." "Being from a rich family," another delegate replied, "a member of the family of Joseph Kennedy, former ambassador to Great Britain, he got some advantages over the other candidate in that he traveled a great deal, had a good education and, no doubt, has met a great many influential personages while in Europe. These kids were brought up among politicians and no doubt have a good knowledge of politics both state-wide and nation-wide."

Some delegates described what they liked best about Kennedy more succinctly. "The fact that he is a Kennedy." "Because of his background." "A fabulous background." "First family." "Comes from one of America's greatest families." "Family ties, ability to win, a Kennedy running in a former Kennedy position." Some believed that Massachusetts would benefit if Kennedy were elected because of his brother's position. One delegate who replied that Kennedy was "personable" and "intelligent" also noted that he was "a man of influence due to the fact that he is the President's brother." "I feel," another wrote, "he has important contacts in the White House that can be beneficial to the state." "He can afford to run," observed a supporter. "His brother is President and himself from Massachusetts so that to make Ted look good Jack has to help Massachusetts." "If Kennedy wins the Senate race," one delegate replied, "we in Massachusetts should be on top of the world; with his brother as President we must prosper." Another liked Kennedy best because of "his knowledge and the fact that he has access and advance knowledge of government needs."

* * *

Edward McCormack campaigned as "The Qualified Candidate" — the crime buster, the civil libertarian, the experienced, mature, and well-educated candidate, who, in the best tradition of American politics, worked hard for the party before seeking high public office. He was stereotyped, however, by many pro-Kennedy respondents as a typical Massachusetts politician, intimately associated with parasitical professionals and therefore unable or unwilling to ferret out wrong-doing. The McCormack family was characterized by many Kennedy supporters as déclassé while the Attorney General was typed as a sure loser — a lazy, ineffectual, unaggressive, and colorless man who maligned his opponent, the President, and the Kennedy family.

A member of the Kennedy brain trust suggested that delegates and voters in Massachusetts frequently evaluate candidates in terms of their family background and associates. Certainly this is true, as we have seen, in the case of Edward Kennedy. Thirty-six per cent of the pro-Kennedy respondents, when describing what they disliked about McCormack, wrote that the Attorney General was a professional politician, that he was surrounded by unsavory types. "His workers and associates," one Kennedy delegate noted, "appear to be low-class types. His pressure in past contests on delegates — strong arm tactics. Background of his father leaves something to be desired — his mudslinging prior to the convention." Another Kennedy supporter objected to "his typical attitude toward problems of national magnitude that one would expect from South Boston Irish. His identification, both personal and ideological, with the city of Boston branch of the Democratic party." A Kennedy delegate disliked "his dependency on elements of the party for which I have little respect. His main support seems to come from those who are job seekers and those with a low level of civic morality." Another reported, "I don't like the men who surround him." "His father's arrogance, certainly, is beyond his control," was one response, "but a son does have loyalty to his parent and this man has, without doubt, made a living at politics." McCormack's supporters were characterized in several ways: "He is committed to the old guard." "His connection with machine politics." "His political parasites." "The people around him, especially 'Knocko,' Uncle John and the rest of the ward heelers." "Too many obligations to professional politicians." One Kennedy supporter objected to McCormack's "attachment to present politics in Massachusetts." Another believed that "He seems educated in the spoils system of ward politics." "I feel he is arrogant," reported still another; "he has too much of the old-time political hack about him. Crude bull tactics went out when the voters learned how to read." The theme that McCormack was an old-style politician — not unlike the Speaker — was variously expressed: "He dances to his uncle's tunes and again Boston politicians." "He is a younger version of the Speaker who, to me, has been a good practical politician but never a statesman like the Kennedys." "He's a Boston pol — a dirty city politician." "At the present time he would be considered a Boston politician and not acceptable to the voters with the issues created in the past few years."

Alhough McCormack, as attorney general, successfully prosecuted more public officials than had any of his predecessors, many delegates and voters, believing that corruption was extensive in the Bay State, apparently assumed that he had failed to execute the duties of his office. A law enforcement officer who is stereotyped as a ward heeler among ward heelers is immediately suspect. Approximately one out of every ten Kennedy respondents believed that McCormack had failed to combat corruption. "He had an opportunity to clean up crime and corruption in Massachusetts," a Kennedy delegate responded, "but failed to do so until he was forced to take action by an indignant public." One delegate believed that "As attorney general, he swept corruption under the rug unless somebody else exposed it." Another Kennedy supporter believed that "as the top law enforcement officer in the state during the corruption scandals he must share a great deal of the responsibility."

Although McCormack realized that the President and the Kennedy family were objects of veneration in Massachusetts, he did suggest prior to the convention, and then in vague terms, that Kennedy was a serious candidate only because of the fact that he was the brother of the President and the Attorney General, and a Kennedy. A small number of Kennedy delegates countered McCormack's charge that Kennedy was a serious candidate only because he was a Kennedy by claiming that McCormack's political success was based on his family name and his uncle's power and prestige. One Kennedy delegate objected to McCormack's "statements about the Kennedy dynasty when all his political gains have been made on his uncle's name and not on his own ability." "Where the hell would McCormack be," another Kennedy supporter responded, "if it wasn't for his uncle? Do you think he would be Attorney General if his name was not McCormack?"

Without equivocation, McCormack stated that his opponent utilized the power and prestige of the White House to pressure delegates, but he failed to "document" these charges as he said he would. Since Kennedy supporters perceived their candidate as aristocratic, honest, and a dedicated non-politician, it is not surprising that they saw McCormack's charges as "mudslinging" and the McCormack campaign as "dirty." Forty-five pro-Kennedy respondents (18 per cent) disliked McCormack's pre-convention campaign tactics. "I disliked the accusations he made about pressure," one reported, "and then refused to prove it. I also think it seemed ridiculous to accuse Kennedy of having Washington help, when he is imparting [sic] so his uncle to help him."

Kennedy delegates referred to the McCormack campaign as "unwarranted," "dirty," and "filthy" and to the Attorney General as a "sorehead" and a "crybaby." One Kennedy delegate, who responded very much like the majority of those who voted for Kennedy in the primary, wrote that McCormack did not "show any respect toward his opponent but instead made remarks about him and was, above all, discourteous." Several Kennedy supporters objected to McCormack's referring to his opponent as "Teddy." If one perceives Kennedy as aristocratic, McCormack's failure to "show any respect" or his references to "Teddy" become irreverent and highly objectionable. If one perceives the President and Edward Kennedy as non-politicians, McCormack's charges of pressure politics appear to be not only absurd but also outrageous and embarrassing. "I didn't like his way of trying to bring in dirt and always complaining about pressure being put on by the White House," a Kennedy supporter responded; "they wouldn't do it." Another objected to McCormack's "willingness to embarrass the Massachusetts President by wild statement — that is not disciplined political responsibility."

McCormack's *personality* was unappealing for 17 per cent of Kennedy's supporters. One of them felt that McCormack "lacks wide personal public appeal. His poor performance as a campaigner, his laziness and his long time association with . . . elements in the Democratic Party. I consider him a colorless character lacking in stature." Others objected to McCormack's "lack of human feelings — a cold person," and his "lack of gregariousness." Several delegates referred to McCormack as "a cold fish"; others disliked "his South Boston accent"; one reported that "he talks out of the corner of his mouth and doesn't look straight at you when he talks to you." One Kennedy delegate objected to "his cold, analytic, military way," another to "his attitude of superiority" and his "artificial smile." When describing what he liked least about McCormack, one Kennedy delegate asked, "Did you ever shake his hand?"

*   *   *

Edward McCormack was described by his supporters among the delegates, however, as an experienced and dedicated public servant who worked his way up the party hierarchy — a sincere, honest, warm, intelligent, and hardworking attorney general whose record qualified him for the United States Senate. More than half of the pro-McCormack respondents (57 per cent) referred to the fact that he had political experience or were of the opinion that his record as attorney general was a distinguished one. These twin themes were repeated in a number of ways. "Ed McCormack has given good service to his people and under very trying conditions. The rotten people who were grafting were sometimes Democrats and it made it tough for him, yet he went after them." "McCormack is qualified by training and experience in legislative and administrative offices at city and state level. He had acted positively in performing his duties. He has manifested good judgment in dealing with sensitive matters." "I believe in rewarding performance and not promises. There is no substitute for experience in politics. The office of Senator should not be presented to anyone who has not had political experience."

The Attorney General's record as a civil libertarian was cited by 14 per cent of the respondents who preferred McCormack. One of his supporters liked best "his record on social issues such as civil rights and civil liberties, capital punishment, etc. and his proven ability to attract the most capable people in the Commonwealth into its service." Another believed that McCormack was deeply concerned with personal liberties: "His willingness to publicly express what I know to be his deeply felt concern to safeguard personal liberties. His restraint in handling prosecution . . . using the courts and not the headlines as the place to fix the blame. His intelligence — he has unfortunate speech and facial mannerisms but he is a bright guy." Another wrote, "He's sensitive about civil rights of all citizens." One delegate noted, "Excellent background — good lawyer — courage on controversial issues." Most McCormack supporters who mentioned his record on civil rights when describing what they liked best about the candidate merely replied, "Civil rights and civil liberties."

The positive worth that McCormack's supporters attached to the candidate's political experience and public record suggests that they regarded prior public service and a lengthy apprenticeship in the party as necessary prerequisites for higher office. Unlike Kennedy's supporters, they approved of politicians, placed a high value on party regularity, and believed that there was no substitute for political experience. They also felt that one should not "start at the top" or conversely that one should "work his way up the ladder." Although one out of every ten pro-McCormack respondents explicitly referred to their candidate as a loyal party man or replied that he had worked his way up in the party hierarchy, these values may well underlie the judgment of another 13 per cent who believed that he was qualified and of many who regarded his experience as a positive asset. For example, one delegate who stated that the Attorney General was "qualified" also reported that he "is an intelligent, honest, capable person who has come up through the ranks of the Democratic Party, has proved his vote-getting ability in previous elections, has an obviously sincere concern for civil rights and liberties, has long indicated his wish to be a senator, and is thus deserving of the endorsement of the convention. He is probably as liberal a person as it is possible to elect to high public office in Massachusetts." Another delegate believed that McCormack "has earned the right to seek the office by starting rather low in the political ladder and working his way slowly upward. He has never double-crossed, as far as I know, and he seems to be able to retain all the people he started out with in politics. He is not a Johnny-Come-Lately." One supporter approved of "the fact that McCormack has been a valid and bona fide member of the Democratic party, has 'earned' his shot for promotion and by reasons of service and

experience deserves the backing of the Democratic party. Granted
that he is a member of a politically prominent family — he has
earned his spurs."

A small number of McCormack delegates referred to the fact
that the Attorney General had consulted city and town and ward
committees prior to making appointments. One delegate who
considered McCormack "qualified" also approved of his "loyalty
to rank and file Democrats" and "his recognition of city and town
Democratic committees as being important enough to consult
when an appointment is made by the Attorney General's office."
"The fact that he started from the bottom and rose through the
ranks" impressed one delegate: "he is also a strong party man who
consults local Democratic leaders." Another referred to "his fairness in dealing with city and town committees." The related
themes of party loyalty, apprenticeship, and experience were repeated: "A good Democrat." "Proven public servant." "Record
of achievement." "Party regularity." "Earned his way up the ladder." "I believe a person doesn't start at the top." "He labored in
the vineyards." "Service to the party." One McCormack supporter expressed the two fundamental values shared by most of
the others: "He has done a good job in any office he has been in.
He knows politics and you have to know politics to represent
people properly."

Approximately one-fourth (24 per cent) of pro-McCormack
respondents referred to the candidate's personality. He was perceived most frequently as sincere, competent, intelligent, and
warm.

*　*　*

The majority of Edward McCormack's supporters regarded
the candidacy of Edward Kennedy as a disgraceful attempt to
elect an inexperienced, incompetent, and presumptuous young
man who would be ignored if he were not the brother of the President of the United States. In view of the fact that they valued
political experience, it is not surprising that more respondents in
the McCormack camp (37 per cent) referred to Kennedy's lack
of experience than any other "negative" aspect of his record, personality, or background. Most of those who mentioned Kennedy's

inexperience believed that he was a serious candidate only because he was a Kennedy. One respondent objected to Kennedy's "lack of experience, his youth, his cheating at Harvard, the fact that he has lived in Massachusetts only one year and he's running on his brother's coattails for nobody would give him a second thought except for his connections." Another disliked Kennedy's "lack of a public record. I sincerely resent the fact that Mr. Ben Smith sat as a bench warmer for two years until Ted reached the age to qualify as a candidate." One respondent replied: "If some thirty-year-old kid by the name of O'Laughlin or Singer wanted to run for the Senate, the people would laugh at him. It's a good thing his father was born before him."

The bitter and resentful tone of these comments is typical. Others said: "He seems to think because he's a Kennedy he would be the only person that could do a good job as Senator. He discounts previous political office or experience in general. Lawyers have to be admitted to the bar, professors have to earn a degree, doctors serve an internship, tradesmen serve an apprenticeship." "The fact that he is running in his brother's shadow. He claims to be running on his own merits and is receiving no help from his brother, the President. If he has brains enough to be a senator he must have brains enough to know that this is not true. If his name were not Kennedy, and he was not the brother of the President, he would not get one hundred votes against McCormack. He claims to be running for the good of the party. He has caused more disunity in the Democratic party in five months than any previous candidate in Massachusetts. I have always had to work for any advancement I received and I believe he should do the same thing. Why should the Kennedys have a corner on political brains?" "If his name was other than Kennedy he couldn't qualify for dog catcher."

Approximately one-third (31 per cent) of the pro-McCormack respondents believed that Kennedy was presumptuous, arrogant, or overweeningly ambitious. These attitudes were expressed in many ways: "'He's arrogant, cheats on exams, too many Kennedys already, starting at the top." "His conceit is believing that because his brother is someone he should have top position in the state." "He's too ambitious, too quick." "I just think he has a nerve to come back to the state only one year and think that he should be elected to this important office." "Gall, audacity, presumptuousness." "His overweaning personal and familiar ambition and his basic scorn for the ordinary citizen." "His lust for power." One McCormack delegate disliked "his unmitigated gall and his apparently correct assumption that people respond like sheep and can be handled accordingly."

Kennedy also violated the belief of many respondents that one should work one's way up in the party. Almost one out of every five McCormack supporters (19 per cent) pointed out that "He didn't start at the bottom of the ladder, not even halfway up. Without his brother being the President this would be impossible." "He should creep before he walks; no qualifications but the name." One delegate objected to Kennedy's "desire to orbit the moon before he has learned to pedal his tricycle." "Will they start him off as Crown Prince?" "He's shooting too high. Let him start at the bottom of the ladder like Eddie did. Let him run for state representative." One respondent expressed the attitude of many McCormack delegates when he replied that Kennedy demonstrated "total disregard for the established customs of political practice."

Eight per cent of McCormack's supporters referred unfavorably to "the Kennedy dynasty," 5 per cent unfavorably to the Kennedy family, 4 per cent disliked Kennedy's wealth, 3 per cent mentioned his cheating in college, and 3 per cent stated that Kennedy was unintelligent.

Psychologists, sociologists, and political scientists have noted for many years that man's image of reality is frequently a distorted one. The concern of these scholars with public opinion, perception, and stereotypes followed naturally from their interest in democratic theory and the role assigned to the public by it. Citizens, according to the classic democratic theory, are presumed to be well informed about political affairs. They are supposed to expose themselves to the propaganda of competing parties and candidates and to know, with some degree of sophistication, the positions taken by those who would govern. They ought to per-

ceive reality fairly accurately if they are to make rational and
meaningful decisions — decisions that will enhance their self-interest. Democratic theorists, in other words, assume that the public, or at least a significant portion of the public, is discerning
enough to separate shadow from substance, sham from reality.

During the past decade, students of voting behavior and
political campaigning have focused their attention on the problem of political perception because knowledge of how the public
sees the campaign, the parties, and the candidates is important if
we are to understand the dynamics of so-called free elections.
Their interest in perception also reflects the fact that many who
plead the democratic case are concerned that campaign managers,
in association with artful public relations men and motivational
research experts — equipped with sophisticated techniques for discerning the opinions (conscious and unconscious) of the public
— can use their knowledge to manipulate voters and "sell" the
false in place of the genuine. Inferior candidates, they fear, can
be merchandised like inferior soap, if the product is attractively
packaged and advertised. The impact of reality on voter opinion,
the campaigners' ability to manufacture "favorable" issues and
"fictional" candidates, and the voters' extravagant expectations
and need for illusions are therefore problems that vitally concern
political theorists and pragmatic politicians.

*　　*　　*

The positive and negative attributes of Edward Kennedy and
Edward McCormack as perceived by approximately one-fourth of
the delegates to the 1962 Democratic State Convention make a
portrait of the political landscape in stark and contrasting colors.
Almost every respondent believed that his candidate was emi-
nently qualified for the United States Senate and that his opponent was unfit. Many pro-Kennedy respondents voted "against"
McCormack as well as for Kennedy. Almost every Kennedy delegate, however, voted "for" Kennedy. Very few McCormack respondents failed to comment, in acid terms, on Kennedy's qualifications. The Edward Kennedy who was perceived by his supporters as intelligent, knowledgeable, aristocratic, energetic, and

statesmanlike appeared to McCormack men as a fictional character — a phantom invented by public relations men — neatly packaged and sold to gullible or frightened delegates. Most of the Attorney General's supporters considered Kennedy simply a conceited and unqualified young man whose candidacy would be utterly preposterous if he were not a member of the first family. McCormack, a highly qualified, experienced, and well-educated party regular, according to his delegates, was stereotyped by Kennedy men as a lazy, shiftless, cold, incompetent South Boston politician — an ineffectual attorney general who was discredited in the eyes of the public. Kennedy and McCormack delegates appear to be living in separate and distinct political worlds — worlds that have no common substance and no generally recognized properties. One might assume that delegates fabricated candidates to fit their conception of the ideal office holder, or that they placed a positive value on the characteristics of their man and a negative value on his antagonist, i.e., they redefined their ideal office holder to conform to their candidate's personal attributes. Whatever the facts of political life during the summer of 1962, delegates apparently evaluated them according to different standards and perceived them selectively.

CHAPTER 3 ⊠ *He Can Do More for Massachusetts*

The identification of the Kennedy family with the Catholic Church is so great that really Ted is a Prince of the Church in this state, no matter what he does . . . you can't touch this guy. You can't lay a glove on him.

— A LODGE CAMPAIGN AIDE

THE DEMOCRATIC STATE CONVENTION endorsed Edward Kennedy on June 8, 1962. The next necessary step was again to defeat Edward McCormack, this time in a closed primary election on September 18. The candidates, therefore, had approximately fourteen weeks to raise money, establish a campaign organization, and appeal to the hard core of Democrats, those who customarily vote in party primaries.

That Kennedy was the endorsed candidate greatly enhanced the likelihood that he would defeat McCormack. Few endorsees in Massachusetts have lost the primary election, but Kennedy's endorsement was particularly significant for him because it made him appear to be less of an "outsider." Party regulars had now placed upon him their stamp of approval. Although many of the old "pros" had hoped McCormack would win at the convention so they would have an excuse for not supporting Kennedy, they now were "forced," at least publicly, to join the Kennedy camp. Without doubt, Kennedy was now a "legitimate" candidate, and the senior member of the Kennedy brain trust took note of this fact when he suggested that Kennedy's endorsement "put him . . . in the stratum of recognized political contenders."

As the endorsee Kennedy would receive additional, albeit minimal, benefits from the state party — the support of Democrats who take the convention seriously, although they are few, the support of the Democratic State Committee, ineffectual though it may be, and the "official" support of Democratic ward and town committees, which amounts to little or nothing, since these committees are basically inactive. The endorsement, however, did entitle Kennedy to first place on the primary ballot. But Kennedy really didn't need the party apparatus because he had unlimited funds, a substantial reserve of experienced manpower—the "Ken nedy Secretaries" — and thousands of citizens who yearned for a chance to do volunteer work for a member of the first family. The party needed Kennedy far more than Kennedy needed the party.

The overwhelming defeat inflicted on McCormack at Springfield — columnist Mary McGrory described the Kennedy organization as "something right out of Univac" — enhanced the mystique that the Kennedys are invincible. At least in Massachusetts, this has become a self-fulfilling prophecy. Party professionals were awed by the precision of the Kennedy operation, the sufficiency of Kennedy money, and the Kennedy penchant for attending to minute detail. McCormack therefore emerged from the convention looking like a loser, and potential McCormack volunteers were consequently discouraged. So were potential contributors to McCormack's campaign fund.

The politics of closed party primaries in which only officially enrolled party members may vote differs substantially from the politics of state conventions and general elections. The politics of Massachusetts state conventions turns, as we have suggested, on the will of perhaps a hundred professionals who are able to name hundreds of delegates and are therefore able to deliver votes. But the influence of these hundred professionals is very limited in Democratic primary elections, when as many as seven or eight hundred thousand secret ballots are cast by citizens, the overwhelming majority of whom not only have no contact with party leaders but do not even know their names. Candidates, therefore, must approach the people who are likely to vote in a primary election differently from the way they approach delegates. The ability to apply political pressure and grant political favors is obviously a critical factor in convention politics. It is relatively insignificant in primary elections. The professionals in Massachusetts play a minor role in primary elections because their local campaign organizations, with rare exceptions, are minuscule, ineffectual, or nonexistent. A candidate may win a primary election without their aid, although if they vigorously support him his chances greatly improve.

Money is a more significant variable in primary elections than in conventions because the candidate must purchase television and radio time, billboards, newspaper space, and hundreds of other items in order to make himself visible to primary voters and those who will vote in November. We do not wish to imply that money is an unimportant resource for state conventions — the convention candidate may spend from $80,000 to $100,000 in part to convince influential delegates that he could finance a primary and a general election contest if endorsed by the convention. The Kennedys could certainly do this.

Perhaps the fundamental difference between convention and primary politics, in terms of appropriate strategy and resources, is that delegates may be browbeaten, intimidated, or otherwise pressured into supporting a candidate, but this will not work with primary voters. The balloting at the convention is public and many delegates seek favors. The balloting in the primary is secret and very few voters seek favors.

The turnout in primary elections is invariably smaller than in general elections. V. O. Key, Jr., for example, discovered that not more than 35 per cent of the potential electorate voted in the primaries of either major party for governor in a sample of fifteen non-Southern states from 1926 to 1952.[1] Well over half of the potential electorate votes, however, in gubernatorial general elections.[2] When a bitter factional fight occurs during a primary, as was to be the case in the Kennedy-McCormack primary, the turnout is larger than usual but still not comparable to that in a general election. With many exceptions, those who vote in primaries are more politically sophisticated, more committed, more active, and more interested than most of those who vote only in general elections. So-called unaffiliated voters, i.e., Independents, are not eligible to vote in closed primaries, and "apathetics" do not vote in primaries.

Political strategy appropriate to primary voters, therefore, must be designed to account for the fact that "those who vote in the primaries do not make up miniatures of the party member-

[1] V. O. Key, Jr., *American State Politics: An Introduction* (New York: Alfred A. Knopf, 1956), p. 134.
[2] *Ibid.*, p. 135.

ship.''[3] The special character of the primary constituency has an influence on the type of person who can be nominated, the type of politician who may lead the party, and the tactics that will be effective for candidates. The unrepresentativeness of those who vote in primaries frequently results in the nomination of candidates who do not appeal to Independents, who in Massachusetts exceed the number of registered Republicans.

Since the candidates and all the voters in a closed primary are members of the same party it is also inevitable (except when the candidates represent divergent wings of the party) that the primary electorate is less concerned with issues and, perhaps, more concerned with "politics" than are those who habitually vote only in general elections. The critical decision for candidates in primaries is the delicate one of deciding just how boldly to attack the opposition in order to win the primary and yet not alienate, for the general election, supporters of the primary opponent.

McCormack, it was thought by his supporters, had a better chance against Kennedy in the primary election than he had had in the convention. The attraction of the Kennedy patronage power was more or less eliminated in a primary contest since few voters seek patronage. The liberals, who were probably underrepresented at the convention, would perhaps turn out in large numbers in the primary and support McCormack because of his liberal record. The party regulars, who do vote in primary contests, had supported McCormack in several previous primaries, and he, more than Edward Kennedy, was one of them. The McCormacks were counting on the party regulars and the support of thousands of citizens who, in their opinion, harbored much resentment toward Kennedy's candidacy. They were not delegates, but they were, to McCormack's mind, likely to vote in September and to vote against Kennedy.

Every election, however, takes place at a particular time and in a particular place. The time of the Kennedy-McCormack contest, of course, was 1962 and the place was Massachusetts. It was a Kennedy year and Massachusetts was a Kennedy place. The

[3] *Ibid.*, p. 145.

particular psychology of Massachusetts voters, the legacy of corruption in state government, and the position of the Kennedy family as the first family of Massachusetts Democrats were bound to affect the outcome — again in favor of Kennedy.

* * *

Modern Massachusetts politics is the history of the gradual displacement of an ancient and supposedly genteel Protestant commercial, cultural, and political elite — Republicans, of course — by a group composed primarily of the sons and grandsons of Irish and Italian immigrants. The new elite understands that political power is a great equalizer, that numbers win elections, and it assumes that politics is a service industry, rather than a mechanism for moralizing society.

Contemporary politics in the Bay State, the setting for the Kennedy-McCormack clash, may best be described in terms of seven major factors: (1) a Republican party, now distinctly the minority party, made up mainly of Anglo-Saxon Protestants, dominated until recent years by venerable Brahmins, and now committed to the Eisenhower brand of Republicanism; (2) a Democratic majority, composed primarily of Irish and Italo-American Catholics and considerably more conservative than its national counterpart; (3) a sizable bloc of unaffiliated voters — so-called Independents — who frequently hold the balance of power; (4) frequent indictments and convictions of elected and appointed officials, both state and local, which have created an aura of corruption; (5) a substantial number of alienated voters — Democrats, Republicans, and Independents who, in response to this corruption, feel politically powerless, robbed of their political birthright, and profoundly cynical; (6) many sophisticated politicians who are aware of the depth of the cynicism and who attempt to take advantage of it during campaigns; and (7) a "first family" — the Kennedys — who are politically powerful and who serve as ego-ideals for hundreds of thousands of Massachusetts Democrats.

Although at least one of the United States senators from Massachusetts has traditionally been a Republican, and the Governor, Lieutenant Governor, and Attorney General are now Republicans, the politics of Massachusetts is dominated by the Democratic party. Since 1955, Democrats have held a majority of the seats in the state House of Representatives and since 1959, a majority of the seats in the state Senate. Between 1955 and 1962 72 Republicans and 88 Democrats were elected to the upper chamber, and 400 Republicans and 560 Democrats to the lower chamber of the Great and General Court (the archaic but official title of the state legislature). Eight of Massachusetts' thirteen congressmen are now Democrats. During the same period 3 Republicans and 21 Democrats have been elected to state-wide office.

As of April 1, 1964, the first year for which such totals were published, 641,588 citizens of Massachusetts were registered as Republicans, 1,033,722 as Democrats, and 914,415 were affiliated with neither party. Most of the precincts in which registered Republicans greatly outnumber registered Democrats contain a sizable majority of middle- and upper-income Anglo-Saxons and Protestants. In these precincts, Protestants, Anglo-Saxons, and Republicans customarily receive a majority of the votes cast for the state legislature, for state-wide offices, and for Congress. The precincts in which Democrats customarily win elections are primarily composed of non-Protestants of lower-middle and lower-socioeconomic status. Voting "for your own kind" is also a Massachusetts tradition. Irish Americans tend to prefer Kennedys, McCormacks, Curleys, and McCarthys. Italo-Americans tend to prefer Volpes and Bellottis. Jews, who are strongly identified with the Democratic party, tend to vote for Jewish candidates, even when they are Republicans. There are many exceptions, but the trend is unmistakably clear and has been documented in several elections.[4]

[4] For an analysis of an election in which Italo-American Democrats voted in large numbers for an Italo-American Republican candidate for governor see Murray B. Levin with George Blackwood, *The Compleat Politician: Political Strategy in Massachusetts* (Indianapolis: The Bobbs-Merrill Company, 1962). The tendency for Democrats and Republicans to cross party lines for ethnic reasons can also be documented in the 1962 gubernatorial election, when approximately 80,000 registered Yankee Republicans supported Endicott Peabody, the Yankee Democrat candidate for governor who opposed an Italo-American Republican. This trend may be observed too in the 1954 election for attorney general, when numerous Jewish Democrats supported a Jewish Republican candidate.

The Democratic party in Massachusetts, as we have said, is far more conservative than the Democratic party in the nation as a whole. John F. Kennedy was forced to transcend the parochialism and conservatism of his Massachusetts brethren before becoming a national candidate. The so-called Al Smith Democrat — a dominant type in the party — is suspicious of governmental authority except when it is used on behalf of the underdog, and then only for limited purposes. He has very little ideological orientation of the traditional liberal sort, particularly when it relates to the planned use of governmental power for long-range goals. He must be persuaded first that planning will result in some immediate benefit to workingmen. Familiar with personal and feudal politics — the politics of ethnic factions headed by party chieftains of a particular national origin and supported primarily by co-ethnics — he finds the abstract, impersonal concepts of the New Deal, the New Frontier, and the Great Society vague and somehow inimical.[5]

A member of the Kennedy brain trust, a most astute observer of Massachusetts politics, commented:

The conservatism of Massachusetts Democrats is a conservatism on international issues and issues of society. . . . On the issue of Communism, the Massachusetts Democrats have much in common with the ideas and position of the late Senator McCarthy. It is a state that is intensely concerned about the Communist menace to the United States, not only in its foreign aspect but in its domestic aspect. And this often pushes great numbers of registered Democrats, and urban Democrats, towards the Republican party. There is also a conservatism in the sense of a fear of strong government. That is, certain strands of negativistic, anarchistic attitude of many people, particularly the Irish, towards government, makes people of Irish-Catholic background have more in common with Republicans than with Democrats. A person who lives in a city and would regard himself as working class or

5 *Ibid.*, pp. 26-30.

underprivileged, or even lower-middle class, would submerge these things to vote for the bread-and-butter liberalism and politics of the Democratic party. But they would still be suspicious of Big Government. This is an inheritance from Europe.

Again, you have to think of the Irish as a Latin people. And when you think of the Irish as Latins, in the way that you think of the French or the Italian voters, you may have a better picture of their political inheritance. . . . And because of their history, they, like the Italians and the French and the Spaniards, have a strong negativistic attitude towards government — any government, you see, which of course accounts, in countries like Italy and France, for the strong Communist vote. Here this conservatism of course doesn't reflect itself in Communism, but it does reflect itself in the small-town philosophy of the Republicans.

If the people of the cities go to a small town, as many do, then they are pushed into the Republican party. Massachusetts has a legacy of religious division, which has divided Protestants and Catholics into the opposing parties. Almost all Protestants in this state are at least nominally Republicans. Almost all Irish Catholics are nominally Democrats. . . . And I would think that a Kennedy or a Stevenson, if religious issues were not present in this state, would probably mean that they wouldn't win. That is, I would think if there were no religious factors in Massachusetts, if there were not in 1960, Nixon would have beaten Kennedy.

* * *

Corruption in public life, real or imaginary, is another factor that influences — and decisively — the outcome of many Massachusetts elections. Prior to World War I, corruption in Massachusetts may have been no more prevalent than in other American states. Flagrant instances of payoffs to public officials and conflicts of interest were unusual, although petty graft was common. The number of investigations, indictments, and convictions of Massachusetts and Boston public officials, however, has sharply increased during the past four decades.[6] Numerous political commentators and hundreds of thousands of citizens of Massachusetts have now come to believe that politics in the Bay State exemplifies the ineptitude and degradation characteristic of many American states and municipalities. Theodore White, for instance, has included Massachusetts among "those states whose politics (excluding the baroque courthouse states of the South) are the most squalid, corrupt and despicable. . . ."[7]

The Massachusetts Crime Commission, in its comprehensive report for 1956, noted the extent of corruption in the Commonwealth.

> Our investigations have shown that corruption in Massachusetts is much more than the giving and taking of bribes and the larceny of public funds. It involves a whole spectrum of actions and attitudes — from the fixing of traffic tickets to the commission of serious crimes. It includes the widespread and dangerous practice of the exaction of campaign contribu-

6 For a discussion of corruption in Massachusetts politics, see:
Ibid., pp. 54–68.
Massachusetts Crime Commission, Comprehensive Report, Vol. I, May 17, 1965.
Anthony Lewis, "Massachusetts Is Aroused by Corruption Scandals," *New York Times,* June 19, 1961; "Massachusetts Turnpike Chief Criticized in Rising Scandals," *ibid.,* June 20, 1961.
Louis M. Lyons, "Boston: Study in Inertia," in Robert S. Allen, ed., *Our Fair City* (New York: Vanguard Press, 1947), pp. 21–24.
U.S. vs. Worcester, 190 Fed. Supp. 548.
Charles L. Whipple, "Dirty Money in Boston," *Atlantic Monthly,* March, 1961.
William H. Wells, "Conflict of Interest in Massachusetts," *Boston Globe,* March 19, 20, 21, 23, 24, 26, 28, 30, April 2, 3, 4, 6, 1961.
Emily Tavel, "Is Massachusetts Worst: Bookies, Kickbacks, Payoffs," *Christian Science Monitor,* August 9, 1961, p. 1; "Public Aroused," *ibid.,* August 11, 1961, p. 1.
"Battle for Boston," *The Economist* (London), March 11, 1961, pp. 952–53.
Hearings of the U.S. House of Representatives Committee on Public Works (subcommittee), March, 1962.
William H. Wells, "Conflict of Interest: How Bad Did It Get?" *Boston Globe,* April 6, 1961, p. 4; "Same Game Played in Town, City Halls," *ibid.,* April 4, 1961, p. 1.
"The Massachusetts Crime Commission, Governmental Indifference, and Public Apathy," *Boston Forum,* March-April, 1966.

7 Theodore H. White, *The Making of the President, 1960* (New York: Atheneum Publishers, 1961), p. 97

tions in return for promised or implied favors in the award of contracts and appointments to office. It includes the spoils system allocation of jobs to political henchmen. It includes the now deeply ingrained view of government jobs and government business as a private preserve for taking care of those with political connections. . . .

When a sizable segment of the political community looks contemptuously on the body politic as a source of plunder — something to be cynically manipulated and exploited — and when, in turn, too many citizens come to look on politics as a dirty business and on politicians as naturally suspect, the fabric of a civilized society becomes dangerously frayed.

In this climate able and honorable men are increasingly unwilling or unable to go into politics or state service. Many of the weaker public servants, whose intentions were at least initially honorable, are gradually infected and play the game as they come to feel it has to be played. They look the other way to avoid being labeled self-righteous do-gooders or troublemakers. They neither oppose nor expose their colleagues, whose votes or help they may need.

In this climate, furthermore, the price of large-scale, long-continued corruption and incompetence is too high for any community, and particularly for Massachusetts, where state finances are a major problem.

Due to financial loss and waste from corruption and incompetence, many urgent needs of the community cannot be met or are met inadequately. The taxpayer pays far more than he should for the results obtained. No estimate can be made in dollar values of the waste and loss suffered by the state in recent years from these causes. It has undoubtedly run into scores of millions. . . .

Although we have far from exhausted the possible investigations, the reality has been worse than we imagined. We have observed with indignation the ways in which some of the most highly placed and powerful political figures in the state have betrayed the public trust. We have noted with increasing concern the moral blindness of so many who have appeared before us, their self-justification and their inability to understand that their conduct was questionable.[8]

8 *Massachusetts Crime Commission, op. cit.,* pp. 2–4.

Many Massachusetts citizens concur. A survey of Massachusetts voters, published in 1962, revealed that 17 per cent of the respondents selected "corruption in government" as "one of the most important" problems in the state, and 80 per cent believed that it was "very important."[9]

Assuming that politicians are corrupt, many citizens have concluded that voting is useless, reform impossible, and the democratic process a hollow mockery of what it is supposed to be. They structure the political world in terms of a sharp dichotomy between the powerful insiders — politicians, contractors, bookies, big businessmen — and voters, who are powerless outsiders. These are the alienated voters, who believe that they are manipulated and exploited by forces they cannot counter or even influence. The feeling of being wrongfully excluded, impotent, and cheated of their political birthright is the essential component of their political alienation.

These voters are hostile to politicians and disenchanted with the political process. They are wary of candidates who spend large sums of money during campaigns. They are skeptical of those who are endorsed by powerful "public" figures, and they regard campaign promises and platforms as empty verbiage. If they vote at all it is for the "lesser of two evils," and against "politicians," against the well financed, and against the powerful. They do not really vote "for" anyone.

Given this condition of extreme skepticism and hostility, or perhaps in some instances extreme sophistication, the traditional vote-getting techniques and the customary political rhetoric are likely to backfire. The candidate who campaigns in an alienated electorate must avoid the appearance of being "a politician," he must not conduct "opulent" campaigns (or he must hide his opulence), and he must convince the voters that he is not corrupt or at least is less corrupt than his opponent.

9 *Massachusetts Voters Talk*, a Statewide Study of Opinion Research Corporation, Princeton, New Jersey, prepared for the Massachusetts Federation of Taxpayers Associations, October, 1962. Eighteen per cent of the respondents selected "state and local taxes" as "one of the most important problems," and 80 per cent selected "schools" as a "very important" problem. These were the only issues mentioned as frequently as "corruption in government."

Signs and hoop-la in the lobby of the convention hotel

McCormack's father, "Knocko," at the convention

Balloting begins in convention hall

Kennedy magnetism

McCormack campaigning

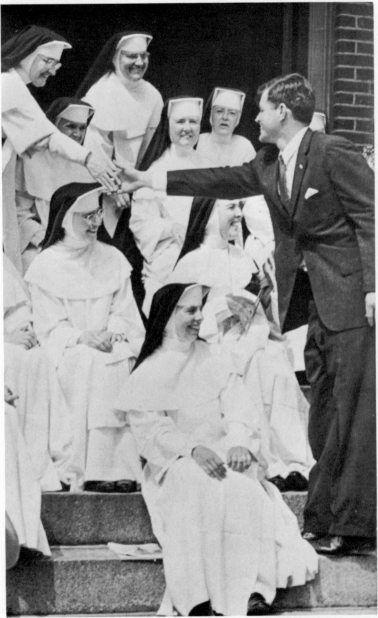

Kennedy campaigning

McCormack meets a voter

"If his name was Edward Moore . . ."   WIDE WORLD PHOTO

WIDE WORLD PHOTO   WIDE WORLD PHOTO

Kennedy and McCormack at the second debate

The McCormacks vote

Victory: Senator-elect Edward Kennedy and his wife

Knowing that alienated voters are plentiful and want information relevant to a candidate's integrity, many candidates respond by proclaiming their purity while castigating the opposition. Mudslinging has therefore become commonplace in recent Massachusetts elections. But the candidates have not fully appreciated the subtlety of the problem. Since alienated voters assume that the candidates are dishonest, they have no reason to believe their attacks on their opponents. As one voter said of a candidate's assault on the opposition, "It takes a crook to know one."

The alienated voter cannot rationally make his choice in terms of campaign speeches and party platforms for experience has taught him that candidates are liars and that campaign promises are hollow pronouncements designed to garner voters rather than meaningful expressions of future intent. Ideology is no longer a relevant criterion of choice. The voter may, however — or perhaps must — cast his vote according to his estimate of the candidate's character or personality, an estimate based on intuitive reactions to the candidate's posture, size, diction, eyes, hair, etc. He may just "feel in his bones," as one respondent put it, that "the candidate is a crook."

Corruption in public life, real or imaginary, and the alienation resulting from it, are therefore critical factors in Massachusetts politics. In recent Massachusetts campaigns, sophisticated politicians have attempted to appear as non-politicians and political innocents. Benjamin De Mott has even suggested that a trend exists in Massachusetts and in the country "toward apolitical politics, partyless and problemless." In the 1962 state convention he noted

. . . an extraordinary consciousness among participants in the gatherings of popular dissatisfaction with politics. A common remark at both conventions was that the best qualifications for any aspirant for State Office was, if not lack of experience, then a lack of identification in the public mind with ward politics, office holding, loyal party labor, or the power of "INSIDERDOM . . ." Every candidate appeared to be engaged in an attempt first to establish himself as a po-

litical innocent, second to link the opposition with professional politics and insiderdom.[10]

For the alienated voter eligible and willing to vote in the primary, the choice was obvious. Edward Kennedy was a political innocent, a "clean" candidate, who had never been elected to any
office. Edward McCormack, however, had been elected to public office — five times. He was Attorney General during a period when many people believed corruption in state and local government was widespread. He was an intimate associate of professional politicians and he was from South Boston. Could he
be easily cast in the role of a non-politician and political innocent? McCormack, of course, according to De Mott, charged "that
Mr. Kennedy was politics itself — politics as promises, things,
postmasterships, federal jobs, deals, men of power lighting each
other's candles."[11]

The trend toward apolitical politics, De Mott suggests, also
can be observed in other states:

Much has been written on the theme of the attractive candidate as a political mute — a set of gestures, a figure in a
myth, a man capable of asking his audience to look straight
into his heart for solutions to community problems (solutions that take the form of lessons in likableness and decency) . . . the minor paradoxes that multiply in such contests need no gloss; the man seeking party endorsement secures it by declaring his scorn for it; the politician seeking
paid political office secures it by noisily despising people who
depend on politics "for a living." But beyond this lies the
less palpable truth that uninterrupted exposure to campaigns organized on this model means the formulation of a
whole new area of taboo. As long as the democratic struggle
to replace suspicion of governors with confidence is given
over, politics itself, the organization of public life emerges as
the Ultimate Unspeakable of human experience.[12]

[10] Benjamin De Mott, "An Unprofessional Eye," *The American Scholar,*
Autumn, 1962, p. 597. With respect to "gut reactions," De Mott wrote that Mc-
Cormack had an "unfortunate slouch to his lower lip."
[11] *Ibid.,* p. 585.
[12] *Ibid.,* p. 599.

The alienated voter could scarcely find a more attractive candidate to support — and thus transcend his alienation — than Edward Kennedy. Alienation was clearly another factor in the Massachusetts political setting, which paved the way for Kennedy's victory and McCormack's defeat.

*   *   *

A significant feature of that setting — perhaps the most significant — was the magnetism of the Kennedy family and Edward Kennedy felt especially by lower- and lower-middle-class voters, primarily of Irish and Italian background. Feelings of alienation and disenchantment with traditional Democratic political types undoubtedly enhance the Kennedy appeal in Massachusetts. Hundreds of people who had an opportunity to be near the candidate attempted to touch him, kiss him, tear off a piece of his clothing, talk to him, comfort him, and urge him on with screams of delight. One McCormack aide, who despised Kennedy, observed him on several occasions and reported:

> I've seen Ted Kennedy get a bigger ovation from the kiddies than Rex Trailer [a television cowboy], who was in the same parade. . . . There was spontaneous cheering among the children, and the women goggled, "Here he comes." . . . The women politely clapped for Eddie McCormack — but all the joy of seeing Ted Kennedy . . . these women just get the chemical reaction when Ted Kennedy comes along, that spontaneous reaction.

Advisers of George Lodge noticed the same phenomenon during the general election. A Lodge man suggested that

> . . . the word Hollywood has been used in connection with Teddy's campaign by a lot of people, and this is the word that I would use myself. There's a tremendous amount of grabbing at Teddy. Teddy is a Hollywood star. Teddy doesn't need the ballyhoo of buses, volunteers, or campaign organization to whip up excitement. . . .

Other Lodge aides suggested that Edward Kennedy should be treated as if he were a cleric. "The identification of the Kennedy family with the Catholic Church," one of them noted, "is so great that really Ted is a Prince of the Church in this state, and you cannot attack a Prince of the Church, no matter what he does. No matter what he does . . . you simply can't touch this guy. You can't lay a glove on him." Kennedy's appeal, he went on, stemmed from the fact that "he is the favorite son of the Irish families. He is *the* example of the successful Irish boy to Irish mothers around this state. They just don't want anybody criticizing any person who is such a prime example of the successful family." A State House political correspondent suggested that the Boston Irish strongly identify with John Kennedy because he was the great success story of all time for them:

> Anyone of similar background looks up to him and hopes that they, at one time or another in their life, will be able to achieve the same thing. But being practical, they know they can't, and therefore attach themselves to him and say, "Well, one of our boys made it and made it big." And so consequently they forget all about McCormack and McCormack's background . . . they forget completely that Eddie McCormack is too an Irish Catholic. It's been said of McCormack . . . he might as well be Jewish.

The enormous prestige of a Kennedy candidate in Massachusetts can be seen in this interview with a trade union official:

> For a period of several days I made arrangements for Mr. Kennedy to visit a series of factories in Massachusetts. . . . I called up a few employers with whom I was not friendly, and I think these employers would take a great deal of delight in turning me down on a personal request . . . bearing in mind also that any time Mr. Kennedy or any candidate visits a plant there is a subsequent loss in production and efficiency for at least an hour and the maximal efficiency of the plant is destroyed for the whole day.
> Well, I called up and I said, "Mr. So-and-So, I'd like to ask a favor of you. Mr. Kennedy would like to visit your plant some time next week" and I gave him the date. "He would be as quick as possible but I must tell you in all fairness that he would walk through the plant, shake hands with people at

their machines, and because he is such an extraordinarily popular person I'm sure that the people will receive him with a great deal of enthusiasm, and contiguous with this enthusiasm would be a disruption of your productive facilities. But I would deeply appreciate it, and so would Mr. Kennedy, if you would allow him to spend a half-hour or an hour visiting your plant." I literally held my breath for the response, fearing that there would just be an Orwellian deluge of invective and animosity. Instead, I was deeply surprised that the three employers who ordinarily would turn me down on any request said, "Why, what an honor, what a prestige, to have a member of the presidential family visit in our plant." They said, "Not only can he visit, but I want to meet him personally if that would be possible, and if you would like, I would be glad to turn off the power and have him hold a meeting right in the plant."

In retrospect, the setting within which this election took place makes a Kennedy victory appear to have been a certainty. Every single factor of significance in Massachusetts politics worked to Kennedy's advantage and McCormack's disadvantage. The conservative taste of many Democrats ran counter to McCormack's liberalism. It was far easier for lower- and lower-middle-class non-Protestants to identify with Kennedy than with McCormack. The alienated voter could easily believe that Kennedy was a non-politician and an innocent whereas McCormack had held elective office and was therefore seen as not so innocent.

The candidates and their campaign managers were forced to operate within this very special setting. Some of the factors we have isolated and analyzed were more or less known to them; others were not. We have the benefit of hindsight; they did not. We conferred with both the Kennedys and the McCormacks during the campaign; they conferred only with themselves. We speak of the Kennedy appeal as if it were an obvious and easily definable entity; neither Kennedy nor McCormack quite understood how powerful a force it was until late in the campaign. We know in retrospect that Kennedy's lack of office holding experience was a distinct advantage for him; both Kennedy and McCormack *thought* it was a decided disadvantage. In other words, much of what seems clear to us now was by no means clear to them then.

The rational candidate, like the rational businessman, will attempt to utilize his scarce resources — time, money, and man-power — as efficiently as possible. He wants to receive the maximum number of votes for a given amount of time, a given amount of money, a given number of man-hours. He must make every minute, every bit of paid and volunteer work count. If his only goal during a campaign is to increase the size of his vote, he will weigh every strategic gambit solely in terms of which is most likely to gain the largest number of votes or lose the fewest — moral considerations notwithstanding.[13]

Professional politicians and public relations men whose specialty is politics claim that experience in many campaigns has equipped them with a political sixth sense — an intuition. It tells them where and how the candidate should spend his precious time, how money should best be allocated, and how best to utilize the efforts of campaign workers. Nevertheless, the efficient allocation of scarce resources is enormously difficult. Whatever public opinion polls seem to indicate, it may not be easy to determine where voters live and work and seek reinforcement, or in what areas large clusters of undecided voters are located. Is it more rational to purchase fifteen minutes of television time, immediately following "Gunsmoke," and engage in a serious discussion of the issues, knowing neither the attention span of the average voter nor his threshold of boredom, or to purchase one-minute "spots," as General Eisenhower did (*"Voice:* Mr. Eisenhower, what about the high cost of living? *Eisenhower:* My wife, Mamie, worries about the same thing. I tell her it's our job to change that on November 4). Should the candidate speak on television as if he were in a living room conversing with a few people or as if he were at a rally talking to thousands? It may not be easy to determine what tasks can be best performed by

13 For an interesting theoretical model of democracy based on this concept of rationality see Anthony Downs, *An Economic Theory of Democracy* (New York: Harper & Brothers, 1957).

hundreds, perhaps thousands, of volunteer workers, whose enthusiasm for the candidate and the cause far exceeds their ability to type. The image of the political campaign as a highly efficient operation, directed by an expert general staff, is rarely true-to-life.[14] Most campaigns resemble a comedy of errors in which the victor prospers primarily because he has committed fewer strategic blunders than his opponent.

The task of candidates and campaign managers is complex and often frustrating. Although they wish to manipulate bits and pieces of reality so as to improve the image of their candidate and worsen the image of his opponent, their ability to do so is always limited by certain facts of the campaign situation that can be neither ignored nor altered by public relations men. These unalterable and unmanipulatable facts of political life we call "givens." Most "givens" are assets as well as liabilities. Edward Kennedy's lineage was an enormous asset, but it was also a liability since a minority of voters in Massachusetts dislike the Kennedy family or fear a Kennedy dynasty. The campaign manager must define the "givens" of his candidate and those of his opponent and evaluate the assets and liabilities of each "given" for both candidates. The advisers, of course, must also determine whether or not their estimate matches that of the majority of voters. A particular "given" may be a liability in the opinion of the candidate's brain trust but an asset in the opinion of voters. Although Kennedy's advisers believed, for example, that his youth, fortune, and lack of experience probably were significant liabilities, a majority of voters apparently viewed them as assets.

The degree to which a particular "given" may be publicized, hidden, disguised, or "manipulated" depends upon how obvious it is, how great is the need of voters to ignore or observe it, and how well the opposition exploits the liabilities inherent in it. Edward Kennedy's "givens," it seems, were seen by a majority of

14 See V. O. Key, Jr., *Politics, Parties, and Pressure Groups* (New York: Thomas Y. Crowell Company, 4th ed., 1958), p. 512: "One may speak of a grand campaign strategy, rationally formulated and executed with precision, but a great deal of campaign management rests on the hunches that guide day-to-day decisions. The lore of politics includes rules of thumb that are supposed to embody the wisdom of political experience as guides to action."

the voters as assets while those of McCormack were viewed primarily as liabilities. However, according to most of the traditional criteria by which candidates in America have been judged, McCormack was a "better" candidate than he could be made to appear to the public, and Kennedy's public image was "better" than his record. From the public relations point of view, it was easy to merchandise Kennedy, difficult to merchandise McCormack.

Political strategy is formulated on the basis of accurate information, misinformation, rules of thumb, hunches, and the availability of scarce resources. The candidate's information concerning voter preferences and prejudices is obviously a critical variable in political campaigns; strategy is based on it. The Kennedys have consistently relied on information gathered by competent professional pollsters — information gathered at considerable expense. Kennedy strategists customarily "move" with a reasonably high degree of confidence because their moves are based on data they regard as valid. The decision to run Edward Kennedy in 1962 was made, in part, because public opinion data indicated he would soundly defeat any likely opponent. A friend of Edward Kennedy reported that

> . . . they've been taking polls all along, and they know they're ahead. And they took polls before Teddy ran and they knew that he could win and that's the reason he's running. I don't believe that Teddy Kennedy would be in this race if they didn't think by reason of polls that he was a winner. I personally know of a poll that was taken before Teddy Kennedy announced his candidacy, which showed him a sure winner over McCormack. And they do it this way.

The difference between the Kennedy and the McCormack approaches to political campaigning is nowhere better illustrated than by a comparison of how the candidates gathered information on which to base strategic decisions. Edward McCormack did not employ the services of a professional public opinion firm. He and his advisers believed that money which might have been allocated to polling could be more effectively spent elsewhere. Several of McCormack's long-time associates, moreover, did not place much value on data gathered by pollsters. Old-style politicians, they still relied on verbal reports from the wards and precincts. Nevertheless, McCormack advisers utilized the services of several college students who interviewed voters, although they had no training in the techniques of interviewing or sampling. A small number of citizens were interviewed at their place of residence or in the streets; some were reached by telephone (every *n*th name in the telephone book). Thus no scholarly attempt was made to interview a truly random sample of registered Democrats. One McCormack aide commented:

> I don't remember all the details of this poll, but I do know this, that there was no way of determining the way in which the poll was conducted, any way of determining the adequacy of the sampling, or the nature of the sampling. As far as I can see, 159 people were called at random. . . .

McCormack's campaign manager reported that no polls had been taken by a professional firm. "I'm not sure," he remarked, "how much McCormack himself believes in professional polls. I myself would have liked to have seen a professional poll of our own early in the game [but] . . . there was opposition from the traditionalists in the McCormack camp." Although McCormack people stated that the techniques they used to gather public opinion data were unreliable and that they placed little credence in them, they continued to compile information. On July 15, just a week after the convention, a McCormack public relations man described the feeling at McCormack headquarters as optimistic:

> I think the basis of their optimism comes not through any scientific sampling, but through the traditional barometric devices that politicians have for gauging political climate. I feel that there is a tide going for Ed McCormack, a tide of resentment, and that he is going either, depending on their own particular assessment of that tide, either sweep in or eke out a narrow victory. . . . Well, basically they consist of talking to people, and in a non-scientific, almost — well, let it go at non-

scientific. A non-scientific way of assessing and divining and projecting from very narrow samples, wider conclusions. And I think traditionally politicians, office holders, people in the political arena, have people that they talk to that to their mind, to their way of thinking, represent an element that they can refer to and say, "Well, I talked to Sam Goldberg and the Jews are with McCormack, or the Jews are with Kennedy." Or "I talked with this guy, and we've got the Lebanese." Or "I've talked to so-and-so and we have this particular strata. . . ." They too often go from the particular to the general and when they do that they do it without any real scientific basis. And they have some validity; I certainly will not decry them to this point. They have some validity, but none of the validity of a real scientific sample that crosses a broad strata of the electorate and has scientific validity as we know it in terms of the science of communications today.

He also gave an example of the type of poll taken for McCormack:

We have certain available data that is not really scientific data, but is based on informal private samplings and polls. Well, basically, for instance, there'll be a guy who was a McCormack supporter who talked to twenty-five different people of his own acquaintance who he feels are a broad-based sample of the electorate, and we can make some determination from this. This is non-scientific at best, and I don't give a great deal of credence to it.

Information gathered by supporters of a candidate is likely to be biased simply because the interviewer is biased and may therefore provide cues to the respondent indicating the kind of answers he seeks, or because the respondent knows the interviewer and his bias. Several Kennedy advisers and a few McCormack aides suggested that since politicians talk primarily with other politicians the information they report tends to be unreliable. One Kennedy aide believed that those involved in the campaign are "the worst judges in the world":

Because they're talking to the same people all the time. This goes for my campaign, my fight, my workers, anybody's.

They're the worst judges in the world. That's why politicians don't pick winners very often. They're talking to the same people and they keep hearing the same answers. They don't realize and stop to think for a minute that they're only talking to pros and semi-pros, and their opinions do not necessarily reflect the opinions of the voters. I think we learn that in many fights now. I think they thought Kennedy was going to win, but I think they were scared to death he wasn't. But certainly nobody in that camp — and I don't know what your poll showed and I don't know what their polls show, but none of them predicted 70–30 or 69–31, or anywhere near it. And they would have signed a contract for 51–49, every one of them, including the candidate, despite the fact that some of the polls, or all of the polls, showed that he was going to win.

McCormack could not have defeated Kennedy if he had had a continuous supply of reliable public opinion data. He apparently had little faith in this technique and insufficient funds to use it. Nevertheless his failure to employ a professional public opinion firm was primarily due to the old-school professionals surrounding him who were skeptical of modern campaign techniques and preferred to operate by arcane rules of thumb and intuition. Still, since McCormack knew that the Kennedys calculate strategic gambits in terms of public opinion data, it is remarkable that he did not follow suit. The national press billed the Kennedy-McCormack contest as a death struggle between two dynastic candidates each with a large entourage of highly skilled professionals. This portrait is to some extent false since many of the McCormack professionals were "old style" and their activities were not very useful.

Edward McCormack and his aides had to make four basic strategic decisions during the campaign. (1) Should the Attorney General attack Kennedy or ignore him, and if attack was deemed advisable, how should it be mounted? (2) How widespread was the stereotype of McCormack as a "Boston pol" (including the view that he had not done enough to fight corruption) and should he attempt to counteract the stereotype or ignore it? If a decision were made to counteract this stereotype, how should he proceed? (3) How could McCormack best take advantage of his record as a public servant, and of Kennedy's great lack of office-holding experience? And (4), should McCormack seek maximum exposure in view of the assumption by many of his aides that his personality and physical characteristics were not best suited to the handshaking type of campaign customarily waged in Massachusetts primary elections?

The question of how to deal with Kennedy was really the fundamental one. McCormack and his aides fully understood the appeal of John F. Kennedy in Massachusetts. It was perfectly obvious to them that he could in no way be criticized. They also sensed how risky it would be to attack the President's brother unless they could separate Edward Kennedy from the President.

In their opinion Edward Kennedy was open to attack and had to be exposed, but in a carefully worded and mild way. The question really was how to attack Kennedy without attacking Kennedy. "You can say he's got money," a friend of McCormack suggested, "you can say he's got the brother, he's got the patronage, you can say all these things. But you can't make him out as a crook, or a bum, or evil, or anything like that — a rat, or a guy that doesn't look right. You can't do that to this kid." Any attack, it appeared, could be based only upon his youth, his wealth, and the fact that he had never held elective office.

McCormack's advisers believed, on this occasion, what they wanted voters to believe. They assumed that Kennedy, at the age of twenty-nine, could be criticized as too young for the job. They assumed that, being a millionaire he could be criticized as a playboy — a ne'er-do-well, who had never worked for a living. And they assumed that since he had never held elective office his candidacy could be portrayed as presumptuous, as violating the log-cabin-to-White-House value system held (they supposed) by the voters of Massachusetts. But, as we have seen, his youth contributed to his image as a political innocent and non-politician, his wealth was interpreted as an indication that he would not steal from the public till, and his office-holding inexperience reinforced his image as a non-politician, a non-member of the Boston political gang, i.e., as a clean outsider. For McCormack, the issue of attacking Kennedy was not simple, but McCormack aides did not fully understand its complexities.

The issue was further complicated by the fact that, as the campaign progressed through the hot summer months, it became clear that Edward Kennedy was seen by hundreds of thousands of Democrats as very special, unusually magnetic if not electrifying. Where he campaigned, not only did large crowds cheer him enthusiastically, scream at him as they do at the Beatles, and want to touch him, but a peculiar kind of titillation swept over the people. In other words, voters now felt the magnetism of the youngest Kennedy. This was not apparent to either the Kennedys or the McCormacks during the first few weeks of the campaign. However, it was patent that to attack a candidate with such obvious appeal was probably suicidal. "To put it bluntly," a McCormack aide noted quite late in the campaign, "our problem is whether or not you can attack God."

Nevertheless, most McCormack advisers were convinced that a substantial number of Democrats and Independents resented Kennedy's candidacy and they urged McCormack to attack Kennedy, utilizing ridicule rather than invective. The Attorney General's public relations counsel said early in July:

I side with doing as much in a so-called anti-Ted Kennedy sense as we can, immediately, and running the risk of running out of steam. I think that there is enough ammunition here so that we will never run out of steam, and I think that our path to victory lies in capitalizing on the fantastic feeling of resentment that I detect in talking to a broad band of people from practically every walk of life, to use the old cliché. There is, I think, a resentment against this young man having the effrontery to run for this position in this stage of his political life, and it crosses the broad spectrum of every class of people that I've had any opportunity to talk to. I think the only way we're going to win this fight is to give enough food to this particular feeling and make it increase. . . .

I think that it can be done in a number of ways. I think that it can be done insidiously, if that's the proper word, by poking fun, if you will, at the effrontery of Ted Kennedy in running for this office. And even more importantly, I think it can be done by trying to relate this particular situation to situations that people can understand and cling to, such as Eddie did in his television show, by drawing the analogy of the boss' brother getting the job that you have trained for and looked toward all of your working career. This is one way; there are other ways. I think that they can be used throughout the rest of the campaign in a manner that will not exhaust any of the ammunition, but will rather let it go in a carefully prearranged time schedule so that the big bombs are thrown at the end.

Almost every McCormack adviser agreed that the Attorney General must "go after the kid." The question was *how?* One of the account executives who handled the McCormack campaign said:

Everyone agrees that eventually this campaign will come down to Ed McCormack's attacking Ted Kennedy on a personal basis, on his various inadequacies, on his qualifications, on his ability and right to run for this office. The disagreement exists, or has existed, much more on the question of when the silken glove was taken off to expose the mail fist. . . . There is one school of thought that says that the big gun should be unveiled right now, that what information we have . . . should be made public. And of course the basic underlying theme of the campaign, his general lack of qualification for the post of United States Senator, should be brought home to the public as dramatically and forcefully as possible. The other school says that this should be done in a statement of the qualifications of Ed McCormack and a kind of dispassionate look at the lack of qualifications of Ted Kennedy. I think I could best probably categorize that as a kind of three steps forward, one step backwards school. . . .

The problem ultimately resolved itself. By mid-August — primary election day was September 18 — McCormack's more objective aides realized that Kennedy had a commanding lead and that the McCormack organization was rapidly disintegrating. At this point literally everyone in the McCormack camp urged the Attorney General to engage in a vigorous attack. Describing the

status of the McCormack organization in late August, a devoted
friend of the candidate reported:

> The general feeling I think was, on the part of most people
> there, that the McCormack campaign was lagging badly.
> There was no sense of urgency among the McCormack work-
> ers. The general feeling within the McCormack camp was,
> well, many people were going through the motions with Eddie
> McCormack, many people, either out of personal loyalty, or
> out of an ideological loyalty for the things for which the can-
> didate stood felt they ought to be doing something for Eddie
> McCormack and so in fact were going through the motions.

A speech writer argued that an attack on Kennedy made
good sense, at this late date, even if it only served the purpose of
revivifying the McCormack organization.

> As a result of this feeling and this general mood of lethargy,
> within the McCormack camp, the first assumption I think ar-
> ticulated by virtually everybody in the brain trust was that
> Eddie McCormack must get himself into a fighting stance. He
> must appear to be the aggressor. . . . Kennedy was out in
> front, and there was a great lethargy in the McCormack camp.
> The only way that Eddie McCormack could overcome this
> lead which Kennedy had and also stimulate his own organi-
> zation was to go on the attack. . . . There was also the reali-
> zation in the McCormack camp that Eddie McCormack is not
> by nature or by temperament . . . an aggressive type of
> fighter. He is much more judicious, much more balanced,
> and much more mild mannered in his whole approach to po-
> litical speeches. . . . So I think there was a conscious effort on
> the part of the strategists around McCormack to anger Mc-
> Cormack, to convey to him their feelings that he must become
> aggressive, that he must fight, that the campaign was slipping
> away from him, and unless he goes on the offensive all will be
> lost. This was the first assumption. Coupled with that, I
> think, was the feeling that Kennedy is relatively inexperi-
> enced, there's some reason to believe he has a relatively low
> boiling point, that he can be angered, he can be incensed, he
> can be baited into counterattacking.

As we shall see, McCormack eventually accepted their advice.

Another serious problem which McCormack had to face was how best to deal with the fact that he was attorney general during a time when corruption in public life appeared to many voters to be extremely prevalent. Kennedy's polls and ours indicated that most of the unfavorable comments of respondents referring to Mc-Cormack had to do with the corruption question. McCormack's more realistic advisers, without the aid of public opinion data, knew that the Attorney General would be stereotyped as a typical "pol" although they believed he had vigorously executed the duties of his office. This problem, perhaps more than any other in this election, exemplifies the difficulties faced by candidates when they must deal with an issue that is both complex and technical and a popular stereotype that is crude, simplistic, and appealing. One McCormack adviser, an attorney and noted civil libertarian, felt that:

> The corruption problem is in abeyance, largely, for the primary. I think it will pop up to be *the* real issue for the final elections, but in the primaries it seems to have receded. However, before the "Meet the Press" it was in full flower, and very difficult because of the tandem nature of the problem, and tendency of the readers and the voters to flail about without any understanding of the technical materials it must go into in a real attempt to cope with the problem of corruption, the amount of time it takes to articulate the technical exposition, and the rather defensive-sounding quality of it.
>
> It means, to begin with, a vast knowledge of the structure of state government in Massachusetts, the nature of a public authority, the fact that it does not have — is not subject to public audit, that public bids are not required, the confusion between it as an agency of government and it as a private enterprise, the way corruption defalcations and so forth come into public attention, the role of the prosecutor, the role of the grand jury, the distinction between the governor's office and the state police and the governor's office and the district attorney's the federal establishment, the state establishment. . . .
> Usually you are given two or three minutes to speak to it,

you can only deal in slogans and it requires a half-hour of very orderly, closely reasoned exposition to lay it out sufficiently and discuss it intelligently. . . .

How do you deal with it? Well, we've spent a great deal of time, I don't think too successfully, in dealing with it, because in two or three minutes you say, "I'm not corrupt, . . . I've gotten more indictments than the last three office holders put together," and so forth and so on. But that doesn't really begin to come to grips with the problem.

McCormack was also at a disadvantage because he, his uncle, and his father were politicians — indeed, South Boston politicians — during a period when politicians were suspect. McCormack's aides were concerned with this problem, which was analyzed with much insight by a member of the Kennedy brain trust.

McCormack is stigmatized by his Boston birth, Boston accent, and by the fact that he has played the game of personalized politics in the usual way. In other words, he is one of the better old-school politicians. This may be unfair; this may not be an accurate assessment; but it would seem to be the assessment of at least the Democratic voters, indeed the voters of both parties in the state. The Boston Irish Catholic has disadvantages coming into a state-wide election for the top position. In fact, an urban politician — Irish, but could be Italo-American or Jewish — has many disadvantages going into this. There is a distinctive way of pronouncing, of speaking, that urban people in Massachusetts have that stigmatizes them. It is an environment comparable to that of England where a person's caste is cut on his tongue — there is a linguistic difference, if you will, between different people. Now, McCormack is stigmatized by his Boston vocabulary, by the fact that he's an urban Boston politician. . . .

But particularly people who have left the urban centers, moving out to the suburbs and small towns, there is a strong irrational prejudice. In the Irish community there is a dichotomy between the urban Irish, often called "shanty Irish" — people who do not speak English as correctly, do not speak with the same cultured, cultivated tones as their suburban small-town brothers, and the legacy of Curley is still very strong in Massachusetts.

To counteract the legacy of Curley, McCormack's advisers decided that the candidate must continuously expose the "real" Edward McCormack to the electorate because, as one of them thought, "McCormack communicates immediately a sense of honesty, a sense of intellectual prowess, an ability to deal with the office." This exposure would show

> . . . the man, Ed McCormack the public official, Ed McCormack the candidate for the United States Senate. And that is a very important thing to those people who think of him as a Boston pol. . . . I think that too many people, way too many people for our good in this particular context, think of Ed McCormack as a typical Boston politician. And I think that those are people who have not been exposed to this man's basic political philosophy, which is the political philosophy of the Democratic party in the highest sense, and which I think communicates itself on television. This is a man who has deep basic feelings about these things, and this is not typical of Boston politicians, and I don't believe that it is, at least in the stereotyped sense; I think it's important that this get across, to the broad electorate.

The case for maximum exposure — particularly on television — however, was not as obvious as he suggested. Several McCormack men thought he projected poorly on television. Said one:

> Physically, Ed McCormack does not come across on television, and in the public mind's eye, as well as his opponent does. Ted Kennedy has the charm, and the Kennedy smile, and the extreme vigor that is characteristic of his family. Ed McCormack, on the other hand, is softer, slower, an approach that is more judicial in its means. . . . I think that in this particular instance it's a disadvantage for him. Also physically speaking, he has a tendency to have a smile that people . . . some people have characterized as sneaky. That is, I think, certainly a subjective judgment on their part and has no basis in fact, but the smile is there, sneaky or otherwise, and we have to deal with it.

Another McCormack adviser said:

> We analyze his mode of expression of a given idea, we take it

apart, try to see what's wrong with it, try to couch it in a way which, in terms of rhetoric, logic, clarity, lucidity, and so forth, comes through most clearly. For myself, I should have liked to have seen him very early take elocution lessons and combine these elocution lessons with substance. It is feared by others that if you address yourself too strongly to elocution, you become too distracted by it at the expense of substance. I think the two can and should be combined. I think a person like Nixon, if he had a speech defect, would probably have gotten up at five o'clock every morning and spent two hours talking about the twenty-hour work week or the common market or Cuba or what have you, perfecting both his knowledge and his expression thereof. But this is not done, and I think that this is our most serious weakness, and may prove to be our fatal weakness. . . . The presence isn't there, and is cut down not only because he's a physically slim, rather glib, and he has no cadence, no body to his voice, and he has a clear South Boston accent. But these are remediable defects. It's too late now. . . .

His despair led him to speculate on the relative importance of personalities and issues to the Massachusetts electorate.

My feeling is that the image is more important to the electorate than what is said. So much the worse for the electorate. That's why I think that what I regard as his defect may well be fatal. That's why I said that if he had been able to combine the notion of powerful presence, assuming that this could have been made up, plus substance, which I'm satisfied with, I think he really would have had something. But I believe that more people pay attention to the presence, which you call the image, and that's bad.

"The more non-interested a voter is," remarked a Kennedy coordinator, "the more likely he is to vote for such personality issues as appearance, presentation, name, identification with someone, i.e., the President. And these are factors in which Kennedy has a real edge over McCormack."

The McCormacks decided upon a two-pronged strategy: McCormack would attack Kennedy, utilizing ridicule rather than invective. He would also wage a "positive" campaign emphasizing

his "successes" as the Commonwealth's chief law enforcement officer, playing up his role as the underdog, and stressing the fact that
he started at the bottom of the political ladder and worked his way
up while Kennedy did not. The most literate expression of the
McCormack candidacy appeared in a letter, written before the
convention and distributed to academics in Massachusetts by
Mark DeWolfe Howe, biographer of Oliver Wendell Holmes, Professor in the Harvard Law School, and a militant supporter of
McCormack.

> . . . For its senatorial candidate the Democratic convention
> will make a selection between a bumptious new-comer and an
> experienced and gifted public servant, Edward J. McCor-
> mack, Jr.
>
> McCormack's academic credentials are impressive in that
> he was first in his class and was Editor-in-Chief of the Boston
> University Law Review.
>
> In the realm of public service McCormack's name has been
> submitted to the voters in Massachusetts thirteen times. He
> has served five years on the Boston City Council — once as its
> President. He was chosen by the General Court to fill an un-
> expired term as Attorney General of the Commonwealth and
> was twice elected to that office, most recently by the largest
> plurality ever accorded an Attorney General of the State.
>
> McCormack has not merely kept the law of the Common-
> wealth in effective operation. He has improved the legal or-
> der in areas where improvement has been sorely needed. Re-
> cently he has completed a comprehensive, two-year study of
> administrative procedure in Massachusetts. The study was
> conducted in cooperation with the Boston Bar Association,
> the Legislative Research Bureau, and members of the facul-
> ties of law in principal law schools of the Commonwealth.
> From this study have come proposals of far-reaching improve-
> ments in the procedures of agencies of State government. He
> has been active in improving ethics in government, serving,
> with notable effectiveness, as Chairman of the Commission
> which has proposed legislation on conflict of interest and a
> new code of ethics for the State. He has also served as Chair-
> man of the Committee on Conflict of Interest of the National
> Association of Attorneys General.

McCormack has taken courageous initiative in safeguarding the rights of those whom our society too often disregards. He was the first Attorney General of any of the states to establish a Civil Rights Division and to appoint, as an officer with comprehensive powers, an Assistant Attorney General for Civil Rights and Civil Liberties, a lead which has been followed by such other states as California, Illinois, and New York. This office prepared and issued the widely proclaimed pamphlet "If You Are Arrested," which officially informs the people of their rights *vis-a-vis* the police, and of which a quarter of a million copies have been distributed throughout the country. The pamphlet is the model upon which the Attorney General of New York, in cooperation with the Association of the Bar of the City of New York, proceeded in the preparation of a similar guide through the maze of criminal procedure. The American Bar Association has designated McCormack, as co-chairman with Thurman Arnold of a committee to develop a similar pamphlet for national distribution.

Of course the efforts of the Attorney General to give reality to civil rights and security to civil liberty have neither outlawed brutality from the Commonwealth nor brought a new era of intellectual freedom. They have, however, established a tone of decency and liberality in government which no successor to his present office can afford to repudiate or disregard. We can expect these same qualities in Mr. McCormack to mark his Senate career with decency and liberality.

Teddy Kennedy seeks his Party's nomination for the Senate simply because he is the brother of the President. He knows as well as you and I know that were he not a coat-tail candidate his name would receive no consideration from any political body for such a high office as he seeks. His academic career is mediocre. His professional career is virtually nonexistent. His candidacy is both preposterous and insulting.

*   *   *

The McCormack strategy and record could not be effectively used without a dedicated organization to support it. After the convention, McCormack's organization was seriously handicapped because potential McCormack volunteers and campaign contributors were so discouraged by Kennedy's complete victory at the convention and so impressed by the Kennedy power and money that they assumed McCormack could not possibly win in September. Many, therefore, refused to contribute their time and money to a cause they regarded as lost. Party "fat cats" concluded that money invested in the Attorney General would be a poor investment and so gave McCormack either a token contribution or nothing.

McCormack men advanced several theories to account for their plight. One aide with extensive experience as a fund raiser suggested that it was considerably more difficult in Massachusetts to raise substantial amounts of money for senatorial candidates than for candidates for various state and municipal offices because senators are unable to dispense the preferential treatment and patronage that serve as bait for most large contributors. According to his theory Democratic candidates in Massachusetts receive the bulk of their financial support from contractors, builders, architects, liquor dealers, realtors, bookies, racketeers, and those who supply goods and services to state and municipal governments. In his view men who seek contracts, commissions, licenses, tax abatements, purchase orders, or police protection may be wise to contribute to mayoralty and gubernatorial candidates or candidates for attorney general or district attorney but they have little to gain by supporting men who run for the United States Senate.

He described what he thought were McCormack's difficulties:

A candidate for U.S. senator, unless he has fabulous family resources, hasn't anything really to offer to contributors. The facts of life are that when persons contribute to campaigns they do it on one or two bases. First because they feel that there is an urgency and a real drive to support a particular candidate and these are people who expect nothing in return for their contributions. Those persons are, unfortunately, from a financial standpoint, idealistic and as a result have very little money. They contribute in the sums of four dollars, five-dollar and ten-dollar bills and two-dollar bills and one-dollar bills. . . . And this is the type of contributors we're getting. We're getting a huge number of contributors, but unfortunately we're not getting the large contributors, and by large contributors I mean contributors who'll contribute five hundred or a thousand or five thousand dollars such as Kennedy is getting. There's a very good realistic reason for running for governor. You can appeal to contractors and others who anticipate the possibility that they might probably require some help from a person holding an office such as governor. On the other hand, the most they can expect from someone who is running for U.S. senator is perhaps a congressional calendar, birdseed or flower seeds and as a consequence there's a reluctance of those who have selfish interests to contribute any substantial sums of money.

Although it may well be true that the majority of those who make substantial campaign contributions do so for purely selfish reasons, the fact remains that many senatorial campaigns are well financed — perhaps because senators are frequently able to influence the distribution of patronage and preferment at the state as well as the federal level. If the incumbent senator is the entrenched leader of a state party, such as Byrd of Virginia or Long of Louisiana, he may control much state patronage simply because he plays a major role in selecting the party's nominees for important state-wide offices. Their debt to him and his influence over them is well known to many significant contributors.

The ability of senatorial candidates to raise campaign funds, however, is not based primarily on the fact that governors and mayors may be obliged to do their bidding. Scores of prominent businessmen and the members of numerous interest groups are concerned with federal legislation while some seek ambassadorial posts or federal appointments. It is perfectly obvious that United States senators, particularly those with seniority or those who are close to the President, may influence his choice of federal appointees and play a vital part in the passage or defeat of legislation that could result in substantial profits or losses to businessmen throughout the country. Congressional calendars and flower seeds do not exhaust the grab bag of senatorial goodies.

According to other aides, McCormack's difficulties had considerably more to do with the fact that he was running against a candidate whose brother was President than with the fact that he was running for the Senate. They frequently intimated and, on occasion, openly stated that many of those who had contributed to the McCormack campaigns in the past and many who wished to contribute in 1962 were simply afraid to do so because of what they believed the Kennedys might do to them.

One McCormack aide, whose views on this matter are representative, remarked that

> . . . a good many people are afraid to contribute to the Mc-Cormack campaign. A good many people who will vote for McCormack don't want their names identified with the Mc-Cormack campaign for fear that there will be some retribution. For fear they will be punished in some way, either by taxes being investigated or by virtue of withdrawing any possible favor or patronage. . . . People who believe that Ted Kennedy is unqualified have contributed to the Ted Kennedy campaign and many more who feel the same way have not contributed to the McCormack campaign for fear that they might offend the party in power.

The fears of retaliation may or may not have been realistic but, like the fears of many delegates who preferred McCormack privately but voted for Kennedy at the convention, they did influence the behavior of many. To support his contention this aide noted that several friends of McCormack assured the Attorney General that they would contribute to his campaign if their names and the amounts they gave were not reported to the Secretary of State, as is required by the Massachusetts law regulating campaign donations. "This would be a violation of the law," he stated, "so we haven't been able to take advantage of that."

One veteran of many Massachusetts political wars, who was friendly with both camps and most of the "serious money" (his description of large contributors), noted:

> Any candidate running against Kennedy would have to have unlimited funds. No one could match Kennedy's ability to raise money. Among their own family and friends and their business associates they can raise a lot of money . . . the President of the United States has got a lot of friends. McCor-

mack is also a good fund raiser. He's got a lot of funds but
you couldn't match the Kennedys'.

I think maybe people are thinking twice about giving
money to McCormack, particularly with this new law which
means that you have to list all the contributions. Well, if
you're publicly listed as a contributor to McCormack, Kennedy and everybody else sees who gave to McCormack. I
would say that it would make it a little harder to raise money.
I have found many people who are with McCormack and with
him strongly, who are not against the President. They're fear-
ful that the President would say that and the Kennedy organization will think they are anti-Kennedy. So I would say that
people of this sort are not anxious to have their names listed
in the paper.

McCormack, of course, had raised large quantities of money
for several previous campaigns. His family was well known and
well connected in Massachusetts, and he and his uncle had been
serving the faithful for years. They had numerous political
debts to collect, but the faithful, according to one aide, conveniently disappeared when about to be approached by fund raisers.
Another aide, a woman, reported:

I was told by one of the two chief fund raisers that the regular
sources had dried up; this was the phrase he used. That they
just weren't getting it where they had always gotten it in the
past. Obviously they never had to spend this kind of money
before. Maybe this was part of the problem. He claimed that
it was because they had gone to the well too often. . . . I suspect that after the convention, there just weren't a lot of
people handing him money, because a lot of people thought
he was going to lose and no one wants to be a loser.

Asked to amplify her remarks and comment on the law requiring candidates to disclose the names of contributors and the
amounts given, she confirmed the reports of other McCormack advisers that many contributors who are "perfectly legitimate sources
of campaign funds" do not want their names made public. In the
past, according to her, they could avoid publicity by contributing
through straws or simply giving cash that was never reported. Referring to the new law regulating campaign contributions she said:

It's a little harder to get someone to do this if his name is going to be published in the newspaper. Perhaps the Internal
Revenue is going to look through the list and say, "Where did
this guy get a thousand dollars to give to a campaign? He just
reported he makes $2,700 a year."

A Kennedy aide agreed that McCormack undoubtedly had
some difficulty raising funds, but in his opinion McCormack was
far from impoverished:

Now, I'm really not that concerned that he doesn't have that
much money to spend. He's got a lot of money of his own. A
lot of testimonials, a lot of tickets, at one hundred dollars a
plate. That's a lot. Six or seven thousand people there, you
can imagine how many tickets he sold. That's a lot of money.
He's spending some money. . . . Other sources that should give
him money in the near future, that perhaps will. All legitimate. . . . Lot of lawyers on his staff who make anywhere
from maybe 10,000 to 30 or 40,000 dollars a year. They've
been assistant attorney generals for a long time and I think
they'll be grateful, they'll be contributing more. McCormack
has never had any real money problems, when he ran for
office, for city councilor or for attorney general, no real serious
ones. I think he doesn't have the money the Kennedy organization has, anywheres near it, but he'll spend as much as
anybody in the state will, with the exception of the Kennedys.

McCormack's campaign manager nevertheless was ever ready
to provide examples of how the organization suffered from lack of
funds:

. . . we did not raise any large sums of money to my knowledge and funds were in tremendous difficulty throughout the
campaign. We had only one type of brochure which we could
afford and we could ill afford much of that. There was a
lot more direct specialized mailing that we would have liked
to have gotten out; some of it was ready to go and we just were
unable to get it out for lack of postage.

He reported that McCormack's treasurer was forced, on occasion,
to cancel orders for bumper stickers, brochures, flyers, pins, and

much of the minor paraphernalia of campaigning because of in-adequate money. McCormack, according to his campaign man-ager, was unable to hire a sizable staff at headquarters — or, for that matter, many headquarters. The Attorney General claimed that he could not pay for large state-wide mailings, extensive tele-vision coverage, or substantial outdoor advertising. McCormack men, in other words, pleaded poverty. In a typical lament: "We can't get our message across as well as our opponent and we can't send brochures advertising the accomplishments of the Attorney General." Or again: "I don't think we had more than five people on television for Eddie, or Eddie himself more than thirty minutes during the entire Senate fight. This is ridiculous, but that's all we had money for."

Lack of funds not only made it hard to "get the message across" but also frequently prevented McCormack workers from carrying out their assignments.

> Assignments were made and in many cases they weren't car-ried out because . . . he lacked the funds or the daytime manpower to do these things. Campaigns take a great deal, and unless a person has enough telephones handy to do the work that has to be done, so that he can contact people in his local area, then you run into problems in organization which can't be solved except in a professional manner, and that takes money. . . .

The McCormack situation discouraged numerous potentially hardworking and sophisticated "daytime" campaigners. As the Commonwealth's chief law enforcement officer McCormack headed a staff of twenty-four assistant attorneys general, appointed by him partly for their political contacts. Many of these men had had considerable political experience and could have formed a working nucleus of an efficient organization. An aide noted:

> Most of the assistant attorney generals were not interested in the campaign. If Eddie had been running for governor I think he would have had their wholehearted support, but he was running for senator, he was going to leave them in the lurch, and they really weren't very much interested in the

whole thing. And an awful lot of them took nice, long summer vacations and just weren't able to be found when we were looking for them.

Poor financial and patronage prospects and minimal hope of victory dampened the enthusiasm of those few professionals who remained with McCormack despite the odds.

A member of the McCormack brain trust who worked diligently for the Attorney General although he did not believe that a Kennedy could be defeated in Massachusetts noted the sense of gloom that pervaded the entire McCormack organization. He said:

> I'll give you a concrete example . . . it was typical of everybody in the campaign. I had a conversation one day with _____, a fellow, I think, with a real sense of loyalty and personal obligation to Eddie McCormack, and who wanted to do something and felt he ought to be doing something in the campaign. . . . He said, well, they made me chairman of the Speaker's Bureau, the Speaker's Committee. I said, what does this entail, what have you done? Well, he says, frankly speaking, I haven't done a damn thing. And I think it's this kind of feeling that pervaded the whole organization.

The McCormack organization was fairly typical of most Massachusetts campaign groups. It consisted primarily of old-style, uneducated, professional politicians of the more affable wardheeler brand who were passionately devoted to the candidate; a brain trust of prominent academics who had little in common with the so-called pros; and a few thousand volunteers many of whom came and went when the maid was at home, when it didn't rain, or when the more pressing business of shopping or babysitting had been taken care of. A colleague of the Attorney General said:

> Well, I think like most of the organizations that I've worked in, in Boston politics, it's a purely personal organization, with hundreds and hundreds of people who are fanatically devoted to the candidate, who would do anything for him, and have

absolutely no stops, no holds barred, as far as they're concerned — where the candidate is concerned. Eddie's group is
singular only in that there are more people who feel this way
than some of the other candidates that I have worked for. He
has a magnificent inefficiency in the organization, dreadful
choice of people to do specific jobs; I cannot think of one person in the campaign, with the possible exception of his own
personal secretary up at the State House, who was well chosen
for the job she did.

The inefficiency of the McCormack organization, according to
this aide, was due in large degree to McCormack himself.

It's almost an axiom in politics, I think, that if you're going to
be well organized, the candidate is going to be well organized,
he must first organize himself, and I sense in Eddie McCormack a great deal of disorganization, a great deal . . . of
inertia and lack of imagination in terms of the internal organization of his own campaign. It would seem to me that
Eddie McCormack is the guy who ought to be concerned
about the fact that he has no real, well-organized brain trust
and research operation which is funneling into him major
and important and well thought-out and conceived policy papers and ideas.

The McCormack organization was hampered not only by
McCormack himself but by McCormack's appointment as his
campaign manager of a Jewish state representative who was a
leading light in the most liberal reform wing of his party. He
was not an old-time McCormack associate. He was not an Irish
American. He was not a typical professional "pol." He was, however, placed in charge of old-time McCormack men, primarily
Irish and professionals, some of whom apparently resented him
as an outsider. One "insider" reported:

The campaign manager, who was brought into the campaign
by the candidate, was somebody who had never actually
worked in a McCormack campaign before, and there was a
great deal of resentment all the way down the line about this.
And therefore this campaign manager was undercut over and

over again. . . . The campaign manager would walk in and he would say, "There will be a scheduling meeting every Friday morning." And he would walk out and five assistant attorney generals would say something obscene and let him run his own scheduling meeting. They'd walk out of the office, and unless they felt like it, they wouldn't come back on Friday morning. . . . And this happened over and over again in various ways, with different people. . . .

The McCormack people are extremely loyal, and they take their memories way back. . . . There's always a certain amount of "We don't want anybody new on the campaign and we like to handle things our own way." But because so many of these people are really old guard and the down-the-line people and they're fighting this last-ditch battle, they don't want anyone else. They're afraid that whoever is coming in is a spy, and really, they watch their step — "This guy I'm sure he's on the Kennedy payroll." The minute anybody dropped a pen, why, he was on the Kennedy payroll. And we were always wondering who it was that was on the Kennedy payroll, in our own headquarters.

To make matters worse, McCormack's campaign manager was a colonel in the Army Reserve and was called up for two weeks of active duty during the middle of the campaign.

His problems were aggravated because he had to compete with McCormack himself, who frequently violated one of the few sound principles of political campaigning by becoming his own campaign manager. McCormack's dual role — as candidate and as super-manager — was regarded by many of his key advisers as a contributing factor to the chaos that characterized the McCormack campaign. A man who had been through a number of Massachusetts political wars commented:

A candidate can't be a good candidate and a good campaign manager at the same time. . . . He hasn't time. Eddie McCormack is a great politician, but he just isn't two people, and he never will be two people. . . . He was exhausted before the end of the campaign. You cannot do this in a major political contest. You have to give up the reins to somebody you trust . . . and then that person has to have an efficient organization. There was not one person who was running that campaign.

McCormack, who said that he had decided to run for the Senate as early as 1960, did literally nothing to prepare for the campaign, an indication of his apathy and disorganization. One adviser noted:

The real organization which Eddie had started building up the first time he ran for attorney general — '56? — and which was a good organization and which had come partially from John McCormack, was allowed to atrophy after he actually became Attorney General. He didn't have a real fight two years ago, and he didn't really campaign two years ago. He went to a lot of nice house parties and met a lot of nice friends and had a grand time, and nobody really did anything. And there was no one sitting up in the Attorney General's office as a paid staff member who was working on keeping the people out in the field going. You had to have a very closely knit organization to be able to fight the Kennedy mystique, and it wasn't there. It wasn't a close-knit organization, it was a group of pals that just couldn't handle the gaff once the gaff started getting thrown at them. They really hadn't been in a high-powered campaign. And I think this is what happened.

The "group of pals" — affable but not very useful — ran the campaign in cooperation with a very large and extremely competent brain trust composed of attorneys and academics. Their relationship to the candidate and the old "pros" and their role in the campaign can be analyzed to illustrate the problems of that hazardous profession known as brain-trusting. During July and August the brain trust continued to meet on a weekly basis except for those members who were vacationing in Europe, Truro, Wellfleet, or Martha's Vineyard. In addition to participating in discussions on political strategy, they advised the Attorney General on the salient issues. One of the most active members described their role:

Our function is to make sure that the candidate understands and is able to articulate the issues of a senatorial candidate.

Secondarily, the function is to see what these issues are, and decide what the articulation, how it is coming across. . . . We are dealing with a candidate who is extremely bright, very retentive memory and capacity to understand quickly what he hears and to get the real substance of the matter. On the other hand, he is very inarticulate, and I suppose the public view of our candidate is cast largely in terms of his capacity to express himself, and therefore this quick intelligence of his is largely lost. I myself, before I got to know him, saw him as a rather slow-witted fellow. . . .

When I got to work with him, I found very quickly that I was quite wrong. . . . But . . . his verbal level coupled with what is often described as a speech defect, which I think is a South Boston accent, gives the impression of a sort of a slow-witted pol out of Southie. And what we are trying to do is to deal with both of these elements. . . . What this man has done is surround himself with . . . a collection of . . . knowledgeable, committed people who have no particular ax to grind except to get an intelligent, liberal, and apparently committed person into office and to make sure that he's soundly grounded in the issues and the facts behind them.

He also described the manner in which the brain trust operated and how it communicated with the candidate.

As you may know, our basic pattern is to just sit and talk like after-dinner table talk. . . . We sit, and Eddie sits, and he listens, and because . . . he's very quick on the uptake, he absorbs very rapidly. We also collect data through the news media, particularly the *New York Times* . . . all of these ideas are taken down, they're taped and gotten back to the candidate. . . . We meet regularly at three-thirty on Thursdays every week, and the attendance is pretty good.

One member suggested that the brain trust was most effective when it had to deal with an immediate problem. He reported that

Prior to the "Meet the Press" program, the brain trust — we sat down, and worked out the big issues of the world, no less, and discussed them for hours at a time. We sat there all day one Saturday, for instance. We did try to anticipate what the moderator and others on the "Meet the Press" panel would ask the candidate. We listened to tapes and examined transcripts of what had been asked Teddy and George. We tried to analyze the bias of the panel — the big issue at the time was corruption in government, the dynasty, and federal aid to education, so we thought. We were discussing sometimes so-called position papers which we prepared . . . on corruption and civil rights and the like . . . on Southeast Asia too, . . . on economics. These things were read, too, read and digested. . . .

We would then discuss the issues, question him, and have him question us, then we would go to mock panel. We'd say, "Mr. Attorney General, Mr. Kennedy has stated that his views on federal aid to education are such and such. Do your views materially differ?" And then he would answer, and we would look for order of importance in stating these views, because, after all, a very tricky issue like that has to be very carefully stated, carefully qualified, and restated, and so forth. And so, too, with corruption.

Frequently candidates advocate positions in private that are more liberal or conservative than their estimate of the public's stand. The rational politician will, of course, alter his public position so that it resembles that of the electorate as closely as possible. Some candidates face a moral crisis when pragmatic considerations suggest repudiation of their deepest beliefs. According to a member of the brain trust, McCormack had in the past taken positions that were known to be unpopular with the bulk of Massachusetts voters. Although he apparently modified his private stance on some issues during the campaign, he nevertheless did advocate positions that most of the brain trust believed lost votes. When asked to comment on whether McCormack faced a conflict over his private beliefs and what he considered to be the "correct" vote-getting position on issues, a brain truster remarked:

Well, that's a good question. The only one that really has that is one in which the candidate had already stated his position before it came up, so that it was obviated. I, for instance, think that in federal aid to education he would really get the Protestant-Jewish vote in great part if he took the

President's stated position in respect to federal aid to education: no aid. . . . Years before, in fact, the Attorney General had stated the position that he ultimately took, and so the real question of trimming on the hottest trimming issue never arose. He did not agree with me or others in the trust, and all we did was to help him fashion his position papers so that he could be darn sure that he did not have a Spellman position of no aid to parochial schools, no aid, period. . . .

Actually, on questions of recognition of Communist China, say, I suppose his position is more realistic and liberal. I say liberal — a liberal position is to concede that recognition does not mean approval. And left to his own devices, he'll probably come out for recognition as a matter of diplomatic necessity, as something in the best interests of the United States. But I think that this is a politically unsupportable position now, and so on that issue he will take it as far as he thinks he politically can go, which is about as far, say, as Joe Clark or some such senator would go, but I doubt that his position for the public records is wholly foursquare with his private belief, and this is an important issue.

I suppose the same would attach to admission of Communist China to the United Nations. I have an impression that on nuclear testing he has more reservations about the wisdom of these tests, in the iodine, fallout, and all the rest, than he could express safely politically. . . . But I suppose — and this is an impression; he certainly hasn't said so — I suppose that his private beliefs are somewhat more adventurous than his public statements, but his public statements are still sufficiently daring, as I say, for Hughes himself to admire them, and for some of the more discerning supporters of Hughes — since I talked to a great deal of them, I know this to be a fact. . . .

The composition of the McCormack brain trust was unstable because several members went on vacation during the campaign. A few others were forced to absent themselves for business reasons. One member said:

I think it has been a disadvantage for the McCormack campaign, because I think, in the first place people were not in on all the basic policy discussions and considerations on a fairly permanent, continuing basis, I think, were then thrown into this situation, I think, oftentimes making judgments, forming opinions, doing things on the basis of incomplete understanding, incomplete information. I think too if you're going to bring people up, it's also very time consuming and wasteful. Because oftentimes what you're doing is merely trying to bring these people, who've just come into the picture, bring them up to date on what led you to reach some of the conclusions, decisions that were made in the past. You really have to fill them in before they're able to operate and intelligently discuss current problems or current strategy. So I think it's very time-consuming, it's very wasteful, and I think it's been very damaging to the candidate.[15]

This critic also suggested that the brain trust talked more than it acted so that the overwhelming support McCormack received from the intellectual community in Massachusetts was seriously dissipated. He also believed that, although Kennedy was supported by very few academics, they were effectively organized and productive.

But to my way of thinking, there are too many people in the McCormack campaign who are willing . . . to just sit back and throw out ideas, . . . there were too few people who were willing to put anything down on paper, and there are even fewer people who are preparing for the candidate well-reasoned position papers with factual data and information. Whatever factual information and data are imparted in these . . . brain trust . . . discussions . . . come out very informally and are not often well considered. So it seems to me that while Eddie McCormack is . . . widely supported by all kinds of intellectuals in Massachusetts, he's not really tapped this potential for getting the kind of imaginative and factual data and research that he ought to have. I see relatively little of this in the McCormack campaign. What you tend to get

[15] The brain trust apparently had considerable impact on the candidate. One member noted, "I think that a large part of his ideas either come from them or are sounded against them, and as I listen to his public pronouncements, I can directly relate them down to so many words. This man deals very closely with the brain trust, he listens to what they say. It's a great well of ideas. Sometimes more of ideas than working materials. No doubt about it."

from people who are advising him and who have all of the academic qualifications to advise on issues tends to be more opinion rather than data and facts. . . .

I have been struck by the relative lack of organization of the McCormack inner sanctum or higher-level brain trust group in particular. For example, . . . apparently there is some research, some basic research, available somewhere within the McCormack operation. At some points various people have contributed their own basic research and their own sense of direction on issues in terms of memoranda and data of various kinds. But there is no real research director, nobody was able to co-ordinate the activities and pull together the basic research which has been done. . . . I pointed out that we were on the eve of Labor Day, . . . could present an opportunity for developing his views on unemployment and for presenting a full-blown policy statement tying in with the labor movement. . . . They do have the names of some very prominent labor people who are supporting the McCormack candidacy which are going to be released on Labor Day. But there had been no effort made, nobody had given any thought to what the candidate himself should say, which could be capitalized upon and used as a full-blown policy statement in an effort to gain some favorable press attention and also to provide an opportunity for developing in a rather full way some of his ideas in the best polished form on unemployment. . . . They were going to prepare some economic data which could be utilized in a speech on unemployment on Labor Day. But nobody really took it upon themselves to go out and develop a full-blown statement. . . .

Despite the ineffectiveness of the McCormack brain trust, one of the more unusual aspects of the campaign was the fact that the academic community in Massachusetts, overwhelmingly in favor of John F. Kennedy in 1960, now supported Edward McCormack with rare exception. A member of the McCormack brain trust described why he and his colleagues backed McCormack when most of them assumed the cause was hopeless.

I talked with a large number of professors, Independents, and Republicans. Many of them are committed to Eddie not because he's a great man but because he has certainly done a pretty good job, and as Massachusetts office holders go. . . . But the commitment to him lies very deep among these people, not on the basis of his own attainments, but of a revulsion, a real revulsion in the most literal sense of that word, to Teddy's candidacy. I don't understand why the President should do this; the cheating episode in college, backed up by — at most charitable — the lack of candor, in fact the continual lack of candor in respect to what was said in his statement announcing his candidacy. . . . He said that he had voted in every election since he was twenty-one. The records show he had voted in two elections, when Jack ran for Senator in '58 and when he ran for President in '60. . . .

Professor Mark DeWolfe Howe, of the Harvard Law School, whose letter to the academic community we quoted previously, appeared on the television program "The Open Mind," when "The Candidacy of Teddy Kennedy" was the subject. Howe made the following opening remarks:

I don't think there's any question but that on any achievement of his own, Ted Kennedy, at the age of thirty, is not qualified to seek such a high office as he is seeking. I cannot believe that were his name not Kennedy, were his brother perhaps not in the White House, and perhaps also his other brother in the Department of Justice, that he could under any circumstances have put himself forward as candidate for the United States Senate. So whatever his native gifts may be, and perhaps they are considerable, nothing has yet happened to show that he has those gifts. Without the affiliations, without the name, his candidacy would have been, as it continues to be, in my judgment, wholly preposterous.

Beyond that I think it is not only preposterous but outrageous. Seeking an office in the United States Senate, while his brother is in the White House, seems to me to represent a total misunderstanding of the responsibilities of a United States Senator. To have a rubber stamp senator is to me an offense against the whole tradition that there should be a separation of powers in our government.

So it is not simply a question of his lack of qualification or at least his lack of proven qualification. It is in fact the total inappropriateness of his seeking an office in which he is unable to exercise that kind of independent responsibility which it seems to me a senator of the United States must be expected to fulfill.

Later in the program he said:

One of the great qualities of this present national administration, at least in its pretensions, has been its emphasis on intelligence. What seems to me to be shown by these figures is that when the chips are down and a member of the family is in a political race, intelligence is not considered to be an important factor. The campaign is directed to the majority of voters and intelligence is to be cast aside.

The anger felt by academics is probably related to the fact that they supposedly are trained to separate image and reality and to make judgments on the basis of concrete data rather than emotional appeal. Training for the academic profession involves a lengthy period of disciplined study, and advancement usually depends, not on contacts and influence, but on experience and productivity. Public relations men are skilled in manipulating reality so as to create favorable or unfavorable images. They evaluate the work of their colleagues and competitors in terms of their ability to appeal both to the consumer's mind and to his emotions by emphasizing or de-emphasizing aspects of reality, ignoring reality, or creating a "false" reality through slogans and oversimplifications rather than careful scrutiny of the facts. Candidates, of course, if they are rational, are willing to work with and indeed seek out public relations men and advisers who are adept at selling a "package" that may be more attractive than the product itself.

Some academics were galled by the disparity between their understanding of the "facts" of Kennedy's candidacy and the "image" of Kennedy, which in their opinion was constructed by public relations men out of whole cloth and sold to a naïve public. Knowing that the "real Edward Kennedy" was young, had never been elected to public office, was starting "at the top," and had been forced to withdraw from Harvard College because he had another student take an examination for him, they were irked that he should be perceived as experienced and fit for the Senate by voters because he grew up in a "political family" and was widely traveled. His campaign slogan — "He Can Do More for Massachusetts" — violated their belief that merit and experience are the hallmarks of a qualified man. They were revolted, therefore, by what they interpreted as the shameless exploitation of his family and fortune. Their anger also stemmed from the fact that Kennedy's face, family, fortune, and accent — irrelevant considerations, in their opinion — were probably more important to the electorate than his experience and academic training.

Although the academics and professional politicians who advised McCormack were united by their dislike of Kennedy, the former did not have the fanatical sense of devotion and loyalty to McCormack that many of the "pros" did — that very special sense of brotherhood that grows out of the sharing of common experiences in several political campaigns. The professionals, almost to a man, were totally unconcerned with the so-called issues of the campaign. Some of them, however, were dependent on a McCormack victory for patronage. The brain trusters were professional men, most of whom had tenure in universities or successful law practices. They had little or no interest in political plums that might fall their way if the Attorney General were elected. They supported McCormack not for reasons of political expediency but because they were outraged by Kennedy's candidacy and because McCormack espoused most of the liberal positions they advocated. This difference in interest, experience, and expectation led not unexpectedly to some differences of opinion between the brain trust and the professional politicians about how the campaign ought to be conducted and why it was being waged.

McCormack's campaign manager, who knew both of these worlds, did not think "there was much conflict between this brain trust and myself." But he remarked that

> . . . it never got to the point when there was any rancor about it — but certainly street politicians had one idea and the members of the brain trust had another idea as to approaches. . . . I think there was some feeling that Eddie was overemphasizing civil rights and civil liberties and that type

of thing, and others felt no, that you had to do something about it.

Brain trusters and the "old pros" agreed that McCormack must attack Kennedy; they disagreed, however, on the position McCormack should adopt on disarmament as well as civil liberties. McCormack's campaign manager commented:

> I think probably it might be in this area where there was some conflict between the so-called professional pols and brain trusters. . . . The brain trust took a position that you've got to do something to stop the spread of arms, and I think the professionals, many of them, felt that this was a dangerous area to get into.

From a strategic point of view, the "pros" were probably right to suggest that McCormack not take a strong position in favor of disarmament. An analysis of "Letters to the Editor" in several Massachusetts newspapers indicates that, with the exception of McCormack's attacks on Kennedy, anti-McCormack letter writers objected most to McCormack's statements on arms control. Analysis of interviews with registered Democrats and Independents indicates that McCormack's position on disarmament was the only issue that attracted any attention and that McCormack was criticized for it by every Kennedy respondent who voluntarily mentioned the issue. Very few respondents who planned to vote for McCormack mentioned the issue.

This melange of old pros and academics directed the McCormack organization, which performed some of the customary tasks of primary campaigning and performed them in a perfunctory manner. When not otherwise occupied, the candidate mounted the hustings, shook hands, spoke at occasional rallies, and delivered, in comparison to Kennedy, a small number of television and radio spot announcements. His workers distributed handbills, ball-point pens, and bumper stickers, and his advertising agency purchased billboard space and newspaper advertisements — all in small amounts compared to what Kennedy and his organization did.

The McCormacks did not conduct a massive drive for signed

pledges of support; the McCormacks did not mount a full-scale registration drive. The McCormacks did not purchase more than a few minutes of videotapes for showing on television. Why? They couldn't afford to and they did not have the manpower to do so.

*   *   *

The Kennedys, in contrast to the McCormacks, approached the campaign as they customarily do — by first employing the services of a reputable and professional public opinion pollster who sampled the electorate. According to some Kennedy aides and a few of the more sophisticated "neutrals" whom we interviewed, a poll taken for the Kennedys, months before Edward Kennedy's announcement, indicated that the President's brother would easily defeat McCormack or any other Democrat in a primary contest and any likely Republican in a general election. Although Kennedy's campaign manager refused to show these public opinion data to the author, the results of the first poll were apparently so one-sided that the members of the Kennedy family who in the beginning were not favorably disposed to Edward Kennedy's candidacy became convinced that he should run.

The President's original attitude is shrouded in secrecy. Some newspapermen suggested that he, and several White House aides, were at first strongly against the idea while Joseph Kennedy and Edward Kennedy were in favor. However, at no time did the President publicly oppose his brother.

Although the pollsters provided data on the strengths and weaknesses of both candidates among various subgroups in the population and in various sections of the Commonwealth, Kennedy's strategic decisions were made primarily on the basis of intuition, common sense, and rules of thumb learned during John F. Kennedy's campaigns. Pollsters did not play a significant role in the decision-making process although public opinion data were frequently used to confirm the intuitive judgments of the candidate and his staff. The polls, for example, corroborated the suspicion that Kennedy would do well among Irish and Italo-Americans and non-Irish voters of the upper middle class, those of low income, women, and the less well educated. The data also strengthened the feeling that Kennedy was less strong among the more politically sophisticated voters — suburban Democrats who were nationally and internationally oriented, Jews, the well educated, civil libertarians, and academics. These voters were disturbed by Kennedy's youth and inexperience, and the possibility that his candidacy might adversely affect the prestige of the President. They were favorably disposed to McCormack in view of his experience, his academic record, and his position on civil rights and civil liberties. Fortunately, from Kennedy's point of view, the number of potential voters who felt this way was not large.

Public opinion polls were also taken during the campaign. They revealed little or nothing that was surprising, but they gave the Kennedys a basis for knowing that they had pursued and were pursuing a strategy that was not too irrational.

Although Kennedy men readily admitted that his family and his name were the candidate's greatest assets (in this sense Edward Kennedy is another in the long line of Massachusetts politicians who belong to the "name's the same" tradition), they, and most insiders, suggested that Edward Kennedy, in and of himself, possessed qualities that made him a superb campaigner and an appealing candidate. All agreed that he was an indefatigable campaigner who "moved like a pro." "Kennedy's campaigning like crazy," a veteran of the Massachusetts political wars noted. "He's going everyplace. He's a great campaigner. Ted Kennedy, by the way, campaigns like his brother, maybe even better. He maneuvers beautifully, and he goes from the crack of dawn till midnight, and he shakes hands, and he's got lots of charm. . . ." Some Kennedy advisers who campaigned for John F. Kennedy when he first ran for Congress reported that the youngest Kennedy was a more effective campaigner than was his brother in 1948. For these reasons his managers wanted the candidate to expose himself as much as possible to the public. Maximum exposure and maximum handshaking were the twin gambits of the Kennedy strategy.

During the early stages of the campaign it was assumed, and correctly, that the candidate was formidable primarily because of what one aide termed "the royal family syndrome" and because he was a tireless campaigner. His magnetism, however, was not so obvious to his advisers until later on. They were at this time much concerned with what they thought were his liabilities: youth, inexperience, wealth, and the fact that he was "starting at the top." They plainly heard what McCormack said throughout the campaign: that Kennedy was ill equipped to be a senator because he lacked the proper background, training and experience.

The doubts of Kennedy's aides and the fact that they, as well as McCormack, actually failed at first to understand the extraordinary personal appeal of their candidate are dramatically illustrated in the following excerpt from a taped interview with a trade-union official who advised Kennedy on matters relating to organized labor in Massachusetts.

Some of Mr. Kennedy's staff people called me in, and said, ". . . how much do you think this will hurt Mr. Kennedy — the fact that he is a millionaire, he hasn't worked very much, and he has no political experience?" They said, "We are deeply concerned about the fact that Mr. McCormack rose to power from one suspender and Mr. Kennedy did not." And I said, "Gentlemen, you are concerned, and I am not concerned about this at all. We have made thorough studies of this particular syndrome, and we find this: the working people in factories have a great respect for a man who doesn't have to climb up the ladder, for a man who has the ability or the background or the connections or the power to start from the top." And I said, "People in industrial situations have a remarkable respect for the man who doesn't have to work himself up from the dogcatcher to senator, but can start as a United States senator. They respect the power. They respect the initiative. I've spoken with hundreds of people about that in our own factories, and every one of them said, 'Why should the man start out as a city councilman or as a clerk of the court? What good is this going to do anybody? What good is this going to do Mr. Kennedy and what good is this going to do the Commonwealth? I respect a guy who's got the courage and the guts and the power to start from there. . . .' — they tell me — 'a guy like this can do a lot of good because he has that essential power.' People today don't respect the poor little man who saved and saved and saved and finally built up something. They respect the man who has this essential power and this essential movement." So I told the Kennedy people not to be worried about it; if anything, Teddy's starting from the top was to his benefit. They didn't agree with me. . . .

I think the best story that is told in the campaign — and it's very true — it's a true story — that Teddy Kennedy was going through a large industrial plant and was making a big hit with the workers. He was shaking hands with everybody, and everybody literally loved him and was happy that he was there. He went over to shake hands with an old machine operator; the machine operator shook hands with him and Teddy smiled back and said, "I hope you'll vote for me," and the machine operator said, "Wait a minute, Teddy, I want to speak to you." "What is it?" He said, "Teddy, I understand you never worked a day in your life." And Mr. Kennedy became concerned, and he said, "Oops, here it comes." And the fellow looked at Mr. Kennedy and said, "Let me tell you something, Teddy. You haven't missed a thing."

This is so typical of American people today. There is no honor in sweat. There is no honor in breaking your back all your life. People do respect this in Mr. Kennedy. And this I found, that they have a profound respect and reverence for. Mr. Kennedy, with his financial holdings, could be a member of the café society international set. Mr. Kennedy could be the dean emeritus of the white trash of the café society. He could spend his winters in Cannes and his summers in Biarritz. He could be a completely non-contributing member of society with his looks, with his money, with his social connections. But instead he has chosen a life of public service. And believe me, this is what people respect. Not that he didn't break his back all his life, but that they respect the quality of the man that forces him to work hard because he has this very basic felt need to make a contribution to society. People do not condemn him for this; they respect him. And I do, too.

The critical "issue" of this campaign and of many others, was the aura cast by the candidate, not the so-called issues of state, national, or international politics which political scientists are so fond of discussing. This is particularly true where candidates of the same wing of the party compete in a primary. Nevertheless, advisers do spend time preparing position papers and candidates do deliver speeches on the issues — in spite of their belief that few voters care about, understand, or listen to a discussion of the issues. The function of such discussion is latent rather than manifest. The candidate who can spout facts and figures on or demonstrate a wide acquaintance with international, national, and state matters may create the impression that he is knowledgeable, sophisticated, and statesmanlike. It was very important, in the opinion of Kennedy's advisers, for their candidate to wage a campaign that would create this impression.

A member of the Kennedy brain trust who understood the latent function of campaign discussion of issues put the case quite clearly:

> . . . he must sell himself not only as a vigorous person, but also as a person of intelligence, particularly in Massachusetts where people have demanded much more of their senators and their governors than they have of other office holders. So it's a question of presenting the candidate in a mature and sophisticated way . . . giving more formal speeches, giving speeches in depth, discussing issues on a semi-academic level, not so much to educate the people on the issues or convince them of the virtue of the issues or his knowledge of the issues, but broadly to show the person that this is a young man of intelligence. My specific advice in a number of cases has been to even talk above the audience. That is, for some candidates this might not be the correct approach to talk over your audience's head. But in this particular case, and under the circumstances that Kennedy is working under, a highly sophisticated presentation to an audience above their level makes good sense, and is good campaign strategy.

Kennedy followed this advice. While debating on television or giving formal speeches to large audiences he spoke on issues, not personalities. He was carefully briefed by the academicians who surrounded him and he stressed international and national as well as state issues.

When visiting cities in Massachusetts he also spoke on the one or two matters that were of special concern to local inhabitants. Advance men on his staff toured the state and carefully prepared analyses of local problems. In New Bedford, for example, where fishing is an important industry, Kennedy stated that existing federal subsidies for fishing boat construction should be broadened by legislation he would introduce if elected. He also promised that if elected he would seek ways of getting the Food and Drug Administration to approve fish flour for certain purposes and that he would try to secure federal support for highway construction in the New Bedford area. No local nuance was neglected. When addressing a large crowd in the Italo-American section of Boston, he spoke his first words in Italian. "The dialect," the *Boston Globe* reported, "wasn't discernible — nor for that matter was his message — but it was in Italian and it went over big." [16]

The meticulous attention to detail that typified the work of Kennedy's advance men and the approach of the candidate was clear at the Blessed Sacrament Feast in New Bedford, one of the largest Portuguese religious functions in the United States. Kennedy, the featured speaker, praised the indomitable Portuguese explorers of the golden age of Lusitania. "We are fortunate," he remarked, "to have here in Massachusetts more Americans of Portuguese descent than in any other state in the Union. Portugal is one of our oldest allies. Portugal stands firmly against Communism, even to the point of allowing our country to use, free of charge, the Azores base which is the most important air base in the Atlantic Ocean." Kennedy then criticized the Walter-McCarran Immigration Act, which limits Portuguese immigration. The statute, he noted, is "injuring our nation by depriving us of the historical source of strength and growth." [17]

The imaginative character of the Kennedy campaign was also apparent in the way Kennedy utilized his brain trust. To counteract his absence of a public record and to create the impression

[16] *Boston Globe*, September 12, 1962.
[17] *New Bedford Standard-Times*, August 6, 1962.

that he was a statesman rather than a politician, members of the brain trust appeared several times in a taped "panel discussion" type of television program during which they invented a new concept in American politics, i.e., that of "relevant experience." Professor Robert Wood of the Massachusetts Institute of Technology, stated that Kennedy "belongs to the twentieth century." He pointed out that in 1961 only 2 per cent of the bills introduced into the Senate concerned law enforcement — "the area in which Mr. McCormack is most competent" — while nearly one-third were concerned with foreign policy, and the remainder with farm resources, industrialization, and welfare. "It is precisely the national and international experience and qualifications of Ted Kennedy — his years and his life abroad, his time in the West and the far West — that I think become the relevant factors to be considered in this campaign." Referring to the President and Edward Kennedy, Professor James McGregor Burns of Williams College stated, ". . . they have this tremendous interest in policy, in program, and a marvelous interest in the intricacies of these terrible problems." [18]

Despite the fact that Kennedy stressed issues, partly for the reasons we have discussed, the basic strategic assumption of the Kennedy camp was that the primary was a contest between personalities and families, not issues. The real question was whether voters were for or against Kennedy. McCormack, in this sense, did not play a role in the election. "My assessment of the Kennedy campaign," a brain truster remarked, "is that it will be pro- and anti-Kennedy factors, rather than the positive support for McCormack." The problem was therefore to protect the Kennedy image. The brain trusters suggested that Kennedy ignore McCormack, not only because of the need to build up Kennedy, but also because they believed McCormack's "liabilities" would speak for themselves.

Kennedy's advisers knew that their candidate was their greatest asset. They also felt that if he was to put his personal charm to best use, he must shake as many hands as possible, visit

[18] *Boston Globe,* August 31, 1962.

as many factories as possible, and speak as frequently as possible. Maximum exposure was the objective. His campaign manager remarked on August 3, "If I had my way I'd send Teddy out the door, and tell him to keep walking the streets and shaking hands from now to election day."

> Are people interested in Ted Kennedy going on and giving a fireside chat every Friday night? Should he be spending his time doing that or should he be out in the community . . . you know, spending all his time right in the community? And this is what our polls indicate. Issues are not too important. There's a name thing, that becomes a highly personalized thing. The dedication of the candidate, the toughness, the smartness are things that we find come out in polls . . . are factors that are holding Ted in very good stead. . . .
>
> I don't know whether the factor or factors involved in this dynasty issue, silver spoon, guy's an intellectual midget, he's just sitting on his big fat fanny, he's doing nothing, he's going to inherit the whole thing. Now, Ted's gone out and he's worked. First, he's proven that he doesn't want it handed to him, he's out there working. Two, I think he's demonstrated his ability to present a picture of somebody who's highly informed, highly dedicated . . . and this is chipping away at this dynasty.

Kennedy's pollsters, we were told, reported that he was more popular with female than with male voters. He was advised therefore to allocate resources accordingly. When possible he spent time with the wives and daughters of Massachusetts Democrats. Holmes and Hunter Alexander reported:

> Each itinerary includes a number of "house parties" where coffee and cookies are served. The candidate pays a brief visit with his attractive wife, Joan, shakes hands with the dozen or more ladies present and darts off to the next one. The schedule may include as many as nine afternoon stops. This technique was used effectively by Jack Kennedy in his 1958 Senatorial election, which was managed by Ted. It combines snob appeal and the greatest possible exposure of the candidate to women voters.[19]

19 *Boston Herald,* July 25, 1962.

During the closing days of the general election campaign in November the candidate appeared in the morning on television with his wife and mother in several programs entitled "Coffee with the Kennedys." The program was directed to housewives busy with morning chores.

The plan was formulated — maximum exposure and endless handshaking designed to permit the candidate's magnetism to take hold, appearances by Mrs. Rose Kennedy,[20] frequent mention of the President, and use of the slogan "He Can Do More for Massachusetts" — to take advantage of the Kennedy prestige and power. The utilization of the candidate's wife and mother was meant to appeal to the female electorate, while dawn-to-dusk campaigning by the candidate, it was hoped, would counteract the silver-spoon dynasty syndrome. The concept of "relevant experience" was invented to neutralize the fact that that candidate had never held elective office, and the sophisticated discussion of issues and frequent use of quotations from famous Americans were supposed to create the impression of a mature and well-informed contender. The decision not to attack McCormack was taken in part to deny the Attorney General an audience and to make it appear that Kennedy was "above" politics.

The candidate managed to incorporate most of these gambits in a five-minute video tape which was shown on television prior to the primary election. The words spoken or the manifest content appears on the left. Our interpretation of what Kennedy was attempting to imply — the latent content of his communication — appears on the right.

Good evening. In the last few months I've been able to meet many of you in the cities and towns where you live.	I'm energetic. I have traveled to every nook and cranny of Massachusetts.

[20] Mrs. Rose Kennedy appeared several times on television in a brief filmed telecast. She challenged the contention that there was anything unhealthy or undemocratic about family dynasties in politics, referred to the Adams family, and said, "There is no more rewarding career than that of public service. My father and husband spent many years in public service and enjoyed it immensely." She remarked that she hoped her children would enter public service "and my children's children."

Tonight I'd like to come into your homes and talk to all of you, to tell you first why I seek public office, and second, some of the things I believe can be done for our state and nation. I am in this campaign because I care about Massachusetts. I care very deeply about the kind of government we have here.

I am sincere and dedicated.

Our public office holders must be the kind of people our citizens can trust and respect. Unless they are, the future of our state is very much in doubt. In 1962, in this election, the time has come for a new kind of leadership. People who seek public office for money or for power have had their day in Massachusetts.

Aren't you fed up with the old-style "pols"? A veiled attack on McCormack and other professional politicians as a group and an appeal to the alienated voters.

Now is the time for people who want to serve. If you elect me this November, I will not only try to conduct myself in a way in this office to bring credit to the Commonwealth, but will also try to convince more people to come into public life.

An additional appeal to the alienated who want new and clean people in public life. Kennedy gives them hope. He will attract other clean and dedicated non-politicians: professors, businessmen, etc.

It is only with good people that we can have good government,

This is precisely what the alienated voter believes. It is also an accurate statement.

and if we work together we can restore to Massachusetts its rightful reputation for clean and effective government.

An appeal to the pride of Massachusetts citizens in their distinguished past. This statement might well appeal to disgruntled Protestants and Republicans as well as alienated Democrats.

In the last five years I've had an opportunity to get close to the problems of people in every part of the Commonwealth . . . who have a stake in what government does. Workers whose job security may depend on developing new skills. Children whose chance for a college education depends on federal scholarships. Older people in retirement, who cannot pay their medical bills. In the coming months and years, the U.S. Senate will be making important decisions to each of them and to each of you.

Our state needs in the Senate its most vigorous champion.

An appeal to several groups on the basis, not of generalities, but of their specific felt needs. Kennedy's campaign is personalized in this way. He is talking to you about what you want and need.

President Kennedy frequently used the word "vigor" and pronounced it with a flat Boston "A," (vigah). He was often spoofed about the way he pronounced the word — in a friendly and humorous way. It has become a word associated with the Kennedys. The use of the word "vigorous" by Edward Kennedy might remind voters of the President — an asset for Edward Kennedy. Certainly through energetic campaigning Edward Kennedy created the impression — an accurate one — that he is vigorous.

We have heard a great deal in recent months about what's wrong with Massachusetts; now is the time to tell what's right with Massachusetts. Our skilled workers, our great universities,

Again, an appeal to the pride of the citizens of Massachusetts, a reminder of the greatness of the past and a promise to return it to that greatness.

our research centers. The fact that this is a wonderful place to live and bring up children.

I will take this message not only to the floor of the Senate, but to the offices of American industry. I will visit personally the highest officials of the largest companies in the United States, which do not now have plants in Massachusetts. I will try to convince them to locate here.

I think they will listen.

I am in this campaign because I care about job security for our people. In the next ten years, to take care of our increasing population, we need 90,000 new jobs. At the same time we must protect the jobs we have from automation. When I was in Fall River, I saw men who had lost their jobs in textile mills, being retrained to be machine tool operators — this under the Area Redevelopment Law. This is the kind of program we need to expand here in Massachusetts. I am in this campaign because I care about young people.

In college I worked in a settlement house in South Boston, with underprivileged children. In the District Attorney's office I served on the juvenile panel.

A reaffirmation of Kennedy's campaign slogan: "He Can Do More for Massachusetts."

These companies will listen to me because I am the brother of the President.

A direct appeal to the unemployed, particularly the unemployed of Fall River, and a demonstration of the fact that Kennedy had been in Fall River, i.e., saw firsthand the problems of people in this city, and, by implication, many other cities. This statement also demonstrates the candidate's familiarity with federal assistance programs, i.e., a "proof" of his knowledgeability and sophistication.

A further proof of Kennedy's good works, particularly his interest in the underprivileged. This statement might also help to counteract what McCormack

I have talked with a great number of boys and girls who have dropped out of high school. I know what can happen when opportunity is denied. Seventy per cent of our high school graduates do not have a chance to go to college. This is our share of a national problem: the waste and neglect of the talents of our youth, to which solution I will devote my energy in the Senate.

And I am in this campaign because I care about peace, I want to see a world not just free from war, but free from the fear of war.

I have been behind the Iron Curtain; I have seen how Communism works.

And it is clear to me that peace can best be won if America is strong. Strong militarily so no one will outdo us; strong spiritually to hold high the torch of freedom.

As the great American patriot, John Dickinson, said 200 years ago, "whenever the cause of American freedom is to be vindicated, I look toward the province of Massachusetts Bay. She

aides called the "silver-spoon syndrome," i.e., Kennedy's birth.

An appeal to the liberals and those who might prefer Stuart Hughes.

A reaffirmation of the stereotype of Kennedy as a worldwide traveler and a firsthand observer of international problems. Statesmen visit foreign countries and talk to foreign dignitaries; Boston "pols" do not.

An appeal to what is probably the dominant view of Massachusetts residents on this problem, using one of several clichés in this speech.

President Kennedy frequently quoted fairly obscure American men of letters and political theorists. Although the average citizen of Massachusetts probably never heard of John must, as she has hitherto done, first kindle the sacred flame." Once again, the job we do here in Massachusetts will help build the strength of all America, and keep as well the peace of the world.

The primary is in September; the election is in November. The question before you is very simple: who will be the best senator for Massachusetts? Who has the ideas? Who has the program? Who has the energy and the vigor to work most effectively for our state? The decision is up to you.

I would like to end on a personal note. We are talking about something much more important than just an election or a political office. We are talking about the future of our country. I have two small children, a daughter two and one-half, and a son a year old. They mean a great deal to me, as I'm

Dickinson, who wrote *Letters from a Pennsylvania Farmer 1767–1768,* the fact that Edward Kennedy can quote Dickinson may indicate to simple-minded people that the candidate is literate, serious, and sophisticated — all of which helps to create the image that his advisers wished to create.

By employing the talents of a very bright cadre of academics who wrote sophisticated speeches for him, Kennedy created the impression that he had ideas and a program. By campaigning vigorously he did create the impression that he is energetic. The fact that he is the President's brother means that the probability is high that he will be an effective senator. Kennedy, unlike McCormack, did campaign vigorously. The argument that "He Can Do More for Massachusetts" is, in view of his relationship to the President, a very plausible and therefore vote-maximizing gambit.

The idea that we — the candidate and the people — will join hands may again create a sense of identity between the people and the candidate. The people therefore become, in a sense, a part of the candidate.

sure your children do to you. If
our children can live in a better
world in the years to come because of what we do, then all
our burdens will have become
blessings. So join with me beginning tonight. Together we
can do the job. Together we can
build the future of Massachusetts. Good night.

* * *

The campaign organization that implemented the Kennedy
strategy was among the largest, and certainly among the most efficient and affluent, ever placed at the disposal of a candidate for
the U.S. Senate in Massachusetts and perhaps in any other state of
comparable size. The Kennedys purchased more television time
and more radio time than McCormack, Curtis, Hughes, and
Lodge combined. They bought time on nine television stations,
including stations in the states of New York and Rhode Island,
and with rare exception it was prime time. They bought time
on over fifty English-language radio stations and more than
twenty foreign-language radio stations. They had 139 minutes
of documentary films and video tape for showing on television
— more than McCormack, Curtis, Hughes, and Lodge combined.

They purchased advertisements in all the larger newspapers
of Massachusetts and several dozen local and foreign-language
newspapers. They purchased prime billboard space throughout
the Commonwealth. They provided automobiles on election day
throughout the state to drive voters to the polls, and when convenient they rented airplanes to transport the candidate. They
employed the services of a highly reputable firm to sample the
electorate prior to the convention and during the primary campaign. They purchased or were provided with space for headquarters in twenty locations in the city of Boston and in most
cities and towns in Massachusetts where substantial numbers of
Democrats and Independents live. Most Kennedy headquarters
were open from mid-August through Election Day. For each

one the Kennedy organization either rented or was supplied with typewriters, telephones, water coolers, signs, electricity, janitor service, insurance, and office furniture.

Kennedy aides estimated that at the very least 300,000 telephone calls were made on Kennedy's behalf, that approximately 500,000 bumper stickers were bought, that at least 200,000 written pledges of support were gathered, and that not less than 1,-500,000 pieces of mail were posted in support of the Kennedy candidacy. Envelopes and letterheads were printed in three colors. Kennedy's advertising agency arranged for the publication of an eight-page rotogravure handout, printed in two colors, entitled "The Ted Kennedy Story." According to Kennedy's campaign manager, copies of this handout were distributed by volunteers to "almost all the homes across the state."

Roughly 160,000 citizens of Massachusetts who were not registered to vote were contacted through the mail via a printed postcard, and Kennedy headquarters estimated that at least 25,000 responded to the call. Special project groups created to work with labor, the elderly, Jews, and various ethnic and religious groups were established, and special mailings were prepared for each group. Area co-ordinators were recruited for every senatorial district, leaders for every major city, virtually every ward, and thousands of precincts. In some large cities where streets run for several miles, block leaders were enlisted to contact voters in apartment houses and housing projects, block by block.

The Kennedy organization also purchased abundant supplies of buttons, streamers, promotional pins, sashes, ribbons, signs and displays, and flyers, and during the closing stages of the primary campaign, when the candidate held several outdoor rallies on the same evening, it rented sound trucks and searchlights.

Kennedy's campaign manager claimed that several thousand volunteer workers executed most of these tasks. The Kennedy payroll included several secretaries in the four-story main Boston headquarters and approximately seven "administrative types," as one Kennedy aide described them. Kennedy treasurers reported about $56,000 solely for salaries — about $20,000 less than Mc-Cormack treasurers reported for his entire campaign. The only campaign of comparable size ever waged in Massachusetts, according to several political reporters, was that mounted for John Kennedy, when he defeated Henry Cabot Lodge in 1952.

No Kennedy aide suggested at any time that any expenditure deemed necessary by the candidate or his key staff members was curtailed for lack of money or manpower. Despite the superabundance of resources, the candidate's advisers were "staggered" by the size of Kennedy's plurality in the primary. In an election postmortem they suggested that the candidate rather than the organization was responsible. "They concede that he started off with some unusual assets," wrote Cornelius Dalton, the political editor of the *Boston Traveler*. "But they contend that the record turnout and the extent of his sweep prove that Ted Kennedy deserves more credit than he has gotten. He had a name, but nobody knew him. . . . He had to go out and sell himself." [21]

Edward Kennedy was the arch upon which the Kennedy organization was built. Commenting on the efficiency of the campaign, a co-ordinator suggested that "an organization can really go only as far as the candidate.":

If they're going to set up a tremendous organizational chart, and people taking him in different areas, and great volunteer workers, and if the candidate's going to go up and give a temperance speech in front of the liquor dealers' association of Massachusetts, this organization is not going to be that effective on election day, because the candidate is destroying what they're trying to do. . . . You have a good political candidate. . . . Mr. Kennedy is physically attractive, which you can never underestimate in an election in any state; he's a tireless worker, excellent speaker — he kept the issues relatively simple, didn't confuse them too much; and he is of course — and perhaps above all in the state of Massachusetts — a Kennedy. He looks like one, he talks like one, he acts like one. This of course is a great asset. And I don't think that can be minimized. I think with a lack of money, though, a lack of organization, you can't exploit these natural attributes. And that's where the part of money plays such a great part. . . .

The task of the organization, according to Kennedy's advisers, was made quite easy because the candidate was so salable. "You don't need a lot of signs if you're a Kennedy," one of them reported.

The only need for billboards is to put across what your general theme of the campaign is. In other words, "He Can Do More for Massachuseetts." Of course, great expenditures were made for billboards for this purpose. . . . The great advantage here is when Ed McCormack, for example, appeared at the gates of a General Electric factory in central Massachusetts and shook hands, no one knew him, by looking at him, who he was, and half an hour later, after they had thrown the card away, there would be great confusion concerning whom they had just shaken hands with and spoken to. When Ted appeared — I mean, ten miles away, as they were walking to work, they could say "There's a Kennedy waiting for us." There was no question at all, and it was something they went home and talked to their wives about and their relatives when they came in for dinner the following Sunday. This was a Kennedy.

"I think that candidates are very very important," remarked Kennedy's campaign manager, "but I think that 5 or 6 or 8 per cent difference is going to come about by the class of the organization."

In 1961 a rudimentary organization was set up for Edward Kennedy in John Kennedy's apartment in Bowdoin Street, and the future candidate began speaking throughout the state. This phase of the campaign was described by an early Kennedy supporter:

In November or December of 1961, Teddy went to South America. At that time, when he was in South America, every previous delegate to the preceding three Democratic state conventions received a personally addressed postcard from — I believe it was Caracas, Venezuela — to him saying, "Best regards, Ted Kennedy." This, for 90 per cent of these people, was the first personal communication they have ever received from any member of the Kennedy family. Some people have framed these and put them on their mantelpieces, for others to look at, put them in their drawers; very few threw them away as an obvious campaign gesture. Immediately preceding that, his return from that trip, the organization was in full force, up to a year and a half ago. Small headquarters were set up, breakfasts were set up with different state senators, state representatives, laying the foundation for the state convention. Different Democratic leaders in the areas were contacted; you had lunch or breakfast or dinner with Teddy, depending on the schedule; he spoke at many college commencements a year in advance, at any type of commencements, in high schools, all over the state. . . . This all adds to a solid foundation. In terms of straight organization, the headquarters were set up a year and a half in advance of the primary, a small one by the State House; there were mailing lists, a cross section, cards were filed on previous delegates; everything was set towards the convention. . . .

About five or six girls and two or three fellows, at this time — a year and a half in advance. Most important, of course, the former area secretaries for President Kennedy were contacted . . . and an organizational chart at that time was roughly set up. And then proceeded a tremendous mailing list; letters were sent out to organizational Democrats all over the state, to leaders of ethnic groups. . . . A film was made in Italy showing his trip there — everything from giving pennies to Italian children in the street to an audience with the Pope — which was then distributed to Italian clubs for showing all over the state. You would just call and say the club in such-and-such an area would like to see the film, and a man would come down with the projector and the film, the works, to show it to the club. To do this on a large scale costs tremendous money. But this is what was done.

The organization had six major tasks: (1) the recruitment of senatorial, city, town, ward, and precinct co-ordinators and volunteer workers; (2) a signature drive for pledges of support designed to give signers a sense of belonging, to gather information, and to recruit volunteers; (3) a registration drive to enroll new voters — particularly young ones who were pro-Kennedy; (4) mailings to hundreds of thousands of voters designed to advertise the candidate and maintain good will; (5) the creation of special project task forces set up to contact ethnic, religious, and occupational groups; and (6) a telephone campaign to reach possible stragglers.

An effort of this magnitude required considerable manpower, large amounts of money, a refined division of labor, and intelligent direction. Kennedy had all of these. The men and women who joined his camp included a small hard core of top advisers, with two members of the family, a brother-in-law, Stephen Smith and a first cousin, Joseph Gargan; a handful of academicians who formed a brain trust; area co-ordinators for senatorial districts; city leaders for larger cities, ward leaders, and precinct captains; several full-time workers in the Boston headquarters; advance men, pollsters, and advertising men; Mrs. Rose Kennedy and Mrs. Edward Kennedy; and thousands of volunteers.

One Kennedy worker, familiar with operations in the Boston headquarters, described the staff:

Well, the paid staff is — there's three types really. First, there's girls that have been on the payroll for years. Well, not years, but a year. Some of them have been on the payroll for a year and a half, others have been on the payroll for six months. There's quite a few of them. They make anywheres from $75, $80, $85, $100 a week, depending on their jobs. . . . I've never counted them but there's . . . say, thirty on the payroll, something like that, maybe a few more. These are secretarial type. Maybe another five or six that are administrative type, make a little bit more money.

Then, number two, the second type of the paid staff is lawyers or insurance men who are married and have families and are taking a year off, or six months off, or a year and a half off in some cases, to help his campaign. They're getting paid salaries to support their family while they campaign with Ted from the organization. This goes on in almost any campaign where people are valuable to have around, they have a family to support, you've got to pay them, or they can't work . . . something like that. A dozen, fifteen. Yeah. Maybe a little bit more, maybe sixteen or seventeen, right around there.

Third type is a very interesting type, they're people who are on leave of absence with pay from different private institutions or firms. And these are people — mostly, I would say, in fairness, that have known Ted for a period of time, have gone to college with him, met him someplace, personal friends of his, and work for companies who feel this is good public relations to keep a fellow on the payroll and let him work for a political candidate, if he were running for governor, or something like that. Then of course, if it's the brother of the President, it's very good public relations. . . .

But those are basically the three types of ways of the top members of the campaign staff. Whereas, newspapermen are either on a personal payroll or on a leave of absence with pay, depending on their newspaper's feeling. This, of course, is supplemented by people like myself who — I'm not getting any money. I run up an expenditure of a lump sum of over $100, then I'll send it to him and let him pay for it, but generally it's a small thing. Telephone calls cost fifteen- twenty dollars, well, I pay for it . . .

On Kennedy aide minimized the importance of the proletariat and extolled the role of the vanguard:

When you take the hard-core professionals — I'm a great believer, perhaps, in politics that — say, Lenin's theory of how to overturn a state has some application. If you take a small, dedicated, hard-core, practical, sophisticated group of men — let's say thirty in the state of Massachusetts — and then you are able to entice great numbers of volunteer workers whom you can then direct into the correct channels — this is the proper way to run an organization. If these top thirty are of sufficient quality and the volunteers are of sufficient quantity, then almost anything can be done. And this is the ideal of the Kennedy organization. Now I don't want to be misquoted into saying that the Kennedy organization resembles Lenin's form of Communist conspiracy!

Although a hard core of professionals may well be necessary for success, their political ambitions and their affection for the candidate may run counter to his needs. Candidates may risk becoming victims of the "echo effect." Instead of receiving objective advice and accurate information from top advisers they may be told what they want to hear or what is flattering to them. This frequently occurs because top advisers, who see the candidate as a source of future reward, wish to remain in his good graces. Sophisticated candidates who would rather be surrounded by men who can appraise situations realistically than sycophants must deal with this problem. Edward Kennedy, according to one aide, dealt with it by placing relatives or hired employees in the highest positions and making it quite clear to the employees that their weekly paycheck relieved him of future obligations. One co-ordinator, an unpaid volunteer, described the problem and the Kennedy's solution.

A Kennedy creates much greater interest than does any ordinary candidate in this state, be he Bobby, Teddy, or any relation at all, even the sisters. Now it would seem that those that were brought quicker into the top echelon were people who avoided this outward identification; in other words, people who said, "Okay, I'm with him, and I'm going to support him, and he's giving me $200 a week. I'm going to do my job, and every time he walks into the room I'm not gonna jump up so I can be the first one beside him." The people who took this practical approach were the ones who moved up the fastest within the organization. This is perhaps a point to remember in most campaigns, and perhaps even more in life, that some organizations or some people that have everything in a practical sense are more impressed by people who aren't outwardly always trying to be with them or next to them or driving them in the car. This is true in any campaign, I think, but especially in the Kennedy campaign there is so much fighting to be near the candidate or next to him or to bring him into the hall, that sometimes seven or eight co-ordinators are trampled in the rush to get to the door fast to bring the candidate down the main aisle. I think the top echelon basically fought this down and said to themselves, "Okay, now we all know Teddy, we all know he's gonna win, and we're gonna try to help him win, and let's not get in each other's way to see who he's going to name the first postmaster in East Byfield, Massachusetts. Let's not worry about those things right now." I think basically the top echelon was made up of those people.

Relatives in key positions were particularly valuable, according to Kennedy's campaign manager, because their familial status had the effect of making "people feel that they're not just listening to some broken-down pol."

The overwhelming majority of academicians in Massachusetts who declared themselves publicly supported McCormack. According to Robert Healy, political editor of the *Boston Globe,* Professors Samuel Beer and John Plank of Harvard University, James McGregor Burns of Williams College, and Robert Wood of the Massachusetts Institute of Technology were "the only charter members of the Kennedy club from among the teaching set." Although two other members of the university community joined the Kennedy brain trust, candidates actually need only a handful of professors to organize a workable brain trust or to give the public the impression of university support.

One Kennedy brain truster noted that the Democratic party in Massachusetts was drastically in need of reform and that Edward Kennedy was the only person who could and would take remedial steps:

> Again, a person who has the capacity to make the system work can make a much greater contribution to the Democratic party in this state. In terms of vigor, in terms of youth, in terms of being separated from the older form of personalized politics. Now this doesn't mean that you can have someone who has only integrity. You must have someone who can play the game but yet has a sense of direction and can break out of this vicious circle of old-school, personalized politics. Times have changed in Massachusetts, and we think that Kennedy may well be a sign of change.

The brain trust advised the candidate not only on the issues but also on political strategy. Its role, according to one member who had served several candidates in previous elections, was "larger than I've ever seen before," because it was utilized as a clearinghouse through which ideas from other components of the organization filtered and were evaluated. In this capacity brain trusters vetoed the proposal of some "old pros" that Kennedy

. . . hit hard on the personal attacks, about his family and his inexperience, and I think the judgment—that this was not a useful kind of procedure . . . in terms of what we thought was possible, what we would judge would be the public re- action, and the capacity of getting through in a limited time on a media network an argument of that kind. This was a professional judgment. . . . We didn't think it would deal with what the candidate's prime strength would be, namely, to talk issues, to demonstrate intelligence, and to show ca- pacity. I think this would be maybe the only candidate in the United States in one sense, that I would say the prime need is for him to expose himself and demonstrate capacity and to handle the issues. And in that sense we thought it was terribly important that he stay on an issue campaign basis.

One academic suggested that the professor, unlike the politi- cian, does not seek future political favors but hopes rather to increase the rationalistic and programmatic element in politics.

A prudent academic can take two or three views of the brain trust role. He can think of himself as a man who will give the candidate his ideas, his status, and his goal and would provide him with solutions to problems in a rationalistic way. I think people who enter this role are bound to be disappointed if they think they will become closer to the candidate, if they think they will generate for the candidate threads of alliances that will continue throughout a successful candidate's term of office. . . .

The problem that an academic faces typically, but not al- ways, is that he is unable to engage in the negotiations or make bargains that are readily understandable to the readily available typical candidate. By that I mean, he is not able to say I will do this if you will give me a job because generally he doesn't want a job. He is not able to say I would like this kind of role because if he is a good academic he doesn't want to divert that amount of time to that kind of role.

This scholar also noted that

. . . the academic community has for a variety of reasons arrived at a place where it has some impact on public affairs. That, one, it should not expend it excessively in every campaign in every election, and two, it should expend it with some of the same calculations and motivations of the other political actors, if indeed it has become an actor of some note. What concerned me at the beginning on the Democratic side was the fact that all or the majority of the academics were . . . going with McCormack. . . . It seems to me it was bad in principle that if the academic community represents something about rationalistic programmatic policy, advice, and guidance, that this should be assured as a component in what other candidate won. . . . I also think it is a tragedy for the academic community to be identified as predominantly Democratic.

Now what I would hope to see emerging from these successive experiences in the brain trust is not a breakthrough of one great candidate with a set of brilliant men behind him that can make his star rise but improved cohesiveness and communication within the academic world itself. So that whatever star rises, access to and influence upon the political actors in official capacity exist and that we do this not as supplicants trying to bend their ears and not as people who stand on the fringes and throw books and newspaper articles to him but that in which we have sufficient political sagacity ourselves so that our point of view and our particular posture gets heard.

Many of the strategic decisions taken by the candidate, his top advisers, and the brain trust were executed by campaign co-ordinators — one for each state senatorial district — who were assisted by hundreds of ward leaders and thousands of volunteer workers. Several weeks before primary election day, Kennedy's campaign manager reported that the organization had succeeded in recruiting a ward leader for every ward in Massachusetts and a precinct captain for approximately half of the state's precincts. On August 3, he said:

We've broken the state up into certain areas. . . . [In our main headquarters] We have one girl handling Suffolk County and we have one girl handling the area south of Boston, another girl handling the far west, another girl handling north of Boston. . . . These girls read the newspapers from those areas, . . . anybody has any kind of a problem from North Andover, they call in . . . if it's a sign problem, if it's a speech problem, if it's an appearance problem . . . rather than look for Joe Jones, Joe Smith, Mary Brown who handles the specific thing, they talk to the one girl. . . . This is a tremendous . . . labor saver for us because they're not running all over. At the end of the day the girl has a check sheet of many things that have to be done. She just very dispassionately walks to the different people and . . . gets the answer and the following day she calls these people back . . . other campaigns that I've been involved in, I mean, you have this tremendous problem of "Oh, wait a minute, let me find out. I'll connect you with the guy who handles the signs or I'll connect you with the guy. . . ." So this is a very simple thing. . . . In each one of the cities who has a leader or contact man, and in each one of the wards we have somebody and in each one of the precincts we have somebody and now we're working on the workers within the precinct, so that if you ask me now about, say ward 1, precinct 2 of the City of Boston, I'll be able to pull the card and tell you who the . . . who the ward contact man is, who the precinct man is that's working in that precinct to get Mary Smith, Joe Brown, Joe Green, Joe White, that it's an Irish Catholic district . . . longshoremen, some freight handlers, some truck drivers, so that again we have the whole state broken down so that we know what we're supposed to do in ward 1, precinct 1, or ward 1, precinct 2. Like any campaign, you have initially, you have a lot of confusion. We've gone over . . . I think the convention was a tremendous help to us because it made us build up a tight organization and an organization that would fight over two votes.

On August 26 Kennedy's campaign manager reported:

In the last three weeks we've set up headquarters in 80 per cent of these communities. We've set up seventeen, eighteen, nineteen headquarters. We've gotten our organization off the ground in Boston, here. We're starting to work on ethnic groups, Italian groups, Jewish groups. . . . You first find out who are the ethnic groups, who their leaders are, what communities they're located in, who has influence with them,

who they'll follow, who they'll listen to, what their attitudes
are toward Ted Kennedy. This has all been culled, and now
we're just working on them. We're starting our effort with
labor groups. . . . We've been working. We conducted a
pretty strenuous registration campaign, sent out about 150,-
000 cards, 160,000 cards. And we got some pretty good results
on that. We've been out, going across the state recruiting for
primary day, building an organization which we don't have,
or didn't have. Well, you go into a community such as Natick, for example, where there'll be a relatively good vote,
4,000–5,000 votes. We have some people who indicated their
favorableness toward Ted, we contact them. We hope that
they, in turn, will contact other friends. Then, after this contacting back and forth, we hope that each one of the precincts
— I believe there's seven precincts in Natick — we will have
one individual in charge of each precinct. And he, in turn,
will have six or seven or eight or ten people working with him
together in the precinct. So that they conduct a signature crusade, they will do a telephone campaign, and on primary day
we will know that in Natick, in precinct 1A we have an effective organization, somebody to man the polls, somebody to
telephone, somebody to deliver a brochure if it has to be delivered. And we hope to be able to do this in the major communities. And you do it the same way in Natick as you do in
Boston.

One Kennedy ward leader described the operation on the local level — the signature drive, the registration drive, and the telephone campaign:

To begin with, let's start on the telephone campaign. The
city publishes a list of all the registered voters. . . . Each
ward is provided with a list of all the registered voters, complete and up to date. They are then provided with a telephone directory listed by streets. Girls will sit down and take
all — we only approach the Democrats, not the Independents
or the Republicans. Then the phone number is transcribed
from the telephone book onto a list of registered voters, and
every single person that has a phone is contacted. They are
called and they are asked if they would not consider Mr. Kennedy as a candidate. At the end of the conversation they are

asked if they need a ride to the polls. The volunteers for driving them to the polls — it's strictly a volunteer thing, using
their own cars, and of course they're not reimbursed for the
expenses involved. . . . I would say 90 percent of those
registered Democrats who had telephones were called. And
of course you may get a family with four or five in the house,
so that they were called in essence also. But for example, let's
say ward 5, which is the Kenmore Square-Beacon Hill area. I
would say that approximately 6,000 people were called. And
this in my opinion is one of the big, big deciding factors, this
personal element of receiving a phone call in such a manner
that it is a message from the candidate to the voter. . . .

We had a registration drive. We had a list of every unregistered voter in the state. They were first sent a letter, and this
of course was handled by the Democratic Registration Committee in conjunction with our organization. They received a
postcard when and where they could register, and then they
received, a lot of them, actual personal contact by solicitors
going from house to house ringing doorbells, informing these
people once again to register, and then as a final thing they
received a phone call to register. . . .

We had a signature campaign before the primary date in
which workers went house-to-house getting everyone — Democrats, Republicans, the like, asking them if they would care
to put their name on a signature card merely stating that they
are endorsing the candidate Mr. Edward Kennedy. And each
one of these people who signed the sheet with their address
received a letter from the candidate thanking them very much
for their support.

Now, from the date of the primary to the election there will
be a leaflet distributed to every house in the state, and it will
be in the form of a brochure. The background of Mr. Kennedy, pictures, his work, what he's done, his policies. And
these will just be put into the mailboxes. And then, of course,
we will again use the phone to contact all the registered Democrats. And if we get through the registered Democrats . . .
if there is time to spare we'll try calling some of the independent voters.

The Kennedy headquarters apparently assumed that local
leaders should have a good deal of freedom in determining how

the tasks assigned from headquarters should be carried out. City co-ordinators and ward chairmen, it was believed, would have a greater sense of participation under these conditions. Headquarters, however, did provide the necessary materials.

Well, a ward co-ordinator works under the unit head or the city head. . . . But the ward co-ordinator is given policy by the city heads — what we are looking for and the general approach. . . . For example, let's try the telephone campaign. He is told what the end result is to get the voters out; as far as what he wants his individual telephone workers to do, that's left up to the ward co-ordinators. . . . The ward co-ordinator solicits his own volunteers by personal contact, friends, people who have come into the main headquarters and signed a volunteer card. These volunteer cards from the main headquarters are in turn given to the ward leader . . . and he calls them up and asks them to come down to his headquarters. . . . And they are asked if they can do poll work or telephone work, and usually if it's telephone work they can put in three to four to five hours, and I have found that there is a tremendous amount of female workers — much, much more than male workers. I know in our ward, it's probably 90 percent females and 10 percent males. And so the women do all the telephoning; the men do all the driving, and in certain wards where it's a little rough, such as economic background, we will use male poll workers. In the nicer areas, well-lit and so forth, we will use female workers. . . .

There was a signature campaign. There was a telephone campaign. There will be this leaflet distribution. Each ward co-ordinator will pick up the leaflets and he in turn will distribute them. For example, in our ward we have the municipal parking lot, and in each automobile that is parked, we will put one of the leaflets in the automobile, aside from putting it in the homes. Then of course we'll have a big drive for absentee ballots. We'll contact people by phone in this telephone drive and ask them if there is anyone in their family that needs an absentee ballot. We'll either send it to him or inform him how to get it. Now the main headquarters is taking care of the servicemen. They have a list of all the servicemen and they will contact the servicemen by mail, asking them if they need absentee ballots, and so forth.

There will be poll workers stationed at each one of the polls, to cover it from eight o'clock in the morning to eight o'clock in the evening; there'll be a coffee driver and each of the poll workers will be given coffee during the course of the day; there will be free transportation to the polls; and then of course there will be many phone inquiries that we receive during the course of the day — when the candidate is speaking, and how can they meet him, and a lot of things on this level. . . .

Activities similar to these were also carried out by hundreds of ward committees throughout the Commonwealth. The effort, of course, required thousands of volunteers. Kennedy's campaign manager remarked, a few weeks after the primary, that the organization "was not ideal and we don't have one [precinct captain] everywhere but probably no other organization has ever equaled the number of people at the grass-roots level. Oh, we probably have 40,000[22] across the state actually working at this point." "The volunteer problem does not exist in the Kennedy campaign," a co-ordinator remarked. "You just can't handle them all. You have to have some of them doing jobs that are completely useless, but it keeps them busy, it makes them feel they are part of the campaign, and they don't know the difference if they're putting cards in that'll never be sent out, or not."

The Kennedy organization was so efficient and the number of volunteers so plentiful that headquarters was even able to recruit workers to serve as street co-ordinators and block chairmen. One Kennedy co-ordinator noted, "Sometimes where you would have a group of apartment houses you would have a house chairman. If you had two apartment houses in a block, you would have a chairman for each house. It got to a point where sometimes you would have a chairman and then five workers for a group of potential signatures of maybe twenty-five or thirty people." No other campaign in Massachusetts that we are familiar with ever had so many

22 Cornelious Dalton, a political writer for the *Boston Traveler*, estimated that 3,000 volunteers worked for Kennedy. A senior Kennedy adviser placed the figure at 10,000.

volunteers that it was possible to have a chairman for a large apartment house.

Although advance men have long been utilized in presidential campaigns, few candidates for Congress have had enough money, manpower, or intelligence to use their services. The advance man scouts the terrain before the candidate's arrival and customarily gathers data on local problems, sets up travel routes, and arranges for speeches and meetings. Since money and manpower were in full supply in the Kennedy camp and since the Kennedy strategy called for the candidate to meet personally as many voters as possible, time was, in fact, the critical scarce resource for Kennedy. He had to allocate his time to meet the largest possible number of voters and deliver the largest number of campaign speeches. His travel routes therefore had to be carefully prepared along with his daily handshaking routine. Kennedy advance men took care of this aspect of the operation.

A Kennedy aide, who knew the advance men, described their duties.

There are two major problems involved in Mr. Kennedy's visiting industrial plants. One is that he wants to cause a minimal amount of inconvenience and loss of production to the owner of the plant. The second, and equally important thing, is that this whole campaign is based on meeting a maximum of people throughout the state in a minimal amount of time. . . . I have seen other candidates go into a plant where they expect to spend a maximum of twenty minutes, and walk out two hours later. Now this, of course, can kill a whole day for Mr. Kennedy, and not only kill his time, but ruin all of the subsequent appointments. Not only does he lose his personal time, but thirteen or twenty other factories are left in the lurch, too. This makes enemies. To overcome this problem, I saw a very effective and very unique system invoked. Mr. Kennedy's schedule is made up some days or some weeks in advance. A few days prior to Mr. Kennedy's going to a particular city, a sheet is made out with exact appointments. Nine to nine-twenty, nine-twenty to nine-thirty-five, nine-thirty-five to nine-forty-five — just where he will go and whom he will see. Now, before Mr. Kennedy actually arrives at these industrial

plants or at any location, two advance men go to the spot that
he will visit some time in the future. They meet the employers and the personnel directors of the plant and they
make a very intensive survey of the physical facilities, so that
it is impossible for Mr. Kennedy . . . to make any wrong
move on this tour. It sounds silly, but a whole morning's
work can just go down the drain by opening up the door that
he thinks is the exit and walks into the ladies' room or walks
into a broom closet. This destroys the whole effectiveness.
. . . The papers would have a field day. . . . So his visits are
almost the same as the President visiting someplace. Everything is mapped out in advance: the route, the people he's going to see, the type of people, the type of work done. He is
armed with everything, from the location of the doors to the
industrial situation in general in that particular plant or that
particular area. It's practically impossible for him to make a
mistake.

As we have seen, the Kennedy organization had an abundance
of amateur volunteer workers and highly skilled paid employees,
an abundance of funds, and an enormous backlog of good will and
devotion among the voters of Massachusetts. One aide suggested
that the Kennedy effort succeeded because

> . . . it's a sign of status in Massachusetts to have a Kennedy
> bumper sticker. It's a sign of status if you can work for Ken-
> nedy, if you get a letter from Kennedy, or if you have any con-
> nection at all with a formal or informal political organization
> led by Kennedy or bearing the Kennedy name; it's something
> to talk about, it's a matter for conversation that puts you per-
> haps a little bit above the next guy in terms of many people's
> eyes, anyway. This is one secret psychological reason why the
> drive was so successful.

In retrospect, one might wonder why the Kennedys mounted
such a massive campaign against McCormack. It is important to
remember that much more was at stake for the Kennedys than one
seat in the United States Senate. If Edward Kennedy overwhelmed
McCormack in September and demolished the Republican candidate in November, not only was he likely to be re-elected to the

Senate again and again but a truly dramatic win would enhance the mystique of Kennedy invincibility. The prestige of the President and the "legitimacy" of Edward Kennedy's candidacy were also at stake. If Kennedy won by a substantial margin, his supporters could always rationalize his candidacy by arguing that he was the only Democrat who could defeat a popular Republican candidate. A truly big win, they assumed, would also lessen the feeling that his candidacy was presumptuous. If the Kennedys were ultimately thinking of the White House for Edward, it was certainly necessary to establish a reputation for the youngest brother as an impressive vote getter with phenomenal appeal. The Kennedys wanted to win and win by a wide margin. They spared no expense and no effort to insure Edward Kennedy's election.

Yet, despite this preponderance of money and manpower, Kennedy almost made a calamitous error of judgment during the campaign when he accepted McCormack's invitation to debate "the issues" on television, with results that were quite unpredictable.

CHAPTER 4 ⊠ *If His Name Was Edward Moore*

If his name was Edward Moore, with his qualifications . . . your candidacy would be a joke, but nobody's laughing because his name is not Edward Moore. It's Edward Moore Kennedy.

— EDWARD MCCORMACK, at the close of the first debate

PRAGMATIC POLITICIANS who are underfinanced, who sense that they are likely to lose, or who know that they are less well known than their opponents, should press for television debates — they have much to gain and little to lose in such confrontations. It is always possible that a witty remark, a pointed barb, a flurry of statistics, or a startling revelation can turn the tide or that the front runner may "blow the election," as one McCormack aide noted, by "being stupid, impolite, or who the hell knows what." Televised debates not only present the underdog with a unique opportunity to get in a crippling blow but also provide him with badly needed free time and equal exposure. Professional politicians agree, therefore, that it is wise for the candidate who is behind to debate unless he is hopelessly inept, stupid, or physically repulsive. They also agree that it is unwise for the favorite to accept the challenge.

McCormack did not have the funds to purchase "equal time" on television. He could not or would not meet thousands of voters every day as Kennedy did. He could not even "meet" Kennedy, whose managers kept him away from the Attorney General and other potentially hostile environments. He wanted to confront Kennedy because he thought he could "expose" him as a "name's the same" candidate, a non-voter, a brash young man who was cashing in on his family's influence. Televised debates, McCormack thought, admirably suited his needs.

On July 25 the Attorney General challenged Kennedy to a series of eight televised debates to be held "any time, any place." The following week he suggested that they discuss the major issues of domestic and foreign policy and debate the meaning of their campaign slogans: Kennedy's "He Can Do More for Massachusetts" and McCormack's "The Qualified Candidate." McCormack proposed that the candidates ask each other ten questions with two minutes provided for each answer and one minute for rebuttal. He also proposed that three minutes be set aside for opening and for closing statements and that the debate be regulated by a neutral and essentially passive moderator.

McCormack, in other words, wished to make the debates as spontaneous and unrehearsed as possible. A situation of this kind, he felt, would provide him with the best opportunity to criticize Kennedy or, as he put it, "strike for the jugular." McCormack's proposed format would give him, rather than panelists, the initiative in selecting the questions. Very brief opening and closing statements would prevent Kennedy from "controlling" a substantial portion of the hour by reading a thoughtfully reasoned and literate statement written by a Harvard or M.I.T. professor. McCormack advisers assumed that since Kennedy spoke the words, voters would naturally conclude that the ideas were his own. McCormack wanted to confront a Kennedy lacking his speech writers, his academicians, and his advertising council.

A debate of this kind would, of course, be an almost unique event in American politics because most political events in this country and most political campaigns are carefully planned to avoid the spontaneous and the unrehearsed. Managers attempt to structure and control the campaign as much as possible. The function of the advertising agency, the speech writer, the documentary film maker, and the makeup man is to cut and edit reality so as to publicize the client's assets and hide his liabilities. If they are truly adept in the art of merchandising soap, or in this case candidates, they will attempt not only to cut and edit reality but also to manufacture a largely new reality — a synthetic and celluloid reality in which the candidate appears to be sagacious, sophisticated, dedicated, commonsensical, earthy, or whatever is likely to appeal to the particular market in question. The candidate and his entourage, in other words, will try to set up a counterfeit reality composed of non-spontaneous, carefully rehearsed pseudo or contrived events. The candidate who sees the need, and who has the money employs talented pseudo-event makers and greatly enhances his chances of being elected.

McCormack assumed that an unrehearsed televised debate in

which the candidates were free to ask questions of each other might lead Kennedy to lose his temper and break down. McCormack's public relations man hoped "that in a debate with Ted Kennedy, Ed McCormack can light Mr. Kennedy's extremely short fuse. I think this is a guy who could blow it on television. . . . Ted Kennedy could be angered to the point where he could make a public display of his very famous temper. . . . This would be highly injurious, and accrue to our benefit."

Although Kennedy's campaign manager responded to the challenge by declaring the Kennedy was "very willing to debate and welcomes the idea of debate," the first meeting to discuss details was not held until August 10, sixteen days after McCormack first suggested the idea. "Our candidate," Kennedy's manager continued, "doesn't take the lazy man's approach and just appear on TV. He's out meeting people in the places where they work as early as six o'clock in the morning and we've got commitments to fill." McCormack made use of this response by placing a large sign in the window of his Boston headquarters which read: "I have noticed on several occasions that my opponent has had excuses why he could not face me in debate. As his next-door neighbor I no longer feel that he can find a satisfactory excuse." The number of days since the challenge and the number of days remaining until the election were recorded each morning on a blackboard below the sign.

On August 14, after four days of preliminary skirmishing, Kennedy and McCormack agreed to debate domestic issues in South Boston on August 27 and foreign affairs in Holyoke on September 5. Kennedy, however, refused to accept the McCormack format. His manager proposed twenty-minute opening statements and five-minute rebuttals. A panel of news commentators, not the candidates, were to ask all the questions. McCormack, of course, refused. A McCormack negotiator stated, "What you'd like is an arrangement where your man could read a twenty-minute opening and a five-minute rebuttal prepared by some speech writer in Washington. Well, we don't think that gives the people any indication of the candidate's ability. Neither does it give the people any opportunity to get answers to questions that should be answered."

Negotiations continued for eleven days, when the candidates finally compromised on five-minute opening statements, two-minute closing statements, thirty-six minutes for questions from panelists with two and a half minutes for answers and one and a half minutes for rebuttal. Both sides also agreed that no restrictions be placed on the panelists with respect to the subject matter of questions.

The selection of the panel, however, brought further problems. McCormack's campaign manager presented the names of five newspapermen and told Kennedy's agent to select two and then name the third. The Kennedy forces rejected all five proposed names as "agents of the enemy." Kennedy's aide then suggested five other names, which McCormack's manager rejected for the same reason. The Kennedys then proposed that the publishers of three Boston newspapers each pick one reporter and that the three selected then choose a fourth panelist from radio or television. McCormack's agents found this proposal unacceptable. In the end the campaign managers agreed to select by lot four names from a list submitted by Boston radio and television stations and executives of Boston newspapers.

The *Worcester Telegram* commented that "the attempt to arrange a meeting between Edward J. McCormack and Edward Kennedy . . . is only slightly less involved than the disarmament talks in Geneva." Each candidate, of course, wanted the format he believed would be most advantageous. McCormack hoped to maximize conflict and dialectic since he believed that Kennedy was vulnerable; Kennedy wanted to minimize the risks involved since he believed he was the front-runner. The format finally decided upon made it likely that the debates would actually be joint news conferences rather than debates. Neither Kennedy nor Mc-Cormack was seriously concerned with the problem of how best to make the debate a vehicle for informing and educating the public. The rational candidate makes strategic decisions in terms of political expediency, not civic duty.

McCormack's campaign manager confessed, "I was a little bit surprised when they finally did agree to debate." Several astute politicians in Massachusetts were also surprised. They believed that Kennedy had little to gain and much to lose. The Kennedys' concern with public opinion and the President's positive attitude toward televised debates, however, influenced Kennedy's advisers, most of whom originally wanted no debates. One aide explained his candidate's acceptance of McCormack's challenge as the lesser of two evils for Kennedy:

It was partly political necessity. We had, in a sense, been backed into a corner. Everyone felt in general, I think, as I did, that it wasn't a good thing, but the alternative was to appear to be ducking. McCormack's uses of public relations was excellent. . . . Statements such as "I will be there Monday night and debate with the wall," . . . put us right on the spot, and the public reaction was at least enough to show us that we had to . . . take our chances.

Some Kennedy aides, of course, believed that their candidate projected so well on television and that McCormack appeared so ineffective that Kennedy ought to debate. Kennedy's campaign manager summarized their views:

We felt that it would probably be in the best interest of Ted Kennedy to have the debate. . . . His brother was going throughout the country saying that people running for office should debate. And we felt in the very beginning that Ted has a peculiar amount of stage presence. He does very well when he's in situations which the average individual wouldn't do too well in. And we felt that he's big, strong, he's vigorous. McCormack himself doesn't project too well on television. We thought it would be a pretty good idea to get them both together. The only problem that we had, we just didn't want to spring into this because it seems Mr. McCormack doesn't have too much going for him in terms of organization, or any type of planned effort. . . . Their feeling was we were out in front, . . . and McCormack had a great amount of difficulty gathering any kind of a crowd. And we felt that this would be building him, and I think, in a sense, we did build him. We brought him up to a certain point. There was a lot of coverage, a lot of notoriety to it. . . . And their feelings were that this is not such a good idea, to give him all of this opportunity for exposure. And I think underlying the whole thing was that Teddy does well on television, McCormack doesn't. We felt we had nothing to fear. Some people thought that every ball team, even the Yankees, have one bad day, and it's courting a little bit of danger, but we weighed all the pros and the cons, and the advocates of the debate seemed to win out. And then we just didn't want to get into the position of running away.

For several weeks prior to the debate McCormack's advisers, as we have noted, discussed whether or not Kennedy should be attacked. During the campaign they resolved the problem in favor of a restrained attack. That Kennedy was forced to withdraw from Harvard College was not exploited, but Kennedy was described as exploiting a famous family name and family power, and as a candidate with no previous public service of any significance and therefore unqualified. His candidacy, consequently, was depicted as arrogant, presumptuous, and, so to speak, against the American grain.

The Kennedys, although assuming that some kind of attack would be mounted during the debate, remained with their original strategy. When asked what instructions Kennedy had been given before the debate, his campaign manager responded:

> Well as somebody very tersely stated to him "you in your mind have some picture as to how a United States Senator should act, and think and deport himself with a certain amount of dignity. Just take the high road, and no matter what he says or does to you, or what the crowd does to you, just remain aloof from it all, and you'll come out OK." He was instructed, and he did ignore all the attacks.

His aides also prepped Kennedy with large numbers of facts and figures, dates, and quotations from famous Americans, apparently on the assumption that these would be interpreted by the electorate as indications of Kennedy's profundity.

Although McCormack's close advisers favored an attack during the debate, they were concerned that the Attorney General might not be constitutionally suited to the task. They attempted, therefore, to prepare him psychologically for an effort they feared was out of character but nevertheless necessary. Pre-debate maneuvers were described by the adviser who wrote the original draft of the opening statement that McCormack would deliver:

> I wrote what I regarded as a fighting, aggressive, hard-hitting attack-type speech. Immediately the candidate said, oh, I think that these are too negative. All they do is attack, and I can't. Half the speech has got to be devoted to more positive aspects. I'm going to talk about my record, my background, my position on national and international issues.
>
> Well, my feeling is, you're limited to five minutes in the debate. If you decide you're going to attack then it seems to me you've got to use the five minutes to attack and actually my speech was devoted to doing one thing and one thing alone, to destroying . . . the Kennedy campaign slogan, "He Can Do More for Massachusetts," to examining the full implications of this, to a process of elimination to show that his statement, in fact, could mean nothing more and it was intended to mean nothing more than that Mr. Kennedy has connections, has influence which he can peddle and manipulate to get things done for Massachusetts. . . . You're going to have this slogan thrust down your throat again and again. Well, my feeling was, knowing this, why not attempt in advance to cut the slogan down, and it seems to me this slogan really epitomizes the real basic issue of this campaign. Now you can't say a hell of a lot in five minutes, and you can't go off and hope to accomplish three, four, or five things in five minutes. So you get really fixed in mind what you want to do and — as I saw it on the basis of our conversation and the consensus—let's hit this one issue and let's attack in the opening. And it seemed to me that in the question period you're in a position to become affirmative, to become positive by the answers which you choose to give to questions to show and to indicate that you have a grasp of national and international issues. And then I also thought that in this first five minutes you could set the tone of the remainder of the debate, and to some extent, perhaps so rattle Mr. Kennedy that you would have him on the defensive for the remainder of the debate. . . .
>
> But as I point out to you, these first drafts which were based on the consensus which had been reached the previous day were unacceptable to the candidate and he wanted at least

half of his speech devoted to what I regarded as this unnecessary, meaningless drivel which would vitiate the effectiveness, I thought, of his attack. He resisted very firmly; this was maybe about a week, ten days, before the debate.

In retrospect, it seems to me that what happened is we progressed here as a result of this constant hammering day after day, "Eddie, you've got to go in there and fight, Eddie; you've got to be aggressive," and I think there was some needling done by some people, telling him Steve Smith had said this about you, or the Kennedys are saying you're a lazy candidate, this kind of thing. . . . reminding him from time to time, remember what they said about you, Eddie, every man has his price, and you could have been bought out of this fight. . . . This kind of thing that went on day after day. I didn't see too much of this. I know there was a little bit of it going on. Perhaps even a misrepresentation, maybe even a few lies in an effort to really shake the candidate. But I can see what happened here. There was really a workup period so to speak of maybe a week or ten days, when the candidate's own resistance, and perhaps his own better judgment as to the type of approach that should be taken in the first debate was gradually chipped away at by his advisers, who were determined to get him into an aggressive fighting stance.

Although McCormack's top advisers assumed that a vigorous attack might cause Kennedy to lose his temper and "blow the election," the problem of what McCormack should do if Kennedy ignored the attack was never discussed or apparently even seriously considered. A speech writer noted:

I think it is indeed unfortunate that nowhere, at any time in any of the meetings in which I participated, in virtually all of them prior to the first debate, did any of the brain trust, so-called, ever raise the question, or did the question ever occur to the candidate himself, What do I do in the event that I attack and I'm ignored in my attack? Do I let it up at all? Do I continue on the attack? And how is this going to appear to the general public? So this never entered the mind of anyone. Had it come into the minds of some of us, I think, certainly, we could have evaluated and weighed to some extent, and probably would have said, somewhere after the midway point after you had made some really telling points, if you're not getting any resistance from the kid at all, then it seems that you can't continue to attack, in effect, what the public regards now as a rather defenseless candidate. The failure of the brain trust, of the strategists around McCormack to consider this, and to consider the impact of a constant attack upon an opponent who is not counterattacking, could have been compensated for, I think, by the intuition to some extent of the feeling of the candidate himself, during the course of the debate.

* * *

The first debate, at Kennedy's suggestion, was held in South Boston — an astute move. This Irish enclave of the Hub has spawned many of the legendary figures portrayed in *The Last Hurrah*, including the McCormacks. Perhaps no other section of Massachusetts in the public mind is so closely associated with the stereotype of the old-style Irish professional politician and Irish politics, i.e., the political type and way of life that alienated voters tend to believe is a root cause of the corruption, chicanery, and inefficiency for which Massachusetts is so notorious.

The Kennedys knew that McCormack was attempting to portray himself as David (a poor and weak but righteous underdog) and Kennedy as Goliath (an enormously wealthy, powerful, and somewhat malicious monster). Their proposal that the first debate be held in South Boston, supposedly a McCormack stronghold, was meant to counteract the image of Kennedy as Goliath and to take advantage of the fact that McCormack was from South Boston. "Psychologically," Kennedy's manager remarked, "we purposely put him in a box. That's why the debate was held in South Boston. So that we would be somewhat cast in the role of the stranger, or the visitor, or the underdog, or call it what you will."

A McCormack aide thought the Kennedy gambit one of the most subtle of the campaign:

I think the Kennedys very wisely kept reneging and stalling on these debates until the last possible moment and, I think,

lulled the McCormack camp into the ill-considered acceptance of the South Boston location. . . . Why go to South
Boston? . . . the Kennedys, sensing the strategy here of putting McCormack in his own back yard on a state-wide television broadcast and having reinforced the image throughout
the state of McCormack as a South Boston politician, with all
of the — believe me, harmful connotations which that con-
jures up in the minds of many people in Massachusetts — I
think that the Kennedys seized on this, and that the McCormack camp didn't give it any thought at all. I think they were
just so happy to get a debate that they would have been willing to debate anywhere.

To make matters even "worse," so to speak, the debate took
place in the auditorium of South Boston High School, McCormack's alma mater. The sixty-minute debate was sponsored by
the Boston Young Democrats and televised, without cost to the
candidates. The Young Democrats were supposed to distribute an
equal number of tickets to both candidates but the crowd appeared to be decidedly pro-McCormack.

Erwin D. Canham, the editor of the *Christian Science Moni-
tor,* served as moderator. The panel of newsmen included Leo
Egan, a television newscaster, David McNeil, a radio news analyst,
C. Edward Holland, managing editor of the *Daily Record,* a
Hearst publication, and A. A. Michelson, political editor of the
Berkshire Eagle. With the exception of Michelson, the only
prominent political writer in Massachusetts who was critical of
Kennedy in print, no panelist had publicly expressed cirticism or
approval of either candidate.

The moderator called the meeting to order after some difficulty, spelled out the ground rules, introduced the candidates,
suggested that the debates were in the best American political
tradition, assured the audience that they were likely to be informed and educated, and then introduced Edward Kennedy, who
utilized his opening statement to develop the themes he had
stressed during the campaign — themes designed to convey the
impression that he was knowledgeable, sophisticated, dignified,
and in a position to do something for Massachusetts.

Mr. Canham and Mr. McCormack, members of the press, ladies and gentlemen: I first of all would like to express my appreciation to the Young Democrats for inviting both my opponent and myself here for this evening. Neither my opponent nor myself are old Democrats. And nonetheless, we appreciate this platform to be with people of our generation who are so interested in good government and the future of our party here in this state.

This evening we are in South Boston, but the problems of the office which we seek affect just as well the problems of South Viet Nam, South America, and East Berlin. Decisions made in the United States Senate in these next few years are vitally going to affect not only the future of our state of Massachusetts but the future of the world.

What kind of defense will we have? What kind of space program will we have? What kind of medical care will we provide for our senior citizens? What kind of education will we provide for the young people? Decisions made in the United States Senate will indicate whether the free world or the Communist world will prevail. And if America is to make progress, Massachusetts will make progress. If we are to beat the Russians to the moon, we must do it in part with the help and the assistance of the electronics firms on Route 128. If we are going to have the defense that we need, we will do it with the help of Raytheon's Thor missile, with the M-14 rifle. If we are going to provide the engineers and the scientists we need they will graduate from the colleges and universities of our state. We know in Massachusetts in 1962, we are undergoing a renaissance. Many of the problems that we face are going to be affected by determinations made by the national government. When my grandfather was mayor of Boston, the cities and towns made their own determinations about their future. This is not as true in 1962. For the United States Senate will make determinations whether Boston will have urban renewal that it needs; whether Pittsfield will have the air transportation that it needs; whether Fall River will have the industrial development that it needs. Certainly we know, as far as our growth and development as a state, the key office in this growth is the United States Senate. And, therefore, it is important that we nominate and elect our most vigorous spokesman; someone who will work round the clock; someone who will certainly know not only our problems as a state, but know the problems that we face as a nation; will know the countries throughout the world, those who are friendly to us and those that are opposed to us. We need certainly, as well, to have someone who can be the effective spokesman for our state. I believe that it is essential that we Democrats nominate and elect a Democrat next November, because we know that many pending problems and programs before the United States Senate are keys to our growth and our development as a state. We know that the Democratic party stands for progress on these programs. We know that the Republicans are opposed to them. And we know that many of the decisions which are made in the Senate of the United States are decided by one or two votes. We can look only in this past month and see the defeat of the Medicare Bill. This lost by two votes. I believe that it is imperative that we elect a Democrat; and I want to state here this evening that if my opponent is successful, that I will vigorously support him, because I believe that only with Democrat votes can we as a state make the kind of progress that we need.

And finally, the problem that we face as a state, the internal program and problem that we face which is most important, is that of honest government. I believe that people who have sought public office for money and power have had their day in Massachusetts. I believe that it is time to elect people who want to serve. If I am elected, I will try to conduct myself in a way that will bring credit to the state of Massachusetts and to the country. I ask you to join with me. Together we can build the future of Massachusetts.

Kennedy's opening statement was a masterful bit of public relations in terms of the image that Kennedy forces wanted to enhance. Kennedy's demeanor was dignified and extremely polite. He thanked all concerned and referred to Canham and McCormack as "Mister." (McCormack was later to refer to him as "Teddy.") He flattered the audience by noting that they are "so interested in good government and the future of our party. . . ." He reminded everyone in Brahminesque tones that they were in South Boston and said that ". . . people who have sought public

office for money and power have had their day in Massachusetts."
He focused the attention of the audience first on international affairs, as a dignified and sophisticated senator should. Then,
touching all bases, he raised global questions about defense, space,
Medicare, and education, and, lest the audience forget, reminded
them that the ultimate confrontation was between the free and the
Communist worlds — issues with which South Boston politicians
customarily do not concern themselves.

Overlooking little, he then transferred their attention from
the moon to Route 128, Raytheon's Thor missile, and several state
and local issues. These statements may have been designed to
demonstrate that Kennedy was acquainted with not only the
macrocosm of world politics but the microcosm of Pittsfield's
need for air transportation.

After reminding the audience that his grandfather was mayor
of Boston he restated the glittering generality: the Democratic
party stands for progress. Little was left to say after he attacked
Communism, defended democracy, and asked the people to join
him in building the future of Massachusetts.

While McCormack listened to Kennedy, he must have been
thinking about how strongly to attack the President's brother.
McCormack's major speech writer had written a stinging "indict-
ment" of Kennedy which McCormack was originally quite reluctant to deliver. He apparently changed his plans at the last
moment because he not only utilized most of the original critique
but also interjected invective of his own making.

Thank you very much. Thank you very much, Mr. Canham
and Mr. Kennedy, my neighbors, and my friends. I welcome
Mr. Kennedy to South Boston on the challenge of these debates, and I like to feel that I'm an old warrior on behalf of
the Democratic party. This area is where I was born. I went
to school in this very building, and I'm proud of my close ties
to this district. These are hard-working people here in South
Boston. They are deeply religious and they take their politics
seriously; and they want the issues discussed fully so that they
may choose a United States senator wisely, and I say let's discuss the issues. And the issues basically are not the issues

where Democrats disagree because we agree on the program of
this administration, but those issues that are raised by the
slogan of the two candidates. I say that I am the qualified
candidate and I point to three years in city government, three
terms with one term as president of that body. I point to
three terms as attorney general of this Commonwealth, the
second most important office in this state, and I ask my opponent "What are your qualifications?" You graduated from
Law School three years ago. You never worked for a living.
You have never run or held an elective office. You are not
running on qualifications. You are running on a slogan:
"You Can Do More for Massachusetts." . . . and I say "Do
more, how?" Because of experience? Because of maturity of
judgment? Because of qualifications? I say no! This is the
most insulting slogan I have seen in Massachusetts politics,
because this slogan means: Vote for this man because he has
influence, he has connections, he has relations. And I say no.
I say that we do not vote on influence or favoritism or connections. We vote for people who will serve. This is a slogan
that insults the President of the United States. He can do
more — that means that the President is not now doing
enough — or that the President will discriminate against
someone other than his brother if he is the senator from this
state. And again I say no. I say that the people of Massachusetts will not buy a slogan. And suddenly, my opponent wants
men who will serve, who will care. I listened to him the other
night and he said, "I want to serve because I care." Well, he
didn't care very much in 1960 when he thought of living out
West. Massachusetts is not my second choice. You didn't care
very much, Ted, when you could have voted between 1953
and 1960, on sixteen occasions, and you only voted three
times . . . three out of sixteen . . . and on those three occasions, your brother was a candidate. You don't care very
much about aid to education. While I was serving on the
City Council, trying to bring good schools here in Boston for
our public school children, not once between the period of
1953 and 1960 did you vote for our school committee. You
don't care very much about the 186,000 youngsters who attend parochial schools, because while I want to raise the edu-
cational standards of all of our children, you have said that

you will not vote to extend and expand federal aid to parochial schools.

These are important issues . . . these and issues like civil rights. Do you really care about civil rights? I have been a champion of civil rights. And while I was fighting to eliminate the black belts and the ghettos, you were attending a school that is almost totally segregated, at the University of Virginia.

I say that we don't need slogans. I say that power and money is not the key to getting elected to public office. I say we need a senator with experience, not arrogance . . . and the office of United States senator should be merited and not inherited.

The audience in the auditorium of South Boston High School broke into wild applause. The moderator, who looked bewildered, gently reprimanded them. "Ladies and gentlemen, you are not aiding the dignity of Massachusetts and the cause of this debate by these demonstrations."

McCormack began as Kennedy had begun — restrained and polite. He referred to Canham and Kennedy as "Mister," thanked those present, and flattered the audience. He then proceeded to make his first error. He reminded the audience that they were in South Boston, that he was an "old warrior" of the Democratic party, that he went to school "in this very building." And, as if that was not enough to reinforce his stereotype as a South Boston pol, he concluded on the note that he was proud of his close ties to that special area of Massachusetts, which, more than any other, symbolizes to alienated and cynical voters most of what is wrong with Massachusetts.

McCormack was realistic when he said that since he and Kennedy were both liberal Democrats the election was fundamentally issueless. It *was* issueless. Despite the efforts of academics to interject issues, the contest was one of personalities. The heart of McCormack's attack, of course, was the suggestion that the true issue was, in fact, the meaning behind the candidates' slogans.

By stating that he had started at the bottom and worked his way to the top while Kennedy had not, the Attorney General was

invoking the log-cabin-to-White-House mythology which he assumed voters continued to live by. We have previously suggested
that Horatio Alger values have far less attraction to Americans
now than they had in the past. We believe, however, that McCormack's appeal to the Alger mentality was not as disturbing to Kennedy supporters as his suggestion that Kennedy would make use of
his influence and that, if they voted for Kennedy, they would be
voting for the very thing that Boy Scouts and the 4-H Club are
supposed to condemn: influence, connections, and nepotism. They
would also be voting against what their high school civics teacher
told them they are supposed to vote for: qualifications. We doubt
that Kennedy voters would be pleased by this inference, particularly if they harbored any suspicion that what McCormack said
was true.

The one statement McCormack made that was obviously in
poor taste and clearly unfair to Kennedy was a reference to the
fact that Kennedy attended the University of Virginia Law School
— the implication being that since the University discriminated
against Negroes Kennedy tacitly followed suit.

A. A. Michelson, of the *Berkshire Eagle,* was the first panelist
to query the candidates. He asked McCormack if there were any
differences between himself and Kennedy "on issues other than
qualifications."

McCormack responded, in part:

. . . I feel that a tax cut is justified; and the role of United
States senator is not to determine whether or not it is to be
enacted but how would you vote on it. And I say that I would
vote for a tax cut right now, because I don't feel that this
country is moving as it should. I think our unemployment
figures are too high. I think our gross national product is
some thirty millions, billions of dollars below what it was
anticipated by the President's economic advisers to be if we
want it to meet our requirements. I have also differed with
this administration on matters such as wiretapping, where I
feel that if we're going to invade another's right of privacy
that all of the law enforcement officials should be required to
go to the courts and get a search warrant, in effect, and bring
wiretapping within the purview of the Fourth Amendment.

Kennedy replied:

First of all, I would like to say that I do not support a tax cut at the present time. I don't think that it is appropriate as a candidate for the United States Senate to come up here this evening to say that I believe we need help and assistance in the questions of education; that I think we need more in the training and retaining of the people whose skills have been lost; that I think we need to provide assistance to our fishing fleets, and to also advocate at this time a tax cut. We know that at the end of this year we will have a deficit of some seven to eight billions of dollars. With the recommendation of my opponent, for the tax cut, this would go up to some fifteen billions of dollars. I do not think that we could expect to see and hope to have this kind of deficit and not see inflation, and the people that are hit by inflation the hardest are the ones with limited incomes. I do, however, think and support a total revamping of the tax system, the closing of many loopholes which exist under our 1954 Act; and I think that this is essential, and I think as well, that this will, in effect lower the taxes for those that it could be lowered for, and I think as well that it will provide us with the opportunity as well to equalize some of the injustices which exist.

On the questions of wiretapping, I could just say that on the examples given by my opponent, stating that he does not feel that there should not be the invasion of privacy, we find out very well that the legislation which is before the United States Senate believes that there should not be any greater expansion but there would be a limitation on the United States Attorney General's power, and this in particular in the cases where there is indiscriminate wiretapping today. The only place which would be provided for the United States Attorney General to provide for the wiretaps would be in cases of national security. . . .

The managing editor of the *Daily Record*, C. Edward Holland, then asked the candidates if they could cite any issues on which their positions differ from that of their relatives in Washington and if they could act independently of their relatives.

Kennedy replied that ". . . the basic philosophies of my brother and myself are the same although I certainly would recognize my responsibilities as a United States senator from Massachusetts are quite distinguishable from the President of the United States, who has been elected by some fifty states." Kennedy continued:

The responsibility of the United States senator from Massachusetts would be *from* Massachusetts and *for* Massachusetts. And therefore I think that the areas of responsibility are different. You ask for illustrations that might point this out. I can understand why a President of the United States would support an expanding tariff — the abilities of the President to lower tariff barriers, that we might expand as a nation and cooperate as a single economic unit with the western European countries, and recognize our responsibilities to the developing countries of the world. But what could happen if this should affect our shoe and leather industry? I've talked to Mr. Hallstein about the problems of the expanding common market, and I have also talked with the people and the workers in Peabody and Salem, who are vitally concerned about the importation of cheap shoes; and I feel strongly that if the shoe and leather industry would be an impact-sensitive industry and an import-sensitive industry, that I would certainly champion their cause to put it on a reserve list, or at least to make sure that they got an adequate hearing before the President, who would be making a determination on this important question under the new legislation. I hope that this might illustrate an example at least, and show the different areas of responsibility. . . .

Kennedy did cite one point on which he might possibly differ with his brother — the tariff on shoes. His answer is of interest, however, because of the latent messages it contains, messages implying that he was both knowledgeable and statesmanlike. He referred to "developing countries" and the "expanding common market" — problems that serious senators are concerned with. He "dropped" his first name of the debate — Walter Hallstein of West Germany — which might be taken by viewers as a sign of Kennedy's influence since only important Americans would be in a position to meet Mr. Hallstein. He singled out two Massachusetts cities, Peabody and Salem, and noted their critical economic problem, cheap shoes. This statement demonstrates that Kennedy moved about the state, knew its people and their specific problems, and would do more for them. In other words, it enhances his image as a doer who is familiar with local problems as well as the common market. This is attractive to voters.

McCormack, in answer to the question, stated that his uncle, the Speaker, did not favor an immediate tax cut while he did. McCormack also noted that he and John McCormack differed on the issue of government ownership of satellite communications. The Attorney General, however, failed to cite many facts, names, figures, and problems, as Kennedy had cited them.

Leo Egan, referring to a statement of 175 professors in the Boston area which urged the President to reduce our nuclear stockpile, asked the third question: ". . . Do you agree with the professors, Mr. McCormack, that our stockpile of nuclear weapons is now too big?" The Attorney General responded:

> . . . One of the steps that I have suggested is to stop production of nuclear weapons. We have sufficient "overkill" now; we don't need any more overkill, and stopping of production is one of the suggestions that I have made to show good faith. I feel that we must in the talks in Geneva on the test ban take into consideration what is reported to be the developments in seismographs with the ability to detect underground testing; and we should immediately ban underwater testing and testing in the atmosphere, and if we can agree with these experts that we can detect underground testing without being on the spot, then we should suggest this. If not, then I would support the proposal that has been made that we reduce the number of sites from over a hundred to somewhere between twelve and twenty, and that it be manned by the nationals of that country and the testing be done by neutrals.

McCormack's position may well have been strategically unsound since a substantial portion of those who vote habitually in Democratic primary elections are probably Irish Catholic, militantly anti-Russian and anti-Communist. Senator McCarthy received more than modest support in several predominantly low-income Irish American areas in Boston.[1] McCormack, however, was concerned with the feelings of the pro-disarmament peace groups that were planning to support H. Stuart Hughes, the independent, in the general election. The Attorney General assumed that he needed pro-Hughes votes in the primary to defeat Kennedy. For these reasons and because of his convictions on the matter he strongly favored disarmament. Some McCormack advisers felt that his position would lose more votes than it would attract and they advised him to refrain from advertising it. His stand is an interesting example of the fact that periodically the candidate may face a moral crisis in which his true beliefs run counter to what is probably his optimal strategy.

Kennedy disagreed with McCormack and stated that he did not think that "we can afford any kind of stepping back from our strong position of military posture."

When we talk about the United States today stopping production, I think that this shows a failing of grasping a basic problem. When we realize today that we might have the possibility of "overkill" this is certainly not relevant to the problems at hand. For we know that we have a defense only so that we are going to be able to retaliate to make any attack on the United States a suicidal attempt, and therefore it is important that we have this kind of potential force, only so that we are going to be able to retaliate. This has been the posture and the policy of the United States for the last fifteen years, and I think that it is essential that we continue it. We have seen with every kind of indication, certainly at Geneva, every attempt we have made we have failed to be able to come up with any kind of good faith on the part of the Soviets. And the history of Soviet foreign policy, whether it has been in Hungary, Poland, or in Berlin this past week, is quite clear to indicate that they are not acting in good faith. We should maintain our strength.

David McNeil followed this question on disarmament with a query to Kennedy concerning his proposals for strengthening the United Nations.

[1] Lawrence Fuchs, "Presidential Politics in Boston, the Irish Response to Stevenson," *New England Quarterly,* December, 1957, p. 439.

Well, Mr. McNeil, I think that the history of the United Nations is not so amazing for what it has not done, but is greater for what it has done. I think that the accomplishments of the United Nations have been significant; and certainly I do not feel, nor would I believe that we could ever expect that certainly in the immediate future that we would be able to have a coercive force within the United Nations. We have seen certainly in a number of illustrations where the United Nations has acted with the expeditionary force that went into the Middle East, certainly, and in other examples as well, where it has been able to react and react in a way which has been meaningful and strong. I don't think and I would not be one that would say that all hope is lost for the United Nations. I think in the last few hours, as a matter of fact, in the Congo, we have seen the strong position which has been taken by U Thant, and the determination, the ultimatum that has been given to the Katanga Province, and I think that we have seen, certainly, the Congo today eliminating the threat of Communism as it pertains and exists, and as it threatened, really, the Congo a few years ago. We have seen the United Nations active in assisting also and stabilizing many of the developing countries of the world. I would just say this — that I do not feel that we can expect a compulsory, we should expect to see a compulsory force within the United Nations in the very immediate future. I think that the United Nations should be complimented really for what it has done. I think that we as a nation should do everything we possibly can to continue our support because I believe that it is in the United Nations that the great hope for peace exists.

Kennedy clearly did not answer the question. He did, however, show vague familiarity with several activities of the United Nations and he did follow what might be termed a Kennedy principle for debating on television: reference to immediate news events designed, in part, to demonstrate that the candidate was, as McCormack put it, "on top of the news." Kennedy did use the phrase "the last few hours" when referring to events in the Congo. In response to the previous question, on disarmament, Kennedy had also shown himself *au courant* — by the phrase "in Berlin this past week." Some of these references were relevant to the question asked, others were not. The point is that references to events of the previous day do convey the impression that the candidate is a newspaper reader, is well briefed, and is an alert activist.

Although McCormack in his reply stated that he warmly supported the United Nations he too failed to answer the question. He apparently sensed, however, that he might have lost votes by advocating disarmament or a test ban treaty too vigorously in his previous remarks because he now stated: ". . . As a matter of fact, I feel that we should have one hundred polaris submarines constructed so long as we have no disarmament agreement, and I feel very strongly about this. As a graduate of the Naval Academy at Annapolis, I realize the importance of maintaining a strong military posture."

The candidates failed to answer not only the question on the United Nations but almost every other question, if by an answer one means a direct and relevant response to the question. In most instances they used the questions as a convenient springboard for whatever it was they had in mind, relevant or not. Their "answers" illustrate, we believe, that this so-called debate was not really a debate, a confrontation characterized by cross-examination and relevant rebuttal. It more closely resembled a joint press conference. One of the disillusioning aspects of the event was that no panelist ever remotely suggested that either candidate failed to answer his question.

Following the questions on the United Nations Kennedy and McCormack were asked to state their views on tax revision. McCormack again argued for "an immediate tax cut" and "reform next year." With respect to reform he mentioned only "the plugging of various tax loopholes that the President and many members of Congress feel so strongly about." Kennedy was again more specific than McCormack and better briefed. He proposed a reduction in the amounts deductible for expense accounts and a revision of the laws relating to Americans who "are able to take advantage of foreign tax laws relating to their share of American tax." He also proposed a reduction of the oil depletion allowance from 27.5 per cent to 13.5 per cent, which would still provide depletion allowances for small companies that did limited business from a million dollars to possibly five million dollars, "but I don't think that it is appropriate that we provide 27.5 per cent depletion allowances for large oil companies."

Kennedy's campaign slogan, "He Can Do More for Massachusetts," was used, with "He speaks with a voice that will be heard." A. A. Michelson asked Kennedy what he meant when he said that he spoke "in a voice that will be heard." Like several other answers that Kennedy and McCormack offered to various questions, Michelson's question received a response of a vague sort but it certainly was not an answer.

Well, I think, Mr. Michelson, the whole question goes down to the matter of basic qualifications with which we come to this race. I believe that I have an understanding of the problems that we face here in Massachusetts. I was the campaign manager for my brother in 1958. I traveled throughout this state. I've talked with the fishermen about the problems in Gloucester. I've talked to the shoe and leather people who have worked in the factories in Lynn and Lowell. I believe that I have an understanding of the problems here in this state. I believe as well that a United States senator is going to vote on matters not only of particular and peculiar importance to Massachusetts, but also to the problems that we face as a nation. I spent three months in Wisconsin and have talked to the dairy farmers. You pay twenty-seven cents for a quart of milk and the dairy farmer receives five cents; and yet his income has been declining in recent years. We as senators from Massachusetts are going to be voting on this matter. I spent three months in West Virginia, and talked to the coal miners of West Virginia, and have seen what happens when automation happens in these coal fields, and I have spent some time and continuing study in the other parts of the countries throughout the world. We as United States senators are going to be voting on important matters — how our taxpayers' dollars are going to be spent . . . are we going to support the Upper Volta project in Ghana . . . are we going to certainly support the regimes of Mr. Sekou Touré in Guinea. United States and Massachusetts taxpayers' dollars are going to be spent in these matters, and I think that we can

be a more effective voice for Massachusetts, when we have an
understanding of the problems which we face here in this
state, when we have an understanding of the problems that we
face in the nation, also the problems that we face throughout
the world.

Although the question was addressed to Kennedy, McCormack utilized his three minutes to refer to his experience as a state
official and to attack Kennedy.

Well, first I think the only way you can understand the problems of this state is to have dealt with them, and I have dealt
with them at both the city and the state level. You can't talk
about problems, such as Mr. Michelson mentioned, of pro-
tecting the consumer, without bearing in mind that I established the first Consumers' Council of the nation, right here
in Massachusetts. But the thing that fascinates me is Teddy's
constant reference to his trips, and the fact that he grew up in
an atmosphere where they dealt at the international level. He
did make some trips around the world. He made two European trips and he visited eleven countries in twenty-four days.
In Latin America he visited nine countries in twenty-seven
days. In Africa, he spent fifteen days visiting nine African
countries. Well, certainly spending one or two days might
not make you or I experts, but he picks things up more
quickly than perhaps I would. What has developed from his
trips? In Israel he almost caused — he caused an international incident by straggling across the border. In East Germany he caused embarrassment by giving recognition to the
East German government. In London, he caused a taxi
strike. In Panama, the ambassador said to one of the reporters, or reportedly to him, "It will take me five months to undo
what you have done in two days." And the Irish, typical of
the Irish. . . .

At this point the moderator notified McCormack that his time
was up. David McNeil then asked McCormack if he agreed with
the AFL-CIO proposal of a thirty-five-hour week to help end unemployment.

"I think," McCormack replied, "that the thirty-five-hour work
week should certainly be considered only as a last resort." Taking

a leaf from the Kennedy debate notebook, McCormack then mentioned two great national issues — "unemployment" and "exploding population" — referred to the competition likely to come from the European Common Market, and cited three statistics. He then returned to the attack:

> Let me just finish with the trip to Ireland, because the Irish, I think, characteristically visualize the trip or saw the trip of Teddy for just what it was. This is a quote in the *Sunday Independent* of Dublin, 25th of February, 1962: "Arriving in Ireland today is Mr. Edward 'Ted' Kennedy, age thirty, a younger brother of President John Fitzgerald Kennedy. Why is he coming to Ireland? He's coming because later this year he is due to be involved in a political fight back home in Massachusetts. He is playing the game political in what has now come to be known as the Kennedy method. You do not spend your time in campaigning in your own little patch, . . . you go out into the world far far afield, hit the headlines, hit the American voters in the right way. I think the trips are more political than fact-finding.

Unlike Kennedy, who always referred to McCormack as "Mister," the Attorney General called Kennedy "Teddy." This was probably a mistake because Kennedy supporters, most of whom held their man in highest esteem, if not awe, might well find McCormack's reference to "Teddy" impolite and offensive.

Kennedy, as agreed-upon, ignored McCormack's attack and stated that he did not favor a thirty-five-hour work week. He noted that "the real question is the conflict now with the Soviet system [pause], the economies of the two parts of the world [pause], the free world versus the Communist world." He then noted that the steel industry was producing "between 60 and 70 per cent" of capacity and stressed the importance of a job-retraining program in Massachusetts to relieve unemployment. Thus he increased the number of references to global issues, stated in the form of clichés, and be managed to introduce another statistic, which, by the way, could be utilized to support the position taken by the AFL-CIO.

Leo Egan directed the penultimate question to Kennedy. "Do you believe the United States should send foreign aid to countries behind the Iron Curtain, like Poland and Yugoslavia?" Kennedy responded in the affirmative, referred to several events that had recently occurred, and cited statistics relating to the number of farms in Poland that were independently owned. He then demonstrated that he was familiar with the news of the day.

Well, I would say, first of all, that I would support in the United States efforts, help and assistance — economic help and assistance — to Yugoslavia and Poland. We have seen dramatic examples of both of these countries of some independence from the Soviet system. For example, in Yugoslavia, we have seen actions brought before the United Nations, in which they objected to Soviet interference in their internal affairs. We see today that Yugoslavia is in a defense pact with Greece, which is a NATO ally. We see that Yugoslavia has tried to eliminate at least the threat of the Soviet penetration in the Middle East. In Poland, as well, we have seen that Poland does not jam American radio stations. It also permits the exchange of magazines and literature. Eighty per cent of the Polish farms are independently owned. And, therefore, and I think we've seen some intellectual independence and freedom within the concept of the Polish mind; and I think we have seen and as shown in this morning's papers, where the Cardinal Wyzanski's declaration that the faith is still very much alive in Poland today, that there is a great heritage for freedom, a great tradition and alliance certainly really as far as their culture goes, with the Western heritage, and I believe that if we are going to expect as a nation, if we are going to expect as well that these countries to exert a type of independence from the Soviet system that we should very well provide economic assistance in the form of food surplus to these nations and I definitely would support it.

It is obvious that Kennedy was well briefed for the debate and that he and his brain trust had spent much time gathering, sorting, and analyzing pieces of information. McCormack, like Kennedy, favored aid to Poland and Yugoslavia. He also demonstrated some familiarity with the contemporary Polish politics when he cited the fact, obscure though it may be, that the Polish government planned to nationalize nursery schools and kinder-

gartens. He too supported religion, attacked Communism, and
mentioned, as Kennedy had, the Primate of Poland.

I don't say, Mr. Egan, just what I will do. I tell you what I
have done already. I took the position when the aid to Poland
and Yugoslavia was eliminated from the foreign aid program, I strongly took the position that it should be restored.
I feel that it's imperative that we not just go on the basis of
whether we like or dislike a form of government, or whether
we are trying to help humanity, without losing sight of the
fact that they are Communist nations, and I also took a very
strong position that we should try to use our moral influence
to bring about a stop to the efforts to curb the religious activities in Poland. The government has indicated that it is going
to take over the nursery schools and the kindergartens in
Poland. About two weeks ago I came out with a very strong
statement and I said that we should deplore this here in the
United States. And we should say to this government that we
do not approve of your trying to wipe out religion, because
the religious is the only organization that is combating the
Communistic system of government, and just today this position that I took was reaffirmed by the Cardinal in Poland.

McCormack and his aides were concerned that the subject of
corruption in Massachusetts and McCormack's role as chief law
enforcement officer would be raised. The subject did not come up
until the last few minutes of the debate, when A. A. Michelson
asked, "Mr. McCormack, you've been accused of foot dragging as
a chief law enforcement officer of Massachusetts. Would you like
to comment on that?" McCormack attempted first to explain the
division of responsibility among the various law enforcement
agencies — local and state police, state auditor, district attorneys,
and the attorney general. He then cited the fact that there were
"more prosecutions in my administration than the last three attorney generals combined," and concluded with "I prosecute without fear, without favor, and I don't ask who was involved, what
their party affiliation is or what their social stature might be."
    Kennedy replied succinctly, "I think the Attorney General
should speak for himself about fulfilling the responsibilities of

investigating crime and wrongdoing here in this state during the last four years." Mild applause filled the auditorium.

It was now time for Kennedy's two-minute closing statement:

"Mr. Canham, the hour is close to nine o'clock here, in South Boston. It's close to three o'clock in Berlin, and only in a few minutes the convoys will start on their way down the Autobahn. I wonder tonight whether this convoy will be stopped like it was last night."

After thus noting that he was familiar with an event that occurred in Germany within the past twenty-four hours — that he was very much up to date, as the public probably imagines a senator should be — he utilized the event to draw a classic non sequitur: "I think that this demonstrates quite clearly the problems that we face here in this state and throughout the nation."

Drawing upon one of John Kennedy's campaign slogans the President's brother continued, "The great problems of this election are the questions of peace and whether Massachusetts will move forward or not."

Apparently unable to refrain any longer from retorting to McCormack's jibes at him, Kennedy suggested that what McCormack regarded as the central issue of the election should be ignored by the voters: "We should not have any talk about personalities or families. I feel that we should be talking about the people's destiny in Massachusetts." And encouraged by the substantial applause that greeted his remark, he concluded on a high note by interjecting the name and thought of Oliver Wendell Holmes:

In 1860, Oliver Wendell Holmes said no city had played a greater part in free speech and free press than the city of Boston. I just hope that this program here this evening has provided in this great tradition a fine opportunity for the hundreds and thousands of viewers to help make their determination on whom they feel would be the best senator from Massachusetts. Thank you and good night.

During the last few seconds of his closing remarks, Kennedy's voice cracked. Some of those present in the auditorium of South

Boston High School reported that his eyes became misty and that a few tears fell down his cheeks. The camera did not show a close-up at this moment so it was difficult to determine whether Kennedy actually wept. Many viewers, however, thought so. It was obvious, nevertheless, that Kennedy was in a state of some shock. His condition was bound to affect the audience, and the effect it had was to be a subject of much speculation.

The television camera then turned to Erwin Canham, the moderator, who said, "Now the time has come for Mr. McCormack's final statement." There had been a tremendous burst of applause at the close of Kennedy's remarks; McCormack was forced to decide immediately whether to continue the attack or take the Kennedy approach, which most reporters were to describe as "the high road."

I appreciate the opportunity afforded me to speak to so many people, not only here in this hall, but over the television and radio networks, to ask the people of Massachusetts whether they are going to judge this contest on personalities or on accomplishments, on qualifications of the candidates or on a slogan. Now it's all right for my opponent to say that we keep families out of this and we stand on our own two feet. I favor this. I stand on my own two feet. I stand on a record, a record of almost a decade in elective office. I've worked my way *up* the political ladder. I'm not starting at the top.

At this point in his closing statement McCormack apparently decided to deliver what he obviously thought would be the final crushing blow. He paused. His voice, at first quiet and restrained, became shrill and tinged with anger.

I ask, since the question of names and families has been injected, If his name was Edward Moore, with his qualifications, with your qualifications, Teddy, if it was Edward Moore, your candidacy would be a joke, but nobody's laughing because his name is not Edward Moore. It's Edward Moore Kennedy, and I say it makes no difference what your name is, in a democracy you stand on your own two feet and you say to the people. You have the right to vote. You go behind that curtain, and you vote without fear, without favor, and you vote for the candidate whom you feel is the qualified candidate, and I place my case in your hands.

While McCormack was making his final remarks, Kennedy appeared stunned, rigid and ashen. Apparently he could not believe that McCormack would publicly make such a remark about the brother of the President of the United States. McCormack, of course, was attempting to shock the audience and provoke Kennedy into making an angry outburst that would cost him the election. Although he did not explode, even before McCormack made the Edward Moore comment Kennedy was visibly shaken.

A moment of silence followed McCormack's final words and then his supporters broke into wild applause.

In a post-election interview, McCormack reminisced about his closing remarks in the debate:

> . . . the only time that I was tempted to slow down on the attack was at the very end when Ted's voice cracked — as I understand it, because of the emotion that he was holding within himself, and the audience interrupted a statement he made with applause, to indicate that they felt perhaps I'd been wrong. My position was that — at that time, it's amazing how many thoughts flash through your mind in a split second — that I had gone this far, and I had two minutes left. Was I going to continue the attack? And I felt that I had committed myself to an approach, that is perhaps not the approach of an Eddie McCormack, because in all my political campaigns I've always ignored my opponents, . . . And I said, well, I've gone this far; I'm going to go all the way. That was the only time I felt that perhaps I was too strong.
>
> In the minds of the people you cannot in effect outshine the Kennedys. I had to disassociate Ted Kennedy from Jack and Bob and Jacqueline and the rest of the Kennedy family. I had to try to impress upon the people of this state that the office of United States senator is a terribly important office, and that it should go to one who has had the experience to deal with the problems that will be dealt with at that level. I had for months been saying the exact same thing that I said in the first debate, and nobody seemed to understand what I was

saying. So I felt that shock therapy was in order, that we must shock the people into understanding.

Mr. Canham waited until the audience was quiet and then closed the debate with a masterpiece of understatement:

Ladies and gentlemen. You've heard a very remarkable debate, I don't have to tell you. I don't have to add in my statement of the ground rules that none of the questions which were addressed to the candidates had been made known to either of the candidates or to any of their friends beforehand. They were drawn together at the last moment.

Mr. Canham then made a remark which described McCormack's presentation more accurately than Kennedy's: "This has been an entirely impromptu, unrehearsed, and straightforward affair." Utilizing both cliché and wishful thinking he terminated the proceedings: "We've had an excellent illustration perhaps of democracy in action. The meeting is adjourned."

McCormack's closing remarks stunned many of those present. Kennedy supporters probably could not tolerate the idea that if Edward Kennedy's name were Edward Moore and Edward Moore had no more qualifications than Edward Kennedy he would either not be a serious candidate for the United States Senate or his candidacy would be, in fact, a ludicrous joke. McCormack may have evoked their anger by coming too close to a truth that Kennedy supporters sensed but repressed because it was too painful. This, of course, is only our speculation. In a sense, McCormack spoke the unspeakable, or, as one of his aides said, "Eddie gave all the apples away."

Edward Kennedy's advisers demonstrated a remarkable capacity for organizing manpower, utilizing time to its fullest, and spending money where it counted. Their judgment and intuition were generally excellent. The decision to foster the image of a non-political innocent who, at the same time, appeared to be knowledgeable and dignified was obviously correct. So was the decision to shake as many hands as possible and ignore McCormack. The first debate, however, was *the* dramatic and critical event of the campaign. Nevertheless most Kennedy aides, and ap-

parently the candidate himself, profoundly misjudged the outcome during the hours immediately afterwards. They and Mc-
Cormack's men thought that the debate was a disaster for Kennedy.

Although one Kennedy aide who was present at headquarters
right after the debate described the reaction as "a mixed attitude," and another described it as one of "cautious optimism," a
third remarked that "there were many people who felt that Mr. Mc-
Cormack's attack was just so earthy and so shattering that our
candidate might not be able to bounce back." The Attorney General himself reported that "the Kennedy forces felt that he had
lost terribly." Asked how he knew this, McCormack replied:

> From statements that were made to my people by his people.
> From reactions of Kennedy supporters in conversation with
> supporters. . . . Some of the Kennedy lieutenants felt that
> their candidate had been slaughtered. Our people felt that we
> had in effect been very successful in getting our point across
> and that this was the turning point of the campaign, so to
> speak.

McCormack's colleagues were convinced, at that point, that
the Attorney General had not only not been too strong but that
he had brilliantly and effectively argued his case. They were sure
he had scored a magnificent triumph and possibly even eliminated
Kennedy as a serious contender. One aide described the feeling
at headquarters that evening as "very enthusiastic," although, she
noted in retrospect, "I don't think that it was a considered assessment. I think they had a good reaction to this debate."

> This is the kind of a debate — or the attack that McCormack
> made was something that should warm the cockles of any poli-
> tician's heart. I don't think it would make anybody else —
> well, it obviously didn't make anybody else happy. But to a
> politician there could be nothing any more beautiful than to
> see this kid shown up for what he was. And McCormack did a
> good job of it, he — to us he was a gentleman. Apparently
> this isn't the way he carried through to the great unwashed
> masses, but it certainly was the way he carried through to
> people who were politically involved. Now they started sing-

ing a different tune, very very quickly, and there are people who claim that from the moment he opened his mouth, they knew that he had done the wrong thing. I don't think this was so. I think they were very happy.

A member of the advertising agency employed by McCormack confirmed her judgment. His reaction indicates that account executives do not always fit the stereotype of the all-knowing, ingenious, and subtle hidden persuader:

> I would say that in the large majority, everyone felt that Ed had done a terrific job and that it was a decided step forward in the campaign and perhaps even a turning point in the campaign. People felt that now we had Ted on the run and up until now we were nipping at his heels, that now it was he that had to catch up to us. . . .

Next morning the reactions of both Kennedy and McCormack aides began to change. In our opinion, the most accurate description of the reaction of the electorate was provided by a state representative — a friend of Kennedy who also served as a local campaign co-ordinator:

> Of course my wife thought that McCormack had murdered him. . . . And I got much the same reaction . . . that McCormack had won the debate and had made Kennedy look bad. However . . . two people that I had run into on the way home that night had seen the debate, and they were Kennedy people, but they were furious — this was the first indication that McCormack may have made a mistake. . . . The next day . . . when I got the telephone to campaign on my own behalf, when I made fifty or sixty phone calls asking them to vote for me, not discussing the Kennedy-McCormack thing, it was almost impossible to talk to them without them saying, "What did you think of the debate?" And the first few people, I told them, I says "Well as you know I'm very pro-Kennedy and I think that — you know, perhaps McCormack did win the debate," and then they started to lacerate McCormack. . . . [They said] He was a South Boston politician, a couple of them made reference to the fact that he brought religion — the South Boston people are religious people — they thought

that McCormack made a terrible mistake. I didn't realize this, Murray. I didn't realize this until I talked to a few more people.

After Kennedy's men in Boston checked with their colleagues in the field, read the newspapers, and analyzed the telegrams and letters sent to headquarters, they concluded that Kennedy had scored a tremendous victory. During the late afternoon of the second day following the debate Kennedy's campaign manager summarized their feelings and their findings.

I think that, in terms of the impact, that Teddy came off and conducted himself as people would feel that a United States senator should, with a certain amount of restraint, certain amount of decorum. He displayed an awareness of the issues. He didn't get embroiled or involved in personalities. . . . it's my very subjective feeling, McCormack got on just like a ward politician speaking out of the side of his mouth and just didn't seem to grow in stature in any respect. I think McCormack was hurt, and hurt very seriously. No matter where you go today, you hear the same thing. This has been our best day, in terms of new people coming in to work, bumper stickers going on. . . . as of noontime we had something like fifty-eight telegrams of congratulations. And I think that it solidified our vote, and I think it's helped us with some women who were undecided. I think it's the first beginning of a breaking-up among this liberal, egghead segment in the community. There's many of them. . . . Out towards Brookline way, many of these people are polite, courteous, wellmannered, and they have been out, some of them have been out working hard for McCormack. Now it's almost like trying to sell a soiled piece of merchandise. . . .

We've checked the headquarters. And the reaction in all the headquarters has been marvelous . . . just intellectually, there are certain points that Teddy did make. I think McCormack got hung up and hung up very badly on this. On the defense status and position. About the stockpiling. . . . And I think that Teddy's restraint was — well, I don't think that I could've been able to do it. Not only his emotional restraint, but the manner in which he handled that question on crime and corruption. You can go out into the street and ask Mickey Mouse, and he'll tell you that crime and corruption is rampant.

Smiling, he concluded the interview with the following remark:

Somebody said today that McCormack was able to make a millionaire an underdog. Number one. But if you take this in a somewhat allegorical manner, he's trying to play the role of David against the Goliath, and I think the American ethic is, they're always for David because he's lovable, or he's likable, or . . . but he just didn't come off on that at all. Rather than coming off as the nice young guy, standing alone against the world, he came off as just a little brat who was throwing rocks and throwing stones, and a lot of people just felt that he threw too many stones and too many rocks.

McCormack and his men were also reading newspapers and talking to people, and coming to the conclusion that McCormack had perhaps not emerged from the debate as victorious as they first thought. Not satisfied with the traditional techniques of local politicians to sample public opinion, they conducted what they euphemistically called a public opinion poll; 150 names in the telephone book were selected at random and telephoned. On the basis of the "poll" they concluded that McCormack won the support of many male voters because he demonstrated his manliness and that he lost the support of many females, who, they felt, favored Kennedy anyway. Given their capacity to rationalize and project, it is not surprising that they really believed voters would rally to the McCormack cause when they finally realized that Kennedy failed to answer McCormack's questions. One aide, who wrote part of McCormack's opening statement, analyzed the impact of the debate six days after it took place.

In my considered opinion, I think the debate did a number of things. In the first place I think it rallied and revivified the whole McCormack organization. . . . In terms of actual votes, I think this is awfully difficult to evaluate. I have always felt that to some extent Eddie McCormack did not have the great appeal, the great personal magnetic appeal that Ted

Kennedy had for women voters. . . . I take this as one of the factors which existed before the debate.

Now, what did the debate do in terms of winning votes? . . . McCormack lost the women vote, the vote of many women, as a result of appearing to be discourteous, impolite, rude. . . . Query: Was there any real net loss to Eddie Mc-Cormack? I don't know. I'm inclined to think there may have been some loss, but I don't think this is as significant a factor as many people would try to make it appear to be, be-cause . . . in my opinion Eddie McCormack really didn't have a substantial or solid block of women supporting him prior to the debate. Now it very well may be true that what he did was to so incense many of the women who were in-clined to vote for Kennedy anyway that he may have bestirred them to greater efforts on behalf of Kennedy and may have incited them to go to the polls. This remains to be seen. . . . I think when all is said and done about the debates and when people sit back and reflect upon them somewhat less emo-tionally perhaps than they did in their initial reactions to it, I think that many people, and particularly the men, are go-ing to be concerned about the fact that there were issues here which were raised by McCormack which were not answered by Kennedy.

*   *   *

It is impossible to determine whether the sympathetic reac-tion of the public to Kennedy was spontaneous or created in part by the press — particularly the *Boston Herald,* which favored Ken-nedy in its news stories. It is not unreasonable to assume, how-ever, that if the majority of the newspapers reported the debate so as to favor one candidate and disparage the other — even by im-plication — the response of the public could be reinforced or pos-sibly altered.

The *Berkshire Eagle* was the only major newspaper in Mas-sachusetts that favored McCormack in its dispatches on the de-bate, although a handful of correspondents on other newspapers did write that the debates were not, in any real sense, debates, clearly suggesting that McCormack raised legitimate and impor-tant questions that Kennedy failed to answer. A few newspapers like the *Christian Science Monitor* described and analyzed the debate without interpretive editorial comment. The headline of the *Christian Science Monitor* was: "Debate Tests Strategies: Viewers Divided." This comment, of course, would be true of any debate.

The interpretation placed on the debate by the *Boston Herald* was fairly typical of the newspapers in Massachusetts that favored Kennedy and chastised McCormack. The *Herald*'s headline read: "Ed Debates Personalities, Ted Debates the Issues." This headline is favorable to Kennedy since it suggests that McCormack did not discuss "the issues" — i.e., disarmament, tax cut, wire tapping, federal aid to education — which is, of course, not true. Although McCormack did attack Kennedy as a person, the *Herald,* by insisting that Kennedy debated "the issues," assumed that Kennedy's inexperience, the implication of the Kennedy slogans, and the fact that Kennedy failed to vote in several elections were not issues. McCormack voters believed they were the relevant issues since Kennedy and McCormack are both liberal Democrats with very few ideological differences of the usual sort. The headline is consequently favorable to Kennedy and unfavorable to McCormack because the public probably believes that debaters are supposed to discuss something called "the issues." If our hypothesis is valid, then McCormack failed to behave in the expected manner while Kennedy behaved as debaters are supposed to behave.

The political editor of the *Boston Herald* wrote in reference to McCormack:

> His assault on Kennedy, and the latter's refusal to be drawn into an Army base brawl, apparently created unfavorable reaction to the Attorney General among many viewers, especially women. . . . Kennedy took the high road, and, although he was battered and mauled by McCormack, probably won a strategic victory with the huge TV audience. . . . Kennedy made his usual good appearance and ticked off a wide assortment of facts and figures which tended to counter McCormack's argument that he was inexperienced.[2]

2 David Farrell, *Boston Herald,* August 29, 1962.

According to this interpretation McCormack is the type who engages in Army base brawls, who batters and mauls, while Kennedy takes the high road, makes a usually good appearance, and is experienced because he can tick off a wide assortment of facts and figures. The Kennedy strategy was working. The relevance of the facts cited to the question asked or to the logic of the answer given is not the critical factor.

Although A. A. Michelson, of the *Berkshire Eagle,* had raised the corruption issue during the debate, most of his columns during the campaign were critical of Kennedy. Despite his partisanship, we believe that his description and commentary are correct. The column he wrote after the debate was entitled "Teddy and Eddie Wage a Battle of Personalities Despite Pious Guff About Discussing the 'Issues.' "

Personalities apparently is a dirty word in politics and in this violent Kennedy-McCormack fight for the Democratic nomination for the U.S. Senate, it has become a real shibboleth or epithet.

The reaction to the so-called debate Monday night between the President's youngest brother and the House speaker's nephew, at least according to the Boston newspapers, was that Ted Kennedy "shunned" personalities, preferring to stick to the "issues," while Attorney General McCormack drew a saber and ran through his opponent with a personal attack.

But the point is that the Teddy-Eddie fight is nothing more than a battle of "personalities." Both are where they are because of their names. As to international and national issues, whatever their differences of the moment, they will undoubtedly vote down the line with the Kennedy administration. The question, then, is who has the qualifications and who deserves the biggest job that Massachusetts can confer upon one of its citizens? . . .

The idea that Ted Kennedy should now insist that the debates between him and McCormack be fought on the lofty plane of national and international issues is ridiculous. Does anyone seriously think that Teddy administered the clobbering job on McCormack at the Democratic State Convention in

Springfield last June on the basis of his thoughts about nuclear stockpiling? Or the present problem in Brazil? Or the
United Nations? Or the dam on the Upper Volta?

Teddy's appeal is based almost wholly on two slogans. He
has been saying that he will speak with a voice that will be
"heard" and that he "can" do more for Massachusetts. . . .
And it is at those two slogans that McCormack directed his attack because the slogans more than anything else, are what
stirred up the imagination of the politicians at the convention. A voice that will be "heard" has no other meaning,
regardless of the presidential interpretation at a press conference Wednesday. It can only mean that as Ted Kennedy,
brother of the President, he will have more influence.

Because we believe that personalities are the issue in this
campaign we asked, as a member of the panel in the Monday
night debate, what Ted meant, in as much as his brother, the
President of the United States, was being clobbered in Congress on such popular issues as Medicare, a Cabinet status for
urban affairs, and agriculture reform designed to save money
for consumers and taxpayers, by saying he would speak with a
voice that would be heard. The answer was that he had talked
to fishermen in Gloucester, shoe and leather people in Lowell,
dairy farmers in Wisconsin, coal miners in West Virginia.
The inference was that because of these talks he understands
the problems and he can be more "effective." In the end the
question wasn't answered at all.[3]

*   *   *

While newspapers may reinforce the judgments of those
who watched or heard the debates, the primary impact on the
viewers probably centers on how the candidate gestures, moves,
smiles, smirks, or frowns, not on what he says. If this is so, televised debates may be "won" or "lost" not in terms of the debat-
er's acumen and knowledge in handling the subjects discussed
but in terms of his television personality.

In his commentary on voter reaction to the Kennedy-Nixon
debates, for example, Samuel Lubell suggested that debates on
television will not only "strengthen the trend toward actor-presi-

[3] A. A. Michelson, *Berkshire Eagle*, August 31, 1962.

dents" but also "tend to lessen somewhat the importance of issues and party and to elevate the significance of personality, particularly on its theatrical side." [4] Lubell, who asked voters, "Did you listen to any of the TV debates?" and "What do you think of them?" reports that "The overwhelming majority responded in terms of how the candidates looked and handled themselves rather than in terms of the issues that were argued about." [5] Kennedy and McCormack aides, after recovering from the initial shock of McCormack's opening and closing statements, agreed that the public reacted primarily to the candidates' theatrical performance, personality, and physical characteristics.

Most of the aides we interviewed were convinced that McCormack offended voters because of the "viciousness" of his attack, the size of his head, his accent, his smirk, and his mouth. They believed that Kennedy pleased voters because of his accent, profile, jaw, shoulders, and "restraint" and "politeness." One McCormack aide who stressed the importance of candidates' physical characteristics suggested that the reaction of the public might have been quite different if the debates had been held only on radio. Although his comments are considerably more sophisticated and insightful than those of his colleagues, they are nevertheless representative.

Television has a much greater impact, simply because you're seeing everything. The obvious is just as obvious and as plain as can be on radio. Radio has impact; but it doesn't have that sort of impact. You're listening to the candidates argue and debate — I'm sure that the people who were listening to this first debate on radio didn't feel quite as sorry for Teddy Kennedy as a great many people felt for him. They could only hear the voice, they couldn't see his magnificent jaw, they couldn't see his forthright Kennedyisms. . . .

The impact upon viewers by television is that you're watching something else; you're watching, your eyes are more sensitive than your ears, you're not listening to what they say,

[4] Samuel Lubell, "Personalities vs. Issues," in *The Great Debates*, edited by Sidney Kraus (Bloomington: The Indiana University Press, 1962), p. 152.

[5] *Ibid.*

you're listening to *how* they say, what they look like, the gestures that are being made, and whatever they say goes for naught in terms of anything that might be important issuewise. Most people I don't think remembered after the TV broadcast what the allegations were against Kennedy; all they knew, that they didn't like the way in which it was done. . . . McCormack has a small mouth, he doesn't open it very wide, while Mr. Kennedy has a big jaw, certainly the Kennedy prototype — it's just my feeling that TV takes away from the actual important issues; radio, you'll be listening to what they *say*. . . . It wasn't Eddie McCormack's voice that anybody disliked; it was his mouth, the so-called sneer. I don't believe it is a sneer. They could not because they didn't see it. On television the impact clearly is one of vision. Mr. McCormack has big shoulders, has a small head, while Ted Kennedy is a little better proportioned in those terms. Eddie McCormack always looks tall with a little head, and I don't think people like tall people with little heads.

Mary McGrory, in her column syndicated in the *Boston Globe,* wrote, "Eddie submitted utterly [to the makeup man] and came on stage as though made up for an early Lon Chaney movie. . . . Whenever he looked off in the middle distance while Teddy was speaking, he suggested the juvenile lead in a silent film scanning the horizon for a sight of Clara Bow."

One McCormack adviser, who thought that "all the Kennedys are very good actors," reported:

It seemed to me reminiscent somewhat of the Nixon Checkers speech; in fact that was my first reaction after watching the first debate that Mr. Kennedy might have been told during the debate to get angry but never to lose his temper, to become somewhat emotional. I think all the Kennedys are very good actors; he certainly evoked sympathy from a great many women. It's somewhat like the two wrestlers. There's a good guy and a bad guy. McCormack assumed the bad guy role, Ted Kennedy evoked sympathy — he is a nice-looking man, there's no doubt about that . . . the crack in his voice, the quiet demeanor of the candidate, certainly evoked a great deal of sympathy for Teddy as a boy. Most mothers I'm sure must have wanted to cuddle him. As in the Nixon Checkers business, Nixon with his oversincere sincerity appealed to the voters on the basis of his honesty, his integrity. Teddy to me looked like a little boy lost at the time, and every mother loves a little boy who's lost and wanted to cuddle him. And to me, I felt the same way, I'm pretty softhearted and an emotional guy, I almost wanted to pick him out and take him home. . . .

One of the few Kennedy advisers who originally favored the debates suggested that McCormack might possibly "trap" Kennedy but

> . . . I think Kennedy looks extremely well on television. If I was Kennedy, I would welcome these debates, and I would debate in every town and city in Massachusetts. . . . What has Kennedy got going for him? That he looks like his brother. That he looks like a Kennedy. That he talks like a Kennedy. That he's got vigor, that he's an excellent and articulate person, and he makes a very strong presentation. And Eddie McCormack, although very capable, has got kind of a bad smile, unfortunately, and a little bit of a lisp — which I got now myself suddenly — and doesn't come through quite as well on television as he does in person.

Most campaign advisers were also convinced that what the candidates said was considerably less important to the public than how they said it. In assessing the public's reaction they dismissed "issues" — with the exception of disarmament — as totally irrelevant. Kennedy aides and several of the Attorney General's people thought that McCormack looked like an old-school Irish ward politician while Kennedy looked like a United States senator. The public, in their opinion, was interested in images, not disputation. A Kennedy campaign co-ordinator expressed the view of almost every respondent when he suggested that McCormack might have been more successful "'if he had used a knife instead of an ax."

> Well, my feelings were that McCormack had made a serious mistake. The issues he brought forth — as defined by him, as issues or qualifications — were perhaps true or not true, de-

pending on how you look at the situation; perhaps more true
than not, but the way he presented them was, in this day and
age in Massachusetts, in this atmosphere of state-wide television, a serious blunder. . . . What he said was true; if he
had used a knife instead of an ax he might have been much
more successful, but he lost all chance of his having the underdog position in the contest by openly attacking — a vicious,
open attack upon Mr. Kennedy — and I think this backfired
quite obviously and was a serious mistake. . . . Mr. Kennedy at all times held his temper; refused to reply, in many
cases because he had no answer to the charges, that Mr. Mc-
Cormack had the figures that he didn't vote in such and such
a year, he couldn't turn around and say "I did," but he just
ignored these charges, but at the same time conducted himself as a gentleman. The general watching audience, especially the women, felt that any type of attack, a personal attack such as this, upon a Kennedy, and in this instance
a young, attractive, articulate, good-looking Kennedy, was
something that was a throwback to the dark ages of Massachusetts politics.

A veteran public relations man who has played a leading
role in several of the more vituperative campaigns of modern
Massachusetts politics suggested that:

When McCormack had his great opportunity to point out
what he considered some inherent weaknesses in Kennedy, he
blew this opportunity by not properly conditioning the public to receive the message that he was putting across so that it
came as such a surprise that apparently, the reaction was unfavorable. He could have said what he said about Kennedy
with greater force if he had pre-conditioned the people, and
I'll illustrate this. For example, when you go to a circus and
you see a clown coming along with an ax and he swings the ax
and presumably cuts off his hand, you have been conditioned
to the fact that this is a funny event, whereas if a man in front
of you in the circus . . . took out an ax and chopped his
hand off, or you thought he was chopping his hand off, it
would be a great shock. So this is the process of conditioning,
and without conditioning, no keynote can ever be put across
successfully. . . . I think that he could have very effectively

put his idea across if he had laid the groundwork prior to the speech. I think that this was the great mistake of the McCormack campaign. . . . He should have, very early in the campaign, established the fact that he was going to talk plainly and bluntly . . . this does not mean crudely, but in a forthright manner. If McCormack had started his campaign, for example, with an ad with a strong keynote, "It's time for a plain talk," then he would have been established as a man who was going to talk in a plain forthright manner and people who listened to him would have accepted and would have expected what he was going to say. The point is that he did not condition people. He posed himself as a gentleman and then stepped over into an area that many people considered rude but if he conditioned the public by his previous establishment of the fact that he was going to talk plain, then they would have considered what he had to say as truth and logic and they would have accepted what he said. For example, McCormack could very well have pointed out the gravity of the situation in the present day, the need for truly great men in the Senate, pointing out certainly with great care, that the office of United States senator is higher than governor and that the difference between us being at war or peace, having prosperity or hard times might depend on the single vote that went into the United States Senate. This would be a situation that called for plain talk and would give him an opportunity to point out any basic weakness that he might feel this candidate possessed and dramatize that carefully over a period of time. If people were conditioned, they would not be shocked.

This man is really talking about political style — the right and wrong way of saying things, the right and wrong image to project, the right and wrong pose to assume. He is suggesting, in slightly different words, precisely what was suggested by the Kennedy brain trust. It was said that McCormack should have used a knife rather than an ax or that he should have attacked Kennedy in a more genteel way. Voters today, many of whom are solidly middle class, probably no longer find attractive the vitriolic outbursts and the slander and libel that characterized many past campaigns. Voters in affluent and bourgeois America probably want more "dignity," "gentlemanliness," and "politeness" in their candidates than did their fathers and grandfathers. The rough-and-tumble professional politician just doesn't fit very well into the good society.

C. R. Owens, the State House correspondent of the *Boston Globe,* sensed this. In his story on the debate Owens suggested that politics in the United States has "undergone a subtle but irrevocable change."

> There was a time when candidates who engaged in public debate were scored according to the validity of their arguments and the one who received the cheers and drew the laughs at his opponent's expense would be the winner.
>
> When Edward M. Kennedy left South Boston High School last night . . . he was tailed by newsmen who wanted to cap a question and answer program with just one more question.
>
> The query Kennedy stopped long enough to answer was unusual in that it was not directed to whether the candidate for the U.S. Senate thought he had won or lost, or scored or didn't. The question was: "Do you think you were treated courteously?"
>
> Kennedy replied that he thought the newsmen who tossed the questions to him were courteous, leaving a question as to the courtesy of his opponent.
>
> The question of how courteously a politician was handled by his opponent may never have been the primary question at the close of a debate before.
>
> But it indicated that the "image" of a candidate may be more important now than his qualifications or how much he can do for the people who place him in office.[6]

Although dignity, wealth, celebrity, status, and a famous family name are among the most salable commodities in contemporary American politics, neither Edward Kennedy nor other candidates can, in good taste, state publicly and in simple and straightforward language that their qualifications are their dignity, wealth, celebrity, status, and family name. Kennedy, for example, could not say openly and directly that since he was a millionaire he was not interested in holding public office for selfish reasons. He was purveying the Kennedy name and the Kennedy charisma rather

[6] C. R. Owens, *Boston Globe,* August 28, 1962.

than traditional qualifications or expertise, but he could not mount the hustings and declare that being a Kennedy made him a worthy candidate and an appealing ego-ideal. Although candidates in Kennedy's enviable position wish to mobilize these sentiments, the traditional rules of the political game and minimal standards of good taste make it necessary for them to do so by innuendo and symbolism, and sleight of mouth.

For instance, Kennedy could remain within the bounds of good taste and say that he could do more for Massachusetts and spoke with a voice that would be heard. But he could not, without giving the whole show away, complete the slogan by stating what Kennedy supporters knew or felt, i.e., that his influence and power stemmed from his having powerful and influential relatives. McCormack, of course, attempted to force Kennedy's hand and embarrass him during the debate by "completing" Kennedy's slogans, i.e., speaking the words and voicing the thoughts that Kennedy wanted understood but only by implication.

A public relations man felt that the Kennedy slogan worked as planned because

> . . . in the present campaign the great strength shown by Kennedy is based on the fact that he has given the people a repeatable keynote . . . whether I would believe or not, I do know that Ted Kennedy has said he will "do more for Massachusetts." . . . I would say that the basic weakness in the [Lodge and McCormack] campaigns is the lack of a repeatable keynote. . . . They have not certainly given a keynote that would follow the test that I always put on any political campaign, and that is, "Could the elevator operator, between the third and the fifth floor of a building going up or down, say what needs to be said, and leave something in the mind of the rider?" If he could not do this, a campaign keynote is worthless . . . you must reach people through their own interests and if you have a basic keynote. . . .
>
> First of all, whether it be attack or whether it be sell, the very first thing that you have to do is build a keynote that has a basis in truth. Then comes the question of strategy. Strategy is what you do with this basic keynote. How many different branches on the tree all stemming from the same root?

For example, if you want to reach people with military background, you have to draw examples built around your keynote that would appeal to them. If you want to reach older people, you have to state your case in such a way that they will listen and think that they understand what you're talking about and if you want to reach younger people, you apply the same principle, and if you want to reach people in a specific field, on the basis of any heritage or background, you must key your keynote to them. . . . They've left no stone unturned to reach every possible voter and they have spoken in the language the average person understands.

Here again, there's a strong contrast between the Kennedy and the McCormack and the Lodge campaign. I think that without being facetious, their campaign has been on the basis of logic, and the Kennedy campaign has been on a basis of emotion. And the emotions always win over the logical appeal. And I think this is easy to understand because the average person is concerned with their own household affairs and their job. Why should they be interested in the politician? Only because the politician shows that he is interested in them personally. Here again is the great appeal of the Kennedy family . . . they have made every family and every group and every individual feel that they are interested in them personally and as an individual. . . .

Politicians, however, need not say things to say things. They may and frequently must utilize accent, mannerisms, and even silence or non-talk rather than direct statements to speak the unspeakable. The implications that will be drawn by voters from what is said or unsaid obviously have much to do with their political predispositions, but the candidate must supply the voter with cues that permit him to find easily what he is looking for. To fully understand what occurred during the Kennedy-McCormack debate — and probably most debates and political campaigns — one must understand the latent as well as overt campaign communications, the hidden or implied messages that are not actually articulated, in a word, the "double talk."

"Double-talk" and "non-talk" were utilized primarily by Kennedy during the campaign and the debate because he appealed to voters, in part, on the basis of his influence and social position — an appeal that must be made but left "unsaid." Mc-Cormack had less reason to resort to "double-talk" and "non-talk" because the log-cabin-to-White House rhetoric he employed is not an "unmentionable." Candidates do talk about their experience but they do not talk about their status and glamour. A member of the Kennedy brain trust wanted Kennedy to give an impression of dignity, knowledgeability, and sophistication. Aware of the uses of "double-talk" and the latent content of campaign communications, he thought that Kennedy should deliver speeches that were probably too sophisticated for the average voter. Clearly, he was less interested in having Kennedy understood than in creating a specific kind of impression.

A member of the McCormack brain trust who wrote part of the Attorney General's opening statement well understood how Kennedy created the impression he and his advisers thought most useful:

Kennedy was much more specific, it seemed to me, in terms of his answers. And in so doing, it seemed to me, combined with certain other techniques which I will mention, I think, managed to convey an impression of a better-informed candidate on national and international issues. I don't really believe Mr. Kennedy is. But I think he created this impression. He did it by utilizing a number of techniques very effectively. The first technique he used, I think, I would call the technique of "currency" for lack of a better catchword. This was a sense of being fully informed and being on top of evolving developments and issues all over the world. Now, obviously, Mr. Kennedy is not. But he created this impression by a very skillful use of a device, namely, referring to the morning papers, or "as we read today," or "as we saw today" or "only today in our morning paper" or "as we heard only today," and he did this once specifically with reference to the declaration by the Polish Cardinal. He said, "As we saw only today in the statement from Cardinal Wyzanski." He did this with his closing device, his closing statement relative to the convoys in Berlin . . . again conveying the impression that he knew from a reading of the morning papers and from being fully informed and on top of events, that the convoy had in fact been stopped last night. This was one of the devices that, I think, contributed to an image as of superior knowledge and superior information and being better informed as to the evolving developments and events all over the world.

Another device which was very effective and, I think, which the President himself has used with great effectiveness in the past, is this device of geographical, what I would call geographical name-dropping. You allude to such things as the Upper Volta Dam in Ghana, just in passing. And, of course, if you utilize this very cleverly, you can throw in four or five or six countries as you go along to give a specific answer to a specific question, which would indicate, even though you never amplified these statements at all, even though you never really indicate to an informed observer that you have any particular knowledge, or specific knowledge as what in fact for example the real issue is in the Upper Volta Dam in Ghana, at the same time, by geographical name-dropping you are able to create an impression that you are really informed about a lot of things which in fact you may not really be tremendously knowledgeable about. It's another device which Mr. Kennedy utilizes and did utilize in this debate that conveys this impression.

And then a third very effective device it seemed to me in the Kennedy debate posture was what I would call, for lack of a better word again, the localization of a general national or international issue. When Mr. Kennedy, for example, would talk about tariffs, and rather than talking about tariffs in a general way, or talking about the issues in any generalized way, Mr. Kennedy would point out that I know because I talked to the textile workers in Lowell and in Fall River, and New Bedford. I talked to the people in Lynn, and by localizing, by tying in a general problem with a specific area, particularly in the light of Mr. Kennedy's intensive personalized campaign which has brought him into many of these areas, and the people in those areas are certainly aware of the fact that he has been there, I think that this device is designed to strike a rapport, to make somewhat more sympathetic the response on the part of the listening public who come from these specific local areas. Rather than discussing it in an abstract way, as Mr. McCormack is wont to do, Mr. Kennedy, by localizing, is able to touch responsive chords in various communities on the part of people who are affected, who work in these industries in various communities.

This McCormack adviser also suggested that Kennedy was better prepared for the debate:

I think these three devices together, plus the fact that I think, in my judgment, and I don't say this to do an injustice to Mr. McCormack, but I do feel that Mr. Kennedy has taken the time to be, and is better organized, and is better briefed and prepped on the specific issues of national and international policy, whereas Mr. McCormack, I think, tends to use his advisers to develop with him more generalized opinions and approaches, rather than the specific factual, rather than using them to give him specific factual data and information. I think this is the difference which I sense in the two candidates' approaches to the use of campaign advisers and intellectuals which I think made it possible for Mr. Kennedy to appear to the general public to be much better informed on issues.

For example, I think again of the Kennedy answer to the specific question of a tax cut. . . . Mr. Kennedy ticked off three specific items which are currently under debate in the Senate of the United States as the Senate is debating tax problems. The question, for example of tightening up on expense accounts. These were things which Mr. Kennedy was able to do, which Mr. McCormack didn't do because I don't think, for example, Mr. McCormack has been frankly following that closely the developments in the United States Senate on a day-by-day basis. I don't think Mr. Kennedy has either. But I think his advisers brought him up to date and gave him the kind of specific factual information which he could use and which McCormack either didn't have or didn't see any necessity for using.

The candidate who follows the Kennedy prescription may well be knowledgeable and insightful. He may, however, be shallow, but well tutored and adept at learning by rote. In a television debate where little or no interchange of ideas actually takes place and candidates have two or three minutes to state their views on complex issues, we suggest that it is difficult, if not impossible, for the intelligent viewer to discern whether the candidate is a robot stuffed with facts or a thoughtful man who has seriously considered the issues. All things being equal, it is probably strategically sound to overwhelm and thereby impress voters with much data and many names of foreign nations and dignitaries rather than glittering generalities. This is precisely what Kennedy did, and with consummate skill.

* * *

The first debate took place on August 27, 1962. The second was held on September 5. By this time McCormack fully understood that his attack on the President's brother had evoked much sympathy for Kennedy. The Kennedys also understood this. The second debate was anticlimatic and dull. McCormack curbed his anger, refrained from violent invective. Kennedy remained calm and polite, ignored McCormack, and executed the Kennedy television technique. Between September 5 and primary election day, September 18, little of consequence occurred. The Kennedy organization, which by this time was supported by thousands of volunteers, continued its daily round of telephone calls to voters, distributed tabloids to almost every home in the state, pre-empted much prime time on radio and television, and carried through on a grand scale the tasks of campaigning that are possible only when expertise is in full supply, volunteers are always available, and money is no object.

The Kennedy effort paid off. The President's brother received 559,303 votes — 69 per cent of the total. The Speaker's nephew received 257,403 votes.

The Kennedys assumed that if they soundly defeated McCormack in the primary they would have little or no difficulty in Democratic Massachusetts with the Republican nominee, George Cabot Lodge, or the Independent candidate, Professor H. Stuart Hughes. Their assumption was well taken. On November 6, 1962, Kennedy received 1,162,611 votes, Lodge received 877,669 votes, and Hughes received 50,013 votes.

CHAPTER 5 ☒ *Serious Money*

You can forget the five- and ten-dollar bills; what counts is the serious money.

— A BOSTON POLITICIAN

IT IS, OF COURSE, no secret to professional politicians that very substantial sums of money are necessary in America to launch a political career and to compete seriously for high public office. Most of the political "pros" agree with the adage that money may not necessarily guarantee victory on election day, but the absence of an adequate campaign fund certainly guarantees defeat. Richard B. Stolley of *Life* wrote:

> Elections have always been "bought" in the sense that it takes big money to run a major campaign, and the side with the most money usually wins. The Organization raises funds by squeezing contractors and merchants who hope to do business with its officeholders. Until recent years, however, rarely has the wherewithal for a campaign come mostly from one source. The Kennedys are the best example of the contemporary trend toward very rich men spending vast sums of their own money, not in order to manipulate governments behind the scenes, as in the past, but to seek power in public office.[1]

A veteran professional in Massachusetts put the matter of money in somewhat different terms: "The bullshit that is thrown around on television and in the papers by the candidates costs a lot of dough, an awful lot of dough. You can forget the five- and ten-dollar bills; what counts is the serious money."

A closely contested campaign for the governorship of a large industrial and competitive two-party state like Pennsylvania or Illinois costs "serious money" — at the very least about $1,200,000. The price could easily run as high as $1,700,000 or $2,000,000. A seat in the United States Senate from one of these states would probably cost no less. A candidate for mayor in a city the size of

[1] Richard B. Stolley, *Life*, May 27, 1966.

New York City, Chicago, Philadelphia, or Los Angeles, who faced formidable and well-financed opposition, could not mount a serious effort for less than $1,000,000. In 1965, John Lindsay announced that he would need a minimum of $2,000,000 to make a respectable showing in New York City, and Lindsay actually reported campaign expenditures of over $2,000,000.

The cost of campaigning, however, may vary greatly from constituency to constituency and from election to election. A candidate for the United States House of Representatives who is extremely wealthy and who is opposing an incumbent in a highly competitive and densely populated urban district may spend as much as $300,000. An incumbent congressman from a safe district, however, may spend only a token $5,000 to keep faithful party workers happy. The cost depends primarily on the candidate's judgment of how much his opponent will spend and how much he believes he needs to win. Naturally, these judgments will be affected by the pool of money available, and perhaps even by the law regulating campaign contributions and expenditures.

What does it cost to run for a major office in Massachusetts? James Doyle of the *Boston Globe,* who spent several weeks analyzing the costs of the 1962 campaign in Massachusetts, reported that aides of Endicott Peabody, a Democratic candidate for governor, estimated that

> . . . it would cost a minimum of $750,000 for him to run. . . . Other leading politicians in the state, who refused to be quoted, estimated that the price tag on a tough fight for the top spots would start at a million. Estimates were obtained by *The Boston Globe* from advertising agencies, printers, mailing companies, radio and television salesmen, sign makers, and others. The total cost for a state-wide campaign estimated by persons who wage such campaigns added up to more than $800,000 for a candidate who wants to win.[2]

A senior executive of one of the largest advertising agencies in this country who heads the firm's Boston office estimated for us the cost of a hard-fought state-wide campaign in Massachusetts. Hav-

[2] James S. Doyle, *Boston Globe,* January 23, 1963.

ing been employed by candidates in Massachusetts, he asserted that a state-wide candidate "would have to spend something between $700,000 and a million plus." In response to a question dealing with the cost of the 1962 senatorial campaign, he replied:

> Well, of course Hughes ran unquestionably the lowest state-wide campaign for office in this state. Lodge ran again a very low-cost campaign — I would guess that Lodge spent somewhere around $350,000. I have no idea what McCormack spent up through the primary but certainly, from observation, he had to spend somewhere around a quarter of a million dollars. . . . I said before, and I think it is a reasonable estimate, the Kennedy campaign cost somebody between $900,000 and a million. In terms of dollars, it was just as elaborate and as widespread and as beautifully financed as anything I have ever seen.

During a discussion of campaign expenditures he said:

> The single most expensive item in any campaign, of course, is the advertising budget, the money that is spent in newspaper space, radio time, TV time, billboards, printed material and the like. For example, if we are talking about Boston now we are talking about three TV stations in the city of Boston. The average prime, night TV spot, a twenty-second or a minute television spot, will run something like $750 . . . depending on the location of the spot and the station. When you consider that for a primary or let's say the combined primary and general election of a state-wide candidate in the city of Boston — he would probably consider, minimum, something in the area of 150 to 200 spots covering that period of time. Candidates, since the early years of television, have been enamored with the so-called thirty-minute documentary program. Almost every major candidate for major office in this state has used one of them in the last eight years. Just as a rule of thumb, the cost is going to be twelve, fifteen hundred, two thousand dollars per minute so you chew up a tremendous amount of money. Billboards, for example, for prime billboard location, and a candidate is running for primary office, picks up his billboards at the early part of the summer and runs them

all the way through the campaign. Prime billboard locations can run $1,500 a month, and that is just one billboard — so this chews up a tremendous amount of money. . . .

Bumper strips — they are very expensive as you know. They have an adhesive back, they have peel-off papers so that the voter can put it on his bumper. I am not an expert in printing costs, but I would think that most bumper strips run something in the area of two to two and a half cents apiece and are turned out by the million — just by the million. A great number of them are wasted — a tremendous amount of printed material in any campaign is wasted. Then the more elaborate things like the multi-colored brochures, the comic strip type of throw-aways, two- and three-colored small printed pieces for various ethnic groups, for laborers, for the urbanists, for the suburbanists — if the candidate gets this involved in his printed material, his printing bill can run $200,000.

Radio costs are another factor, of course, although the preparation of your radio material is not as expensive as it is in television where you have film work. Still it chews up a great piece of money. If you are trying to do a fairly good job — what we call saturation radio, say an eighteen-week period — you could easily spend five to seven thousand dollars a week. This would not be uncommon in the last two weeks of the campaign.

Newton H. Fulbright of the *New York Herald Tribune,* who spent several days in Massachusetts analyzing the costs of the campaign, reported that "People with an eye for campaign costs maintain that Mr. Kennedy, the youngest brother of the President, spent around $1 million in his victorious sledgehammer primary fight against Edward J. McCormack, Jr., nephew of the Speaker of the House."[3] A member of the Kennedy entourage when asked to estimate the cost of the 1962 senatorial campaign replied: "I have had different percentages quoted. But let us say that McCormack spent in the vicinity of $200,000. And it would not be unfair to say we outspent him six or seven to one."

With these estimates from knowledgeable observers, it is

3 Newton H. Fulbright, *New York Herald Tribune,* October 22, 1962.

somewhat startling to look at the expenditures reported by the treasurers of political committees in 1962, as required by law, and the date by which all debts had been paid and/or the accounts officially closed.

Reported Expenditures and Liabilities of
Senatorial and Gubernatorial Candidates
in 1962

CANDIDATE	EXPENDITURES	ACCOUNT CLOSED	REMAINING LIABILITIES
Endicott Peabody (Democratic gubernatorial candidate)	$659,271.18	May, 1964	$2,683.70
John Volpe (Republican gubernatorial candidate)	554,299.53	June, 1964	
Edward Kennedy (Democratic senatorial candidate)	421,442.22	December, 1963	
George Lodge (Republican senatorial candidate)	353,276.55	April, 1964	978.95
Laurence Curtis (Republican senatorial candidate)	181,025.00	April, 1963	
H. Stuart Hughes (Independent senatorial candidate)	165,889.05	May, 1964	
Edward McCormack (Democratic senatorial candidate)	78,765.68	January, 1963	3,425.50

These figures, to which we will return, were reported to the Secretary of State of Massachusetts under the requirements of a statute (Chapter 55 of the Massachusetts General Laws) which had been newly revised at the behest of the Greater Boston Junior Chamber of Commerce, the Secretary of State, and numerous private individuals. The law deals with the reporting of expenses of candidates, political contributions, and corrupt practices relating to elections. The amendments were designed primarily to provide the public with complete information, *during the campaign*, about the amount of money spent by candidates and their committees, the identity of contributors and the amounts contributed by them, and the amounts borrowed by candidates and their committees and the identity of individuals or institutions who loaned money or goods and services. The Massachusetts law requires public semimonthly reports of most of this information during the campaign on the assumption that the information will be of use to the electorate only if it is available prior to the election.

Under the terms of the amended law, a candidate and/or his campaign committees are required to select a depository bank and open a campaign account, either when the campaign organization or polititcal committee is officially announced or when primary nomination papers are filed, whichever date is the last to occur. The candidate and/or the treasurers of a political committee must deposit all contributions, in the form received, in the depository bank by the end of the third business day after receipt of the contribution. The bank may accept deposits only if they are accompanied by a deposit slip containing, for each contribution in excess of twenty-five dollars, the name and residential address of the contributor. If any deposits represent the proceeds of borrowings, the deposit slip must indicate the names and addresses of the lender, persons liable, either primarily or secondarily, for a portion of the borrowings, and persons providing collateral for the borrowers. This information must also be provided for contributions of less than twenty-five dollars if the aggregate amounts from one contributor exceeded the sum of twenty-five dollars during the preceding fourteen days.

Although the law places no limit on how much candidates or

their committees may spend, individuals may not contribute more than $3,000 to a candidate or any one of his committees in any one calendar year. No limit, however, is placed on the amount a candidate may contribute to his own campaign.

All payments for campaign purposes in excess of fifty dollars must be made only from funds on deposit in the designated bank and they must be made by check drawn on the designated depository. Every check must contain a notation to the effect that the check is drawn on the campaign account of the candidate or the political committee involved. All payments in excess of fifty dollars must be made payable to the order of a named payee, who is not a candidate or treasurer. A payment not in excess of twenty-five dollars may be made payable to a candidate or treasurer, provided that checks made payable to a candidate or treasurer do not exceed $500 in any fourteen-day period.

A statement of the purpose of the payment must be printed on the front of every campaign check:

Purposes of Payment
(Check One and Fill in Specific Purpose)

T.V., Radio	Printing	Sign or
Newspaper	Office	Display
Meetings	Travel	Transfer of
		Fund
		Other

Specific Purpose

Campaign checks must also contain the following statement, printed on the reverse side, under which the payee must affix his signature.

The undersigned affirms under the penalties of perjury that he is the named payee of this check or an authorized officer thereof, that he or it performed the services or delivered the goods indicated hereon, that the payment is for the sole purpose of paying for such goods or services and that no person other than the named payee has any interest, direct or indirect, in this payment.

Candidates and treasurers are not permitted to authorize any expenditure unless monies are on deposit in the designated depository sufficient to pay the amount of the authorized expenditure at the time it is made and all other expenditures previously authorized and still outstanding, unless the candidate or treasurer files with the Secretary of State a complete statement of all unpaid obligations then outstanding, the terms of payment, the purpose of the expenditure for which the obligation was made, and the name and address of the person or persons holding the obligation.

The cashier or treasurer of the bank must file a semimonthly report with the Secretary of State which contains an alphabetized list of all deposits and all payments made on the campaign account. This report has to include the name and residential address of every contributor and the amount contributed, and the name of every individual or firm to whom monies were paid and the amounts paid. The candidate or his treasurer must file a monthly report with the Secretary of State which includes a list of all liabilities, loans, and contributions in kind. The account must be kept open and reports must be filed until all debts have been paid. A candidate or his treasurer may continue to file reports indefinitely.

The Secretary of State is obligated to make the reports available to the public. He is also supposed to check the reports for violations, notify candidates and treasurers of violations, and, if necessary, forward the reports to the Attorney General for investigation and possible criminal action. Violations of various sections of the law are punishable by fines, imprisonment, and, under certain conditions, disbarment from public office.

According to the revised Massachusetts law a candidate may have not more than three committees soliciting contributions and making disbursements in his behalf. He must consent to the formation of these committees, of which each must have a treasurer and a chairman. Each treasurer qualifies for his office by filing a written acceptance of the position with the Secretary of State and remains subject to all the duties and responsibilities imposed on him by the law until he files a written resignation of the office. He is required to keep and preserve detailed accounts, vouchers, and receipts. Violation of any of these provisions is punishable by imprisonment for not more than six months or by a fine of not more than $500.

The term "campaign contribution" was defined very broadly to include, in addition to gifts of money or its equivalent (i.e. many other items of value such as contributions in kind — office equipment or office space for instance), payments or promises or guarantees of payment to others for the benefit of a candidate or political committee, loans of property, discounts or rebates not available to the general public, the cancellation of indebtedness, and purchases of tickets and advertisements to testimonial dinners if the purchase price exceeds the fair value of the goods sold or the services rendered. Services rendered by unpaid speakers, editors, writers, and poll-watchers are not considered campaign contributions.

At this point we present first the reported expenditures and liabilities of senatorial candidates for the period covering the primary campaign and then their total reported expenditures for the primary and final election campaigns.

Reported Expenditures and Liabilities of
Senatorial Candidates for the 1962 Primary Campaign

CANDIDATE		EXPENDITURES	LIABILITIES
Laurence Curtis	(Republican senatorial candidate)	$181,025	$ 0
Edward Kennedy	(Democratic senatorial candidate)	121,535	0
George Lodge	(Republican senatorial candidate)	116,234	56,291
Edward McCormack	(Democratic senatorial candidate)	78,765	3,426

Reported Expenditures and Liabilities of
Senatorial Candidates for the
1962 Primary and General Election Campaigns

CANDIDATE	EXPENDITURES	LIABILITIES
Edward Kennedy	$421,442	0
George Lodge	353,276	$979
H. Stuart Hughes	165,889	0

As noted previously, persons thoroughly familiar with the cost of waging major state-wide campaigns in Massachusetts estimate that an absolute minimum of $750,000 is necessary to mount a competitive six-month campaign for the convention endorsement, the primary nomination, and the final election. No knowledgeable person whom we interviewed placed the minimum cost at less. A number of advertising executives, fund raisers, and political reporters, however, argued that a really substantial campaign — a campaign utilizing several television documentaries, for example — would cost not less than $1,000,000 nor probably more than $1,300,000 or $1,400,000.

It is curious, therefore, that in 1962 only two state-wide candidates (gubernatorial) reported campaign expenses ($550,000–$650,000) that even approach the minimal estimate of $750,000. Edward McCormack managed to wage, and for six months, one of the most bitter convention and primary fights in Massachusetts history for about $79,000. Edward Kennedy, who waged three of the most impressive campaigns in the memory of many political observers — convention, primary, and final election — reported less than one-half the amount that experts assume a really big Massachusetts campaign would cost. Treasurers for George Lodge, whose campaign, in the opinion of all political reporters we interviewed, was substantially smaller than that waged by Kennedy, reported only about $68,000 less than did Kennedy's treasurers.

It is also interesting to note that in 1962 no senatorial candidate, according to our analysis, reported any contributions in kind — that is, free headquarters space, or free typewriters or stationery, or any other free goods and services. The law requires "each . . . thing of value expended, contributed or promised," be reported.

Perhaps the most singular aspect of the 1962 financial reports is that the treasurer for Professor H. Stuart Hughes, the Independent peace candidate, whose campaign was tiny in contrast even to that waged by McCormack, reported expenditures of approximately $166,000. Professor Hughes incurred no expenses for a convention endorsement because he did not seek any endorsement. He incurred no expenditures for a primary nomination because he was not a candidate in any primary election. He did incur expenditures, however, in connection with a drive for nomination signatures. Hughes had about five full-time paid workers and one headquarters (of any size). He posted no state-wide mailings. He purchased relatively little television time in comparison with Lodge and Kennedy, and no documentary films of the traditional sort. He rented a few inexpensive billboards and one sound truck. Some political observers in Massachusetts suggested that the Hughes campaign resembled the Kennedy campaign as a fly-by-night tent circus resembles Barnum and Bailey performing in Madison Square Garden. Most correspondents regarded the Hughes campaign as a curiosity.

The total amount of checks drawn on Hughes' depository bank as reported to the Secretary of State by the cashier of the bank came to approximately 40 per cent of the amount of the checks drawn on Kennedy's campaign account. We were allowed to compare the amounts reported by Hughes' treasurer for many goods and services with the invoices sent to Hughes by the firms and individuals that had supplied them, the only way to determine the accuracy of the reports submitted. Approximately two years after the election, Hughes, upon our request, showed us the campaign invoices — about $50,000 worth — remaining in his possession. Our examination indicates that Hughes' treasurer did report campaign expenses that equal the amounts billed to various Hughes committees, and the Hughes reports do serve as a standard for evaluating the reports of other candidates.

We asked not only Hughes but also McCormack, Kennedy, Lodge, and Curtis for their 1962 invoices. Curtis did not respond to our letter. Lodge provided us with his canceled campaign checks. One McCormack aide, at the Attorney General's request, telephoned us about the matter and reported that the woman in charge of the McCormack accounts had died, and her husband, in the fullness of his grief, had "burned the invoices." The aide told us he was sorry he could not be of service. Kennedy's campaign treasurer, at the Senator's request, sent us a letter on May 17, 1965, stating that the reports filed by the Edward M.

244 | KENNEDY CAMPAIGNING

Kennedy Committee for United States Senator contained "a complete and accurate statement of all receipts, contributions, and all expenditures, billings and invoices made during the 1962 campaign. These records are on file at the Office of the Secretary of State, and I would suggest that you examine them for the information which you requested in your letter."

As the reported expenditures of the senatorial candidates were made public, some newspapermen and some members of the Greater Boston Junior Chamber of Commerce interested in the law regulating campaign costs questioned the accuracy of reports submitted by some of the candidates. On October 22, 1962, for example, three weeks before election day, the *New York Herald Tribune* published a front-page article on Massachusetts campaign costs with the headline "MONEY AND ELECTIONS — A DISTURBING LOOK." Newton H. Fulbright, a veteran *Tribune* reporter, who had visited Massachusetts at the suggestion of a Lodge campaign manager, wrote that observers believed the primary campaign would have cost Kennedy "several times the $100,000 he reported in expenses."

Fulbright also wrote "That few candidates apparently made full disclosures. That Mr. McCormack had little money with which to wage a major campaign. . . . That neither Mr. Kennedy nor Laurence Curtis, defeated Republican candidate for the United States Senate, bothered to list the full cost of the television they both used lavishly during the campaign. The people who keep tab of the high cost of politicking believe that young Mr. Kennedy paid out almost $1,000,000. . . ."

Fulbright was not the only newspaperman to question, in print, the financial reports of some of the candidates. The *Boston Globe* gave reporter James S. Doyle about a month to study the 1962 reports and write a series of five articles evaluating the problem of campaign finances. Doyle concluded that by August "it became obvious that a pattern of evasion was emerging in some reports." [4] Candidates, and/or their treasurers, according to Doyle, did the following:

[4] Doyle, *op. cit.*, January 21, 1963.

Some treasurers gave the names and addresses of contributors daily in alphabetical order so that the report, which covered a two-week period, listed names in "complete disorder." Large contributions, moreover, could be hidden by splitting them up and reporting them as smaller contributions to the three different committees. In addition, the true recipients of payments were masked by reporting very large sums to advertising agencies, who presumably then paid television stations, newspapers, etc. The latter were, in fact, the true suppliers of goods and services, to whom the checks on the candidate's depository bank should have been made payable. In such cases it is impossible to determine how much a candidate paid a particular television station or newspaper.

Doyle also noted that one widely used device for under-reporting was to permit persons not directly connected with the campaign to "pick up the tab" for some very substantial expenditures.

Perhaps Doyle's most revealing discovery was that "large contributions" were made by "known campaign workers who were drawing a salary even while they made contributions. In one case, a man who was getting paid $100 a week for his campaigning is listed as contributing $1000, or 10 weeks' pay."

Enforcement procedures were lax or nonexistent. Doyle observed that "the law does not offer the threat of vigorous enforcement and investigation necessary to exact compliance."[5] "In summary, the Full Disclosure Law, in its first time out, was a bit of a sham."[6] We agree.

Doyle was impressed, as were we, with the relatively small amounts reported by some senatorial candidates in comparison to what Hughes reported. "Do the figures add up?" he wrote. "H. Stuart Hughes, who ran a shoestring campaign from Cambridge, using a maximum of footwork and a minimum of radio, television, newspaper ads, two billboards, had campaign expenses ($165,996.00) that are astronomical relative to what his opponents got for their reported campaign dollars."[7] On the basis of Hughes'

[5] *Ibid.*, January 25, 1963.
[6] *Ibid.*, January 21, 1963.
[7] *Ibid.*

stated expenditures he questioned the reported payments of several candidates.

The most thorough — and scholarly — investigation of the 1962 reports was undertaken not by newspapermen but by the Greater Boston Junior Chamber of Commerce. A Boston attorney, Bernard Borman, who was instrumental in the movement for a revised law and who is probably the most knowledgeable man in Massachusetts on this topic, spent several months preparing a lengthy and detailed report[8] in which are documented dozens of obvious and not so obvious evasions of either the letter or the purpose of the law by many candidates. Most Massachusetts newspapers have neither the courage nor the manpower to undertake an analysis of this kind.

Four or five of the questions raised in the report and a few examples of the types of data cited are given below out of Borman's perhaps sixty or seventy examples.

Several candidates, according to Borman, obscured the recipients of thousands of dollars by lumping together many expenditures due to many different persons into just a few large reported expenditures to one person. The "person" was usually the candidate's advertising agency.

By doing this, these candidates were able to conceal the actual fees paid to their agencies. They also concealed what these agencies actually did with all the money they spent, and the real sellers of the goods and services never were reported and never signed the required affidavits.

Examples of this practice appear in the reports of several candidates. For example, the committee for Governor Volpe disbursed approximately $389,000.00 to his agency in only eight payments to account for about 87% of his total expenditures through November 30th. Senator Kennedy's disbursements and liabilities to his agency were approximately $272,000.00 in only six payments to account for approximately 54% of his overall expenditures and liabilities as of

8 "The Greater Boston Junior Chamber of Commerce Survey of Depository System," undated, mimeographed, 1963.

November 30, 1962. . . . By comparison, the Lodge disbursements to an agency were only about 8% of his total expenditures.[9]

The Junior Chamber commented on the problem of contributions in kind:

Persons who do not wish to be reported as cash contributors or who regularly sell merchandise of value to the candidate often make contributions in kind rather than in money. For example, gifts of stationery with campaign letterheads or of other printed material are the equivalent of money to the candidate and must be reported as "campaign contributions."

One indication that the reporting requirements concerning contributions in kind may not have been effective appears from an examination of the printing expenditures of Senator Kennedy. Printing expenditures are specifically required to be reported as item number 4 on the Secretary of State's report form. As of November 30, 1962, Governor Volpe had reported printing expenditures of approximately $13,-678.00, George Lodge approximately $27,029.00, Governor Peabody approximately $8,715.00, and Senator Kennedy had reported printing expenses of zero. As of April 15, 1963, this figure still was zero.

Since a substantial amount of Kennedy printed material was observed during the campaign but no printing expenditures were reported as such, it would seem that either (i) this printed material had been contributed in kind but was not so reported, or (ii) the expenditures for printing were wrongly shown under other items and not reported as printing under item number 4, or (iii) printing expenditures were made but not reported at all. Whether any or all of these cases, it seems that the persons filing reports on behalf of Senator Kennedy did not comply with the law in so far as reporting of printing is concerned.[10]

9 *Ibid.*, p. 11.

10 *Ibid.*, p. 6. Kennedy treasurers in fact reported $1,791.77 specified as printing.

On Kennedy's reported expenditures for newspaper advertising, radio, television, and telephone, it was noted:

These reports show that the Senator reported no expenses or liabilities for newspaper advertising until October 1st, and that he had reported no expenses or liabilities for radio and television until November 15th. The Kennedy reports show payment to the phone company of about $4,250 for the period ending July 31st, $4,000 for the period of August 1st–15th, and $2,800 for the period of October 15th–30th. Thus, there are no checks written to the phone company from August 16th to October 15th, or for the month of November. Even though the Kennedy reports reveal the name of a contributor who gave over $3,000, still no questions were asked. . . . In view of these unaudited statistics, either there is something wrong with the reports or there is something wrong with the law.[11]

Borman might have added a third alternative: there is something wrong with the enforcement of the law.

The author also compared the expenditures of several candidates for similar items and concluded:

The comparative unaudited expenses of major candidates give further indication that either the reporting system is confused or certain expenditures simply are not being reported. For example, contrast the telephone bills to November 30th: Peabody $13,400; Kennedy, $11,000; Volpe $4,750; Hughes $4,075; or the television and radio expenses: Peabody $131,000; Lodge $35,900; Hughes $21,500; Kennedy $14,100; Volpe $11,800; or meeting expenses: Peabody $21,-500; Hughes $13,000; Lodge $11,400; Volpe $3,200; Kennedy $712. And, according to the reports, Laurence Curtis had no expenditures or contributions whatsoever from August 1st to August 15th in his senatorial campaign.[12]

There was also a comment on candidates' debts:

A significant device employed by some candidates to delay

11 *Ibid.*, p. 21.
12 *Ibid.*

disclosure was their tardy reporting of campaign debts incurred. . . .

For example, by November 5th, Senator Kennedy had reported only about $247,000 in cash expenditures for the election but his November 20th report for the first time disclosed certain liabilities and these were reported in the amount of $161,000 or about 40% of his total reported expenditures delayed until after the election through the maneuver of delaying reports of debts by one means or another. On July 31st, George Lodge listed liabilities of $55,-579 which he was then required to report every two weeks afterwards if they remained unpaid. However, no debts were thereafter reported by Lodge during the election. Then on December 20th, he reported liabilities of $76,624 unlisted since July 31st, a delay reporting of 20% of his total expenditures.[13]

The author points out that expenditures for the convention may be paid in cash but must be reported. "The reports," he writes, "cannot be double-checked because no campaign checks are required."[14]

Thus, despite the requirement of reporting, several candidates who displayed the products of significant financial expenditure at the pre-primary conventions apparently did not report these expenditures, which leads to the conclusion that they also failed to report concurrent contributions or liabilities which balanced these expenditures. For example, the Volpe committees reported no expenditures or liabilities *at all* prior to July, although substantial campaign material was observed at Worcester.[15]

A spot check of the names of many contributors "would have revealed that some persons were reported as having made contributions that would seem very unlikely in view of their personal financial situations."[16]

13 *Ibid.*, p. 16.
14 *Ibid.*, p. 14.
15 *Ibid.*
16 *Ibid.*, p. 9.

We said earlier that the only absolutely sure way to determine whether or not a treasurer reported the full cost of the campaign is to compare the stated expenditures for various goods and services with invoices for those goods and services. In 1964 the Massachusetts Crime Commission, undertaking a full-scale investigation of 1962 reported expenditures and contributions, asked the known suppliers of goods and services to forward to it copies of all invoices to state-wide candidates. Thousands of the suppliers complied, but, as the Commission noted in its final report, "Two well-known companies refused to provide information requested by the Commission relating to campaign expenditures in the 1962 election." [17] We are authoritatively informed that these companies were John C. Dowd Inc., of Boston, the advertising agency employed by Kennedy, and Buck Printing Company, of Boston, which, we were told, produced much of Kennedy's printed materials and that of other candidates. Because it was claimed that the Commission lacked the authority to require this disclosure, the Commission, according to an authoritative source, considered requesting power to subpoena their records. Preparations for this action were terminated, in part, because the Commission decided that a full-scale investigation of campaign expenditures would divert so much manpower that the other investigations in which it was interested would suffer.

On the basis of the investigation it did conduct, the Commission found: *"There is almost universal circumvention of the provisions of our Campaign Fund Reporting Act in the reporting of contributions and expenditures."* [18]

* * *

We turn now to a detailed analysis of the reported expenditures of McCormack and Kennedy.

The law regulating campaign contributions and expenditures specifies that every payment be classified as to purpose into one of nine categories, which appear on each campaign check. Cam-

17 *Massachusetts Crime Commission: Comprehensive Report,* May 17, 1965, Vol. I, p. 13.

18 *Ibid.,* p. 10.

paign treasurers are not required to report totals for each classification. The following table therefore contains our totals of McCormack's individually reported expenditures in each of the nine categories.

Total Reported Payment of McCormack Committees

Television and radio	$ 6,632.52
Newpapers	579.82
Meetings	3,491.73
Printing	731.64
Office	19,885.02
Travel	3,230.52
Signs and displays	9,432.02
Transfer of fund	261.01
Other	34,521.40
	$78,765.68

The categories "office" and "other" are vague, and the law does not specify the types of expenditures that must be so classified. Treasurers of most gubernatorial and senatorial candidates placed the greater part of their expenditures in one or both of these categories, thus making it almost impossible for the analyst to determine the true purpose of expenditures for hundreds of goods and services. To compound the matter, few treasurers noted the "specific purpose" of expenditures which is required by law in addition to the general purpose.

McCormack's treasurers classified approximately 25 per cent ($19,885.02) of all payments as "office" and approximately 44 per cent ($34,521.40) as "other." Given the fact that they rarely reported the specific purpose of any of these payments, it is literally impossible to determine the purpose for which most of McCormack's money was spent without examining the records in the Secretary of State's office for every payment and then determining the nature of the payee's business. We took eight months to analyze treasurers' reports and were still unable to determine the specific purpose of about $6,400 that McCormack's treasurers reported.

Here is our analysis of McCormack's payments reported as "office":

Telephone and telegraph	$ 7,516.25
Equipment and supplies	2,842.25
Salaries	5,272.02
Unidentified	2,178.79
Postage	856.00
Electricity	468.63
Catering	311.83
Mailings	274.00
Rent	140.00
Janitorial service	20.00
	$19,879.77*

* This sum amounts to $5.25 less than the amount noted above as "office." We could not account for this difference.

McCormack's treasurers, according to our analysis, reported $7,516.25 for telephone and telegrams. Lodge's treasurers reported $7,857.80 for this purpose, Kennedy's about $21,500, and Hughes' about $6,000. McCormack's expenses for telephone and telegraph, then, in comparison to those of other candidates, appear to be very reasonable for a candidate who was defeated in a primary and therefore spent nothing for a general election.

Additional comments concerning McCormack's payments classified as "office" are in order. Although his treasurers reported payment of $856 for postage as "office," they also included payments of $2,043.04 for postage as "other." Total reported payments for postage, therefore, amount to $2,899.04. At the 1962 bulk rate (2⅞¢ per letter), McCormack could have mailed about 100,000 letters for this sum. A mailing of 100,000 would cover the number of registered voters in about six wards of average size in Boston. Boston has twenty-two wards, and Massachusetts had about 1,000,000 registered Democrats in 1962. H. Stuart Hughes' treasurer reported payments of $8,278 for postage, and Lodge's treasurer reported slightly under $10,000 for this purpose. The average Kennedy mailing to special groups like the "elderly" or "labor" was 50,000, and dozens of such mailings were made. Kennedy's treasurer reported about $18,200 for postage. Whether any of the candidates paid cash for stamps or used the postage meter of a supporter cannot be ascertained.

We shall look now at McCormack's reported payments for rental for headquarters. Rent is customarily a substantial cost because many candidates for major office in Massachusetts have, at the very least, forty to seventy headquarters throughout the state. Lodge's office manager, for example, told us that Lodge had sixty-five to seventy headquarters, most of them small and inexpensive storefronts contributed to Lodge rent free — that is, as a contrition in kind, yet Lodge's treasurers reported no contributions in kind for headquarters. It would be unusual, but by no means implausible, for a well-financed candidate to have ninety or a hundred headquarters, i.e., headquarters in most cities and towns with at least 7,000 inhabitants. Kennedy, for example, had twenty headquarters in the city of Boston alone.

McCormack's treasurers reported payment of $140 (as "office") the specific purpose of which was "rental of headquarters," and another $274.40 specified as "headquarters rental" (under "other"). Throughout the McCormack reports, about ten small payments ($60 to $100) are listed to individuals whom we could not identify but who we know were not on the regular secretarial staff. These payments, sometimes noted as "headquarters expenses," may not have been payment for rent but reimbursement for other "out of pocket" expenses. They do not, however, amount to more than about $1,000. Let us assume they are for rent, in which case total McCormack reported payments for rent would amount to $1,414.40. Part of this $1,414.40 is made up of two payments of $137.20 for rent for Springfield headquarters, one payment of $75 for headquarters in Charlestown, and one payment of $65 for headquarters in Boston (Ward 13). We were unable to identify reported payments covering rent for any other headquarters.

During the campaign we visited two McCormack headquarters in Boston, one of them located next door to Kennedy's main headquarters on Tremont Street, which is a main thoroughfare in a high-rent district. We also observed McCormack headquarters in some cities and towns outside of Boston. Massachusetts has 351 cities and towns, 48 with a population in excess of 25,000, i.e., large clusters of voters. Most McCormack headquarters were located in formerly vacant stores and were small and inexpensive — renting for perhaps $70 to $90 per month. Headquarters in large cities, however, customarily rent for substantially more. If it is assumed that McCormack or his supporters rented at least ten headquarters in the Commonwealth — a very small number for a major candidate — and that they were open from June 15 to mid-September, or if McCormack committees were provided with headquarters rent-free for this period, and if it is assumed that the average rental per headquarters was $70 per month (we noted previously that McCormack's treasurers reported two payments of $137.00 for Springfield headquarters) then McCormack would have spent about $2,100 for rent or been given contributions in kind (rent-free space) worth this amount. Contributions in kind are supposed to be reported. McCormack's treasurers reported no contributions in kind.

Some may dispute our estimate. It is necessarily speculative. We did not count the number of McCormack headquarters throughout the state. However, McCormack's campaign manager told us that Democratic candidates for major office who are well financed usually try to have one headquarters per ward in all the large Democratic cities of Massachusetts. Included in this category were Boston, Springfield, Worcester, Lawrence, Lowell, Cambridge, Fall River, Brockton, New Bedford, and Quincy, which together have ninety-six wards. To his knowledge no candidate succeeded in establishing headquarters in all ninety-six wards, but this was the customary goal. He also remarked that attempts are also customarily made in Massachusetts to set up at least one headquarters in all other cities with populations in excess of 25,000. To assume that McCormack had ten headquarters is therefore to assume that he had forty to sixty headquarters less than what a candidate would have who mounted a major effort.

Like other candidates, McCormack probably supplied every headquarters with telephone equipment, electricity, water, desks, chairs, typewriters, wastebaskets, janitorial service, and filing cabinets. Almost every headquarters we have ever seen also has numerous signs and displays — often hand painted, i.e., expensive —

streamers, posters, and blowups of photographs. And McCormack did have these. For example, we know of at least one eight-panel display for windows he used. These must be built to specification, hand painted and constructed. One such display costs about $500. McCormack headquarters also contained about fifty 40 × 50 inch photographic blowups, which cost about $10 each.

According to our analysis, McCormack's payments for electricity ($468.63) under "office" exceed payments specifically reported as rent although rent is ordinarily significantly more costly than electricity. It is interesting to note that McCormack's treasurers reported payments to electric companies only in Boston, although he had headquarters outside of Boston. Either no electricity was utilized for McCormack outside of Boston, or electric bills were paid by supporters — a contribution in kind — and not reported as such. McCormack supporters did report payments to the telephone company in Quincy, Taunton, Boston, and Falmouth.

McCormack treasurers reported $2,269.85 to firms that specialize in office equipment and/or typewriter rentals. One McCormack treasurer reported a liability of $912.30 to Royal McBee, which rents typewriters. We could find no reported payment for this liability. According to our analysis, $2,675 was paid to a firm that specializes in hand-painted signs and displays and about $5,-800 to firms that specialize in billboards. For $5,800 a candidate could rent about nine large billboards in good locations for one month.

Although McCormack treasurers reported about $2,500 for signs and displays and about $5,800 to firms that specialize in billboards, McCormack had numerous signs and displays in addition to those used in headquarters and very substantial "transit" advertising — in subways, in streetcars, and in buses. For example, he had, from mid-August to mid-September, "three-sheets" in dozens of subways and about one thousand 11 × 28 "car cards" for use in transit vehicles throughout the state. These two items, in the quantity purchased by McCormack, cost about $3,000, merely for the space. He also had to pay for the

design and printing of "sheets" with large halftones — we estimate about 200 to 250 such — and for the design and printing
of his 11 × 28 car cards (Dayglo and large halftone) — the production and printing for such items purchased in approximately
the amounts purchased by McCormack costs about $4,000 to
$4,500.

McCormack also purchased about 1500 or 2000 "one-sheet
posters" in three colors with Dayglo and large halftone. He had
to pay for layout, design, photo lettering, prints, pasteup, and
mechanical for these "one-sheets." The total expenditure for an
item of this kind in the amount used by McCormack would be
about $1,500.

McCormack also purchased a substantial number — perhaps 1500 to 2000 — green and white telephone posters. The
cost for design and printing this number of posters would be
about $200 to $300. McCormack also purchased hand painted
auto signs and other hand painted signs which were used in the
Bunker Hill Day parade (June 17) and on July 4.

We now consider payments reported by McCormack treasurers as "other" (number 9 in the Secretary of State's report
form). The sum in this category is $34,521.40, roughly 44 per
cent of total reported payments. The specific purpose of payments reported as "other" as far as we could determine is presented below. Payments to persons or firms we could not identify are listed as "unidentified."

Total Reported Payments of McCormack
Committees Categorized as "Other"

J. D. Pratt (advertising)	$ 3,300.00
Bernard Ostreicher (advertising agency)	6,337.00
Joseph Purcell (public relations firm)	6,000.00
Ingalls Associates (advertising agency)	10,688.08
Unidentified	3,954.18
Postage	2,043.04
Donations	538.50
Bank charges	505.00

Supplies and equipment	470.72
Headquarters rent	274.40
Stationery	132.08
Television and radio	125.00
Photographs	103.40
Transportation	50.00
	$34,521.40

In addition to the $10,688.08 paid to Ingalls Associates under "other," McCormack's treasurer reported payment of $6,572.20 to Ingalls Associates with the notation "television and radio," so that a total of $17,260.28 was reported paid to this firm.

McCormack, and several other candidates, employed advertising agencies to arrange for the production of newspaper, television, radio, and outdoor advertising copy, for the purchase of television and radio time and newspaper space, and for the production and purchase of bumper stickers, envelopes, letterheads, "throwaways," etc. Suppliers of goods and services in Massachusetts usually bill the candidate's advertising agencies rather than the candidate himself or one of the committees. As we noted, several candidates, including McCormack, reported substantial payments in a few large lump sums to their advertising agencies, which then paid numerous suppliers. The Secretary of State, Kevin White, permitted candidates and their treasurers to follow this practice throughout the campaign. We believe their actions and his administrative decision ran counter to the spirit of the law and greatly lessened its utility to the public.

In addition to the $17,260.28 paid to Ingalls Associates, committees organized to solicit contributions and make payments for Edward McCormack used the services of another Boston advertising agency, Bernard F. Ostreicher and of Joseph Purcell, who we understand is a public relations man, and J. D. Pratt. Payments of $6,337 to Bernard Ostreicher, $6,000 to Joseph Purcell, and $3,300 to J. D. Pratt were reported, bringing payments to advertising agencies and public relations counsel, therefore, as far as we could determine to $32,897.28. Of this, 15 per cent, or about $4,933, probably went to these firms as their commissions, leaving about $27,964 available to them for payment to firms and individuals that supplied McCormack committees with goods and services. All payments to Ingalls Associates, Bernard Ostreicher, and Joseph Purcell were listed as "other" with the exception of the payment to Ingalls Associates of $6,572.20 for "television and radio." Outside of this one amount we cannot determine from the McCormack reports to whom these firms disbursed funds. The bulk of their payments probably went to television and radio stations, newspapers, manufacturers of novelties, transit advertising companies, and printers, since McCormack treasurers reported very few payments of any size directly to such firms.

It is possible to determine with a high degree of accuracy the amounts candidates must have been billed for three goods and services for which substantial sums are customarily spent by candidates in Massachusetts: television time, radio time, and newspaper space. Television and radio station rates are public, and monitoring will reveal the amounts of time purchased by candidates. Newspaper rates are also available, and the space bought by candidates may be computed.

Examination of space used by McCormack committees in newspapers indicates an expenditure of about $14,000. A few examples will suffice. On Sunday, August 19, 1962, the Independent Citizens Committee for McCormack for U.S. Senator placed an advertisement in the *New York Times* "Review of the Week" — five columns of two hundred lines per column, or a total of a thousand lines. At $3.02 per line — the public rate — the space would have cost $3,020, and art work (sketches and typographical layout) also had to be paid for. On September 13, 1962 (and/or 14), this committee purchased ads in the following newspapers: the *Boston Herald-Traveler* ($3,150), the *Boston Globe* ($1,800), the *Springfield Daily News and Union* ($450), and the *Berkshire Eagle* ($162). During the course of the campaign it also bought space in the *Boston Record-American* which cost, at 1962 rates, about $3,000.

The records of television stations indicate that television time cost McCormack committees about $6,900. This sum includes, as far as we can determine, almost all of McCormack's production charges. He used no documentary films of the traditional sort, although he did buy a few videotapes. According to our analysis he purchased 120 minutes of television time: for example, five minutes on WBZ-TV Boston on June 28, 1962, at a cost of about $730; five minutes on WBZ-TV Boston on August 8, 1962, at a cost of about $580; five minutes on the same station on September 17 and five minutes on June 30, 1962, each at a cost of about $500; and five minutes on WWLP-TV Springfield on September 17, 1962, for about $190.

McCormack's television budget was very small in comparison to that of other senatorial and gubernatorial candidates, primarily because he purchased relatively little time and no documentary films, which usually cost about $1,000 per projected minute. His budget for radio was also small compared to what some of the other candidates spent. Analysis of thirteen stations indicated that McCormack committees paid about $2,500 for radio time, $1,250 of which was for time on WMEX Boston (the Jerry Williams Show).

Although our review of television and radio time and production charges indicates that they were billed a total of about $9,400, McCormack treasurers reported payments of $6,632.52 specifically classified as "television and radio" (number one on the Secretary of State's report form). Almost all ($6,572.20) of the payments so earmarked were reported paid to Ingalls Associates.

Our analysis of newspapers throughout Massachusetts and New York State indicates that McCormack committees were billed about $14,000 for space. We do not know the costs of preparing advertisements. As already noted, $579.82 was tagged "newspapers" (number 2 in the Secretary of State's report form). If our analysis of McCormack newspaper costs is correct, about $13,400 for McCormack's newspaper advertising was not accounted for as such. We understand that the amount reported paid to Bernard Ostreicher ($6,337) was allocated to payments to the *New York Times* and some other newspapers.

We have now accounted for about $23,400 (television and

radio time and production charges plus newspapers) that we believe was billed to McCormack committees. McCormack's treasurers reported $7,212.34 specifically classified for these purposes. We pointed out that Ingalls Associates, Bernard Ostreicher, Joseph Purcell, and J. D. Pratt had about $27,964 in McCormack money (after commissions) to pay McCormack bills. If these three agencies paid every one of McCormack's television, radio, and newspaper bills, they had about $4,500 left to pay for dozens of other costly goods and services such as printed materials, including bumper strips and leaflets, purchased by McCormack committees and seen by us, hundreds of delegates, and thousands of voters — and for which McCormack treasurers reported nothing, or very small amounts.

McCormack treasurers, for example, reported total payments of $731.64 specified as "printing" (number 4 in the Secretary of State's report form). If McCormack did spend several thousands of dollars for printing (he purchased substantial amounts of bumper stickers, handouts, brochures, letterheads, envelopes, etc.) someone had to pay the bills. Ingalls Associates, Bernard Ostreicher, J. D. Pratt, and Joseph Purcell could only have paid $4,500 for printing if they utilized McCormack money to pay for McCormack television, radio, and newspapers. If they paid the printing bills, on the other hand, and the bills for novelties, and for catering, or any other groups of bills amounting to about $28,000, they could not have paid the bills for television, radio, and newspapers, or any other bills, because they had only about $28,000 in McCormack money.

For $731.64 a candidate in 1962 could purchase and mail (at the bulk rate of 2$\frac{7}{8}$¢) about 5,000 printed copies of a four-page letter in two colors (envelopes and reply cards included). McCormack did purchase approximately this number of copies of the four-page letter written by Professor Mark DeWolfe Howe which we quoted in Chapter 1, and they were mailed to faculty members of colleges and universities throughout the Commonwealth of Massachusetts. Obviously, however, printed materials in addition to Professor Howe's letter were sent out. One McCormack aide, for example, informed us that over 500,000

"Qualified Candidate" brochures had been bought, which, as noted previously, listed numerous McCormack "qualifications" in one column and one Kennedy "qualification" ("Brother of the President") in the other column. Half a million brochures is by no means an unusually large number for a major Massachusetts campaign. Printers to whom copies of this brochure (two colors, 70 pound stock) were shown estimated that the cost for one half million brochures (production costs included) would be about $5,000. This sum for this one piece amounts to almost 6 per cent of McCormack's total reported expenditures, and exceeds the amount his treasurers reported specifically for printing by about $4,200. McCormack aides, familiar with the candidate's advertising budget, also informed us that McCormack purchased about 125,000 bumper strips, which is quite a small number for a major candidate. Bumper strips of the type purchased by McCormack cost, in large lots, about 4¢ apiece so that 125,000 would cost about $5,000; i.e., about 6 per cent of the total amout reported by McCormack treasurers.

McCormack, of course, purchased many other printed materials in addition to his "qualified candidate" brochures and bumper strips; i.e., envelopes, letterheads, press kits for newsmen at the convention, delegates' newsclips, convention posters, several thousand copies of a convention newspaper, several thousand palm cards, news releases, and news release envelopes. Printed materials are always a major item in every large campaign. Lodge's treasurer, for example, reported payments of $38,372.07 for "printing." The Hughes' campaign, which was a minuscule effort in comparison to those mounted by every other contender, somehow managed to spend $12,076.38 for printing. In 1964, Endicott Peabody, according to persons associated with his campaign, mounted one of the largest primary campaigns in Massachusetts history, and spent about $100,000 on printed materials.

McCormack, of course, also purchased envelopes, letterheads, press kits for newsmen at the convention, delegates' newsclips, convention posters, several thousand copies of a convention newspaper, and several thousand handout cards. Printed materials are almost always one of the most costly items in the campaign budget. Kennedy treasurers, for example, reported payments of $1,791.71 specified as "printing" (number 4 on the Secretary of State's report form) and Kennedy, as we will demonstrate, was a major user of printed materials.

McCormack committees, however, bought many other goods and services in addition to printed materials, for which either nothing or very small payments, frequently classified as "office," were listed. They did report payments of $34,521.40 classified as "other," but we have already accounted for about 75 per cent of these, since they were paid to Ingalls Associates, Bernard Ostreicher, J. D. Pratt, and Joseph Purcell. One of the best ways to examine the goods and services (other than "printing") purchased by McCormack is to analyze his operation before and during the Democratic State Convention. According to our analysis, of all payments ($78,765.68) reported by McCormack committees, $31,-505.37 were reported for the period preceding July 31, 1962. The state convention was held on June 8, 1962, so that this $31,505.37 covers the cost of campaigning for about two months prior to the convention, costs incurred at the convention, and costs incurred for about seven additional weeks of campaigning for the primary — that is, costs incurred from the time McCormack began to campaign to July 31, 1962.

McCormack's reported payments to July 31, 1962, are about the same as those reported by George Lodge and the Republican State Committee solely for public opinion polls. Endicott Peabody's treasurer reported half as much in production costs for one fifteen-minute documentary film, as McCormack's treasurer reported for all goods and services through July 31.

The law regulating campaign expenditures does permit payments prior to July 31 of an election year to be made in cash — although all such expenditures must be reported. This is one of the weakest provisions of the law because it is impossible to validate with any degree of accuracy the flow of cash as opposed to payments.

The contest between Kennedy and McCormack for the convention endorsement was, according to veteran political observers, the most bitter and certainly one of the most costly in memory. Newspaper reporters from out of state and correspondents for numerous national magazines frequently remarked on the hostility vented by campaign aides both publicly and in private, and were deeply impressed by the scope and skill of the Kennedy operation. In contrast they were impressed by the amateurish character of McCormack's campaign. The candidates campaigned seriously — and therefore were spending money — for three or four months prior to the convention. Since McCormack opened headquarters during this period, he had to pay for telephones, office equipment, electricity, stationery, travel expenses, rent, postage, and other goods and services. He also had a small paid staff. Large amounts of McCormack novelties, communications equipment, and advertising were in full public view at the convention — streamers, buttons, signs, sashes, pins, displays, metal lapel tabs, hats, balloons, walkie-talkies, sound trucks, press kits, and banners, for example.

The average voter and perhaps many delegates do not realize just how much these specialized convention items cost. The type of sashes customarily seen at conventions and purchased by candidates in lots of 100 cost 60¢ apiece in Massachusetts in 1962, and ribbons, which candidates often purchase in lots of 1,000, cost $90 per thousand. McCormack sashes and ribbons were much in evidence at the convention. Promotional pens of the type used by McCormack — colored barrel with a gold tip and a gold imprint — are generally bought in lots of 10,000 and cost 9¢ apiece. One order of 10,000 would therefore cost $900 or slightly more than 1 per cent of McCormack's total reported payments for all goods and services for the entire campaign. Candidates for major office in Massachusetts rarely purchase less than 15,000 pens and many buy between 30,000 and 40,000. Three-inch-round buttons of the type used by McCormack usually cost about $100 per lot in lots of 1,000, and very few candidates purchase less than 3,000. Metal tabs for lapels of the type used by McCormack (two colors) usually go in lots of 100,000 and cost about $400 per lot. Some candidates get 300,000 to 400,000.

The treasurers for George Lodge reported payments of approximately $10,000 for novelties like these and Lodge did not purchase an unusually large number of them. According to our analysis, McCormack's treasurer reported about $320 paid to firms that we could identify as novelty wholesalers.

McCormack, of course, also had to pay for hotel and motel rooms for himself and his staff, and telephone, and meeting rooms, and catering, and transportation to and from the Springfield convention, and sound trucks — all of which were in evidence and used for McCormack. By our analysis, McCormack treasurers reported about $200 to hotels and motels in the Springfield area at the time of the convention. McCormack headquarters were established in several rooms in the Sheraton-Kimball Hotel in Springfield, and several members of the McCormack staff were lodged there. McCormack's treasurers, as far as we can determine, reported no payments to this hotel.

McCormack treasurers reported expenditures of $78,765.68 for the 1962 campaign. To give this report some perspective, we note that Laurence Curtis, who like McCormack was defeated in a senatorial primary, reported payments of $70,128.21 to one direct mail house.

*   *   *

Let us look now at the reported expenditures of various Kennedy committees. We noted previously that the total amount of checks drawn on Kennedy's depository bank was $421,442.22. Kennedy's treasurers classified their payments as follows:

Reported Expenditures of All Kennedy Committees

Television and radio	$ 14,139.93
Newspapers	16,851.21
Meetings	422.74
Printing	1,791.77
Office	86,078.02
Travel	4,622.71
Signs and displays	13,151.45
Other	284,384.39
	$421,442.22

The $86,078.02 for "office" (number 5 in the Secretary of State's report form) represents approximately 20 per cent of Kennedy's total reported expenditures. We classified the specific purpose of expenditures reported for "office" as follows:

Salaries	$56,445.13
Telephone and telegraph	9,765.12
Bank charges	7,573.60
Rent	3,291.00
Postage	2,600.00
Stationery	2,119.31
Unidentified	2,438.53
Hotels and catering	810.65
Electricity	620.98
Supplies	413.70
	$86,078.02

The Edward M. Kennedy Committee for United States Senator reported expenditures of $284,384.39 as "other" (number 9 of Secretary of State's report form), approximately 67 per cent of Kennedy's total reported expenditures. We classified the specific purpose of these payments as follows:

John C. Dowd (advertising agency)	$203,583.65
Unidentified	18,029.06
Postage	15,600.00
Hotels and catering	10,811.21
Telegraph and telephone	11,870.45
Taxes and bank deposits	9,594.03
Joseph Napolitan (public relations)	7,791.06
Rent	3,150.00
Signs and displays	2,374.00
Utilities	789.51
Newspapers	672.42
Television and radio	119.00
	$284,384.39

The Kennedy primary campaign, in the opinion of many veteran newspapermen and professional politicians in Massachusetts, was the most carefully planned, expertly staffed, and lavish in memory. Funds were available to wage an ideal campaign. Kennedy recruited the very best political talent available and hired the most modern equipment. He employed one of America's more competent pollsters, who sampled public opinion in the state more than once. Prime newspaper and prime billboard space in Massachusetts and prime television and radio time in Massachusetts, New York, and Rhode Island were used to the extent he and his advisers thought necessary. There were 137 minutes, we estimate, of videotapes and documentaries on television. Kennedy's workers made more than 300,000 telephone calls, addressed hundreds of thousands of pieces of campaign literature, and distributed bumper stickers, metal tabs, pins, and display signs in vast quantity. The Kennedy organization conducted one of the largest and most successful registration and signature drives in the history of Massachusetts politics.

In addition to the expenditures reported to John C. Dowd (Kennedy's advertising agency) and noted in the previous table, additional sums were stated as paid to this company by other Kennedy committees, and still other payments to Dowd were reported as "office." Total checks drawn on Kennedy's depository bank to John C. Dowd, according to our analysis, amounted to $234,561.03. With the exception of $15,052.21 reported to Dowd and earmarked "newspapers" and $9,369.17 earmarked "signs and displays," all payments reported to John C. Dowd were categorized by Kennedy's treasurer as "other." It is, therefore, impossible to determine to whom Dowd paid the bulk of his money. By reporting very substantial sums to Dowd, classified as "other" and without notation of special purpose, Kennedy's treasurer succeeded, willfully or not, in preventing the public from knowing to whom and for what purpose approximately one-half of Kennedy's reported payments was allocated.

By careful examination of Kennedy's reported payments for "office" and "other" along with an attempt to identify as many payees as possible in all other categories, we were able to estimate the following reported expenses:

Telephone	$18,626.95
Western Union	2,958.22
Postage	18,200.00
Hotels and/or catering	14,311.00
Bank charges	14,547.77
Rent	6,702.77
Taxes (federal and state)	3,324.72
Photographs	1,275.50
Electricity	1,346.19
Stationery	3,628.43
Printers	1,164.46
Signs and displays	2,374.00

Kennedy headquarters were established in several large cities and suburbs in the Commonwealth and in many towns. On election day the Kennedy organization offered voters throughout the state transportation to the polls, and during the last week of the primary and general election campaigns Kennedy's agents rented searchlights and sound trucks for evening rallies, while Kennedy workers distributed eight-page, two-color tabloids. — "The Ted Kennedy Story" — to hundreds of thousands of households. One volunteer told us that he was provided with a toll credit card for telephone calls. Thousands of citizens were entertained at receptions with food and soft drink. Bands played at rallies. Airplanes were rented. Automobiles were rented. Office equipment was rented, and the voters of Massachusetts were reminded of Kennedy's candidacy on billboards throughout the state.

On several occasions, as we have noted, Kennedy's campaign manager intimated that money was not a scarce resource during the campaign; the organization was never forced to curtail any element of its operations for lack of funds. One Kennedy aide, however, commented on the scope and cost of the campaign, particularly "invisible" costs — that is, operations not readily seen by the public. While discussing his theory of timing during campaigns, he remarked: "On a state level you want to try to hit peaks and hold them, just before the election. Lavish expenditure of money, of course, an obvious expenditure has been criticized. Money being spent by staffs, people on a payroll, telephones, organizational equipment — this costs an awful lot of money. This isn't obvious."

In most really big contemporary campaigns a substantial portion of the candidate's budget is allocated to television time and the production of documentary films for showing on television. In our opinion, Kennedy probably spent more money for television time and the production of documentary films than for any other single item. The candidate who advertises extensively on television and utilizes documentary films incurs, in addition to television time charges, numerous production costs of which the general public is probably not aware. He must, for example, pay for the use of the television studios, the services of announcers, directors, and makeup men, slides, tape recordings, music, dubbing, sound booms, and teleprompters, besides the film crew, the film, and the editing. It costs approximately $1,000 to produce one finished minute of documentary film, and the price of fifteen minutes of prime time (8:30–8:45 P.M.) on a Boston television station may be as high as $1,200. The use of a Boston television studio for three hours, a boom man, videotape, and scenery, for example, costs approximately $640.

A well-made one-minute television "commercial" advertisement utilizing music, narration, and five or six actors, and produced in the New York area, usually costs between $15,000 and $25,000. The records of WBZ-TV Boston indicate that thirteen documentary films and/or videotapes were exhibited for Edward Kennedy on that station. The total showing time for eleven of the films is 127 minutes and 39 seconds, but the records of WBZ-TV do not indicate the length of the other two. Since six of the Kennedy films are five minutes in length, we will assume the other two films are also five minutes long. If this estimate is reasonable, the total length of Kennedy films or videotapes is 137 minutes and 39 seconds.

Two of the Kennedy films are rather elaborate documentaries showing the candidate in various sections of the Commonwealth talking to citizens about economic and political problems. Other films and videotapes show the candidate or his mother, wife, and sisters ("Coffee with the Kennedys"), or a prominent politician or group of professors, speaking on behalf of the candidate. This type of film is obviously much less expensive to produce than a documentary. The maximum cost, in a Boston television studio, for one edited minute of videotape is $300, the minimum is $150. Two films of the documentary type, *The Edward M. Kennedy Story* and *Kennedy, the Man for Massachusetts,* are fifteen and thirty minutes respectively in length. Assuming that these forty-five minutes of documentary film cost the customary $1,000 per projected minute to produce, Kennedy must have spent approximately $45,000 for them exclusive of the time charges billed to his committees by the several television stations on which they were shown. This does not seem an unreasonable surmise in view of the fact that Endicott Peabody reported a payment of $15,108 to Vision Associates of New York City for the preparation of a fifteen-minute documentary for showing on television.

Kennedy, of course, had to pay for the production of an additional ninety-two minutes of film, most of it probably on videotapes. If the films were videotaped in a studio and prints were made for several television stations at an average cost of $200 per projected minute — an average cost in a Boston station in 1962 — Kennedy would have spent an additional $18,400 for videotapes. On the basis of these estimates, Kennedy's documentary films and videotapes would have cost approximately $63,400.

We noted previously that a thirty-minute film of Kennedy's travels in Italy was made in 1961 and shown to Italo-American clubs in Massachusetts prior to and during the campaign. Kennedy supplied the film, a projector, and a projectionist to clubs that requested a showing. This film was obviously produced as propaganda for Kennedy's future campaigns. Since it was shown during the campaign one might argue that the outlay for making it should have been reported as campaign expenditure. But this is a moot point since the cost was incurred prior to the time Kennedy filed nomination papers. Three film makers estimated that a film of this type, shot in Italy, probably could not cost less than $12,000 and could have cost much more if many scenes were shot but not used, or if an American rather than an Italian crew were used. In our opinion this film probably is not a "campaign expenditure" and need not have been reported. We take note of it only because it is an extraordinary example of the dramatic pre-campaign buildup that is available to men of great wealth and to no others.

The records of the Federal Communications Commission reveal that Democratic candidates or their supporters purchased 985 minutes of television time for the Democratic primary campaign on Massachusetts channels.[19] According to our analysis, McCormack committees bought 120 minutes during the primary. Consequently, if our analysis is correct, Kennedy and Kennedy committees used 865 minutes, which is 345 minutes more than was taken by both the Republican contenders, Curtis and Lodge. The FCC records also show that during the 1962 general election campaign the Democratic candidate for senator and/or his supporters purchased 495 minutes, the Republican candidate and/or his supporters 234 minutes, and Stuart Hughes and/or his supporters 190 minutes. Kennedy and/or Kennedy committees therefore, by our analysis, bought 1,360 minutes of television time — more than all the other senatorial candidates as a group. The figures we cited, however, are only for time in Massachusetts. Kennedy and/or his committees also purchased we believe about 245 minutes of time on channels in Providence, Rhode Island (WPRO-TV and WJAR-TV), and in Albany, New York (WTEN-TV and WROB-TV). The total, then, according to our analysis of FCC reports, was about 1,600 minutes, about 26 ½ hours of television time, for Kennedy.

This, according to our analysis, amounts to approximately $60,000 worth of television time: for example, $12,525 of time (and a few production charges) from WHDH-TV of Boston, part of which was for programs on August 22, 1962 (10 minutes — $1,050); six five-minute programs the week of September 3, 1962 ($1,650); seven five-, ten-, and thirty-minute programs the week of September 10, 1962 ($2,340).

Kennedy committees purchased time on more than fifty Eng-

19 *Federal Communications Commission Report 1963*, Massachusetts television, p. 209.

lish language radio stations and on about twenty foreign language radio stations, at an estimated cost of about $29,000.

Kennedy committees, according to our estimate, purchased documentary films and videotapes ($63,400); according to media records they purchased television time (about $60,000), and radio time (about $29,000). The total amount for these goods and services is $152,400.

Various Kennedy committees reported payments of $14,139.93 as "television and radio" (number 1 in the Secretary of State's report form), of which $13,955.73 was reported to Pike Productions, of Newton, Massachusetts, a documentary film maker.

We assume that Kennedy's agency, John C. Dowd, paid some of Kennedy's television, radio, and documentary film charges. Checks to John C. Dowd in the amount of $234,561.03 were reported to the Secretary of State by the cashier of Kennedy's depository bank. Of this sum, $15,052.21 was earmarked "newspapers" and $9,369.17 was earmarked "signs and displays." The remaining payments to Dowd were classified as "other." It would appear, therefore, that Dowd would have $210,139.65 in Kennedy funds available to pay for television and radio time and production charges, or to take care of any other Kennedy costs. However, after Dowd received its 15 per cent commission on gross billings — the standard advertising agency commission — Dowd would have about $179,000 in Kennedy monies to disburse to television and radio stations, to documentary film producers, to whoever did the Kennedy videotaping, or to any other supplier. We estimated Kennedy television and radio costs to be about $152,400. Kennedy's treasurer reported $14,139.93 for "television and radio," which, if our estimate is correct, leaves an unpaid balance of about $138,260. If our estimates of television and radio costs are reasonable, and if Dowd paid the remaining $138,260, Dowd would have $40,740 left in Kennedy funds to pay for numerous goods and services normally purchased through an advertising agency, for which, as we will indicate, Kennedy treasurers reported small or no payments clearly designated for such purposes.

We turn now to the payments reported by Kennedy treasurers to newspapers and the cost of Kennedy newspaper advertising as revealed by an analysis of space purchased by Kennedy committees or Kennedy supporters. Various Lodge committees reported payments of $10,413.48 for newspapers. Hughes committees reported $16,149.74 in payments for newspaper advertising although Hughes was not a major candidate.

According to our analysis of space used and the standard rates per column inch, Kennedy committees spent approximately $19,000 for newspaper space: for example, about $5,500 for space in the *Boston Globe,* about $3,100 for space in the *Boston Record-American and Daily Advertiser,* and about $205 for space in the *Portuguese Daily News.*

Kennedy's treasurer reported payments of $16,851.21 for "newspapers" (number 2 in the Secretary of State's report form). Of this sum, $15,052.21 was reported to John C. Dowd, whose commission we assume was 15 per cent, or about $2,257. Dowd, therefore, actually had about $12,795 in Kennedy money to pay the newspapers.

In many large-scale campaigns the cost of outdoor advertising (billboards and transit advertising) is exceeded only by the cost of television, stationery and printing, and possibly salaries for staff. It would not be unusual for a major senatorial or gubernatorial candidate in Massachusetts to spend $20,000 to $35,000 for outdoor advertising solely in the Boston area. We noted previously that a large billboard, in a prime location in Boston, would cost $1,200 a month.

Our travels throughout the state during the campaign indicate that Kennedy committees purchased outdoor advertising in the Worcester, Fitchburg-Leominster, Palmer markets, and in the Boston, Brockton, Plymouth, Taunton, and Haverhill markets; also in the Lawrence and Lowell, Newbury, Merrimac, Amesbury, Salisbury, Newburyport, Ipswich, Rowley, and Gloucester markets; also in Springfield, Holyoke, Greenfield, Northampton, and Westfield, and in the New Bedford area. The number and location of Kennedy billboards suggest to us that they cost about $41,000 including agency commission fees. The Edward M. Kennedy Committee for Advertising reported payments of $9,369.17 to John C. Dowd specifically for "signs and displays." Another

$3,782.28 was reported by the Edward M. Kennedy Committee for United States Senator for "signs and displays." Total payments reported for "signs and displays" therefore amounted to $13,151.45 (number 7 in the Secretary of State's report form). Lodge's treasurers reported payments of $25,107.90 for this purpose.

We have dealt only with outdoor advertising (billboards). During the campaign Kennedy was also a major purchaser of window and interior signs for headquarters, signs for rallies and meetings, automobile signs, building signs, and signs for the convention. Of the $25,107.90 reported for Lodge signs and displays, about $3,000 can be identified as payment for signs other than billboards. Let us assume that Kennedy committees spent twice as much, $6,000, for signs, headquarter signs, convention signs, automobile signs, etc. Kennedy, we will suggest, had roughly sixty headquarters (twenty in Boston), all of which presumably had some signs or posters.

We shall look now at the cost of Kennedy printed materials and postage. Chapter 3 described the signature drive undertaken by the Kennedy organization after the convention. Kennedy's campaign manager reported that approximately 300,000 pledges of support were collected and that a thank-you note was sent to every person who was solicited: that means 300,000 envelopes (in three colors), and 300,000 letterheads (in three colors), mailed at the bulk rate of 2⅞¢ per letter. He also said, on September 1, that special mailings were sent to various ethnic groups, youth groups, the elderly, and labor groups — "about half a million" letters — that is, 500,000 envelopes, 500,000 letterheads, and 2⅞¢ postage per letter. During August the Kennedy organization also conducted a state-wide registration drive which resulted in an estimated 25,000 new voters. Carl Johnson, the Kennedy aide who directed the drive, estimated that 160,000 three-penny postcards were mailed to unregistered citizens throughout the state.[20]

C. R. Owens, of the *Boston Globe,* reported:

A voter registration is an expensive matter for an individual to undertake. Johnson's efforts were limited to twenty-one

[20] C. R. Owens, *Boston Globe,* August 27, 1962.

of the larger communities, yet it cost $4,800.00 for the post-
cards alone. Added to this would be the cost of printing, lights,
writing materials, etc. . . . Johnson is laying the groundwork
for a state-wide registration drive after the primary. Boston
will then be included, he said; the fall drive will be a whing
dinger, said Johnson.[21]

If we assume that the fall registration drive was no larger than the
August registration drive, the Kennedy organization would have
purchased additional postcards for $4,800, and the cost of both
drives therefore would have been $9,600 for postcards. This esti-
mate is, of course, minimal. Since Boston, we were told, was included in the second registration drive, it is highly likely that
substantially more than 160,000 postcards were mailed during the
fall drive.

Some idea of the number and size of Kennedy mailings may
be gleaned from the following description by a Kennedy aide:

... volunteer and paid workers have expanded to over a hundred, did nothing all day but bang out letters to different
people. . . . During the campaign, you'd get from three to four
letters in a seven-day week from Kennedy headquarters saying
everything from "Get down to a meeting right away in Suffolk
County" to "At six-fifteen and seven-fifteen or eight-fifteen,
three days from now, Rose Kennedy is going to be on television with tea." And thousands of things in between. These
were going on, day after day, all over the state. And each letter was red, white, and blue — addressed on the outside, said
Kennedy with the name of the headquarters, and inside a picture of the candidate — red, white, and blue — "He can do
more for Massachusetts," and the rest of the business . . . hundreds of thousands of people who signed . . . all followed by
personal letters. . . . Let us say, on an average mailing, there
were 50,000 people. . . .

As we have already noted, Kennedy's campaign manager estimated
on September 1, seventeen days before the primary election, that
"about half a million" letters had been mailed to special groups

21 *Ibid.*

and that about 300,000 additional letters had been sent to those who participated in the signature drive. Let us assume that no more than 700,000 letters were mailed between September 1 and election day, November 6, since we are making what we consider modest estimates. At the bulk rate (2⅞¢) the postage for 1,500,000 letters would have amounted to $43,125. To estimate the total cost of postage, however, we must add the $9,600 expended for postcards for two registration drives — and the total for postage comes to $52,725. Kennedy treasurers reported payments of $18,-200 earmarked "postage." An estimate of $52,725 for postage for a campaign as important to the Kennedys as this one was, is not, in our opinion, unreasonable, since postage, even at the bulk rate, costs more than twice what we estimate the stationery cost. Hughes, whose campaign was tiny in comparison to Kennedy's, reported $8,278 for postage. And Hughes had no convention fight and no primary fight.

Indeed, our estimate of the cost of postage may well be somewhat low, based as it is on the assumption that the Kennedy organization posted no first-class letters at 5¢ apiece.

A mailing of 1,500,000 letters means 1,500,000 envelopes and 1,500,000 letterheads. We noted that the Kennedy envelopes and letterheads were printed in three colors; the letterhead contained a photograph of the candidate. Three large stationery supply houses quoted the following prices for these items purchased in large lots: $590 per 100,000 envelopes (three colors) and $615 per 100,000 letterheads (three colors) — that is, about .6¢ per envelope and per letterhead, or about 1.2¢ for each letter. If Kennedy paid this amount and mailed 1,500,000 letters, the cost of stationery must have been about $18,000.

On October 30, 1962, Kennedy's campaign manager reported: "We're in the process now of distributing a tabloid which I believe we will distribute to almost all homes across the state." There were approximately 5,200,000 persons residing in Massachusetts in 1962. Let us assume, therefore, that there were approximately 1,500,000 households and that the Kennedy organization distributed only 1,000,000 copies. The tabloid Kennedy's campaign manager referred to, "The Edward M. Kennedy Story," contained eight pages and was printed in blue and black on very inexpensive white paper. Three printers estimated that 1,000,000 copies of this tabloid would cost in the vicinity of $20,000.

In addition to these pieces of literature the Kennedy organization distributed bumper stickers — we do not know how many — and numerous copies of a "throwaway," printed in three colors on glossy paper. McCormack probably paid about $4,500 for bumper strips — a very modest amount for this item for a major candidate. If Kennedy purchased three times as many — he campaigned about seven weeks longer than did McCormack — he would have spent approximately $13,500 for bumper strips. Mc-Cormack purchased, according to one of his aides, about 500,000 handouts in two colors, some 4 × 9 inches in size and some 8 × 11 inches. The former, according to printers, cost approximately $1\frac{3}{5}$¢ per brochure. McCormack's average unit cost was, we estimate, $1\frac{2}{5}$¢. We assume Kennedy bought at least three times the number of handouts McCormack did because his campaign was longer and because our observation of both campaigns leads us to believe that the McCormack campaign was modest by comparison.

Kennedy, however, must have paid more per handout than McCormack because Kennedy's were printed in three colors, Mc-Cormack's in two. The Kennedy handouts were also more than twice as large (11 × 17, or 187 square inches) as McCormack's, whose brochures were 36 square inches for the smaller size and 88 square inches for the larger. The McCormack brochures were printed on seventy pound coated stock while the Kennedy brochures were printed on eighty pound coated stock which is more expensive. Printers place the cost of 1,500,000 handouts of the type used by Kennedy at approximately $30,000.

Lodge's treasurers reported payments of $38,372.07 earmarked "printing" (number 4 in the Secretary of State's report form), Kennedy's treasurers $1,791.77. According to our analysis, Kennedy's treasurers reported payments of $3,628.43 to firms we could identify as stationery suppliers, and some of the money reported to John C. Dowd may have been used by Dowd to pay printers.

Public opinion polls of the Massachusetts electorate were taken for Kennedy prior to and during the campaign. We know neither the number of polls, the sample size, nor the cost. Several references to polls appeared in the press during the campaign, ostensibly based on "leaks" from Kennedy's aides, and Kennedy's campaign manager mentioned Kennedy polls during our interviews with him. A few months after the election, a Kennedy aide showed us some of the pollsters' reports, which revealed that the polls were thorough and extensive. We know that George Lodge and the Republican State Committee were billed $30,000 by the Opinion Research Corporation of Princeton, New Jersey, for three public opinion polls, two of which were based on 500 interviews taken in the respondents' homes. The third sample was interviewed by telephone. The telephone poll cost $2,500, the other polls $13,750 each. We know that some of the Kennedy polls were taken by a well-known firm not located in Massachusetts. Let us assume that Kennedy had only three large-scale polls at the same unit cost as Lodge's. Given this assumption, the cost would have been $41,250. Kennedy's treasurer reported no payments to any firm that we could identify as a public opinion specialist located in Massachusetts. However, he did report payments of $7,791.06 to Joseph Napolitan Associates of Springfield, Massachusetts, a public relations firm that, we understand, did some public opinion surveying via telephone.

We have not yet analyzed Kennedy costs for pins, metal lapel tabs, ribbons, buttons, streamers, sashes, and other novelties, travel (airplane and automobile), rental for headquarters, rental of office equipment, photographs, sound equipment, insurance, electricity, salaries, telephone, telegraph, withholding taxes, hotels and motels, catering services, bank charges, office supplies, and some advertising agency commission fees.

Let us discuss some of these costs. Massachusetts has 351 cities and towns. Thirty-five cities and thirteen towns have populations in excess of 25,000. A candidate for major office, for whom money is not a major problem and who faces a bitter primary fight, as did Kennedy, opens headquarters in cities, towns, and wards where substantial numbers of potential voters live.

A candidate who has large numbers of headquarters not only incurs substantial rentals but also substantial cost for the rental of office equipment, signs and displays, photographs, "blowups," insurance, utilities, and, in some cases, janitorial services. He must pay rent or be given space as a contribution in kind, and he must have typewriters, desks, file cabinets, mimeograph machines, water coolers, chairs, etc. As noted previously, Lodge's office manager reported that Lodge had between sixty-five and seventy headquarters. The Boston telephone company "Information" listed telephone numbers for twenty "Kennedy for Senator" headquarters in Boston alone.

A Kennedy aide reported that during the primary Kennedy had approximately seventy headquarters and that after the primary, when victory seemed assured, the number was reduced to about fifty-five. We will assume, therefore, that Kennedy had about sixty headquarters. Kennedy's treasurers reported payments of $5,250 for rent for his four-story main Boston headquarters on Tremont Street. If we assume that Kennedy paid an average monthly rental of $90 for each of his other headquarters — or, what is more probable, received headquarters space rent free, i.e., as a contribution in kind — and if we assume that these headquarters were open for three months, then the cost of Kennedy headquarters, or the value of contributions in kind, would have been $16,200 above and beyond the reported cost ($5,250) of the main Boston headquarters.

Furthermore, telephones were undoubtedly installed in every Kennedy headquarters, telephone calls were made, electricity and water were utilized, signs, displays, and photographs were exhibited, and typewriters and other office equipment were on hand. Costs for all this must have been considerable. For example, if the Kennedy organization rented only 120 typewriters for three and one-half months — two typewriters per headquarters — (non-electric typewriters rented in Massachusetts in 1962 for approximately $4.25 per month if large numbers were rented), the cost would have amounted to about $1,785. And there were desks, chairs, tables, filing cabinets, wastebaskets, and office supplies, and electricity, water coolers, and insurance, besides. Let us assume that the average cost per month per headquarters for insurance and all office equipment exclusive of typewriters was $30 and that Kennedy purchased these items for sixty headquarters for three months. The cost would have been $5,400.

Our estimates, made we think conservatively, for only nine of the many items purchased for Kennedy total $422,255.

Television and radio	$152,400
Newspaper advertising	19,000
Postage	52,725
Billboards, signs and displays	47,000
Stationery	18,000
Tabloid	20,000
Bumper stickers and handouts	43,500
Public opinion polls	41,250
Headquarters rent and equipment	28,380

Kennedy's total reported expenditures for all goods and services were $421,442.22. In making estimates of this kind — some of which are speculative — we may easily have over- or underestimated. However, we have not yet considered many other expenditures which candidates must make and which Kennedy made. Nor have we examined some other goods and services for which Kennedy treasurers reported substantial sums. For instance, Kennedy treasurers reported payments of $18,626.95 to various telephone companies and $2,958.22 to Western Union.

We turn now to the cost of salaries for the Kennedy staff. The Kennedy campaign was directed from a four-story headquarters on Tremont Street in Boston. The first floor was occupied by a press secretary and volunteer workers who stuffed and addressed envelopes and distributed bumper stickers and Kennedy literature. The remaining floors contained offices for the men who directed the campaign and space for several secretaries. It is impossible for us to estimate the number of secretaries employed in Kennedy headquarters throughout the state. It is also impossible for us to determine how many secretaries were salaried and how many were unpaid volunteers. One Kennedy aide estimated that approxi-

280 | KENNEDY CAMPAIGNING

mately thirty girls "making from $75, $80, $85, $100 a week, depending on their jobs" were employed at the Boston headquarters.
He also suggested that "maybe another five or six that are administrative types, who make a little bit more money" were also
employed there. The author, who visited Kennedy headquarters
on several occasions, estimates that approximately half this number of secretaries were employed at the main Boston headquarters.

The Kennedy reports from August to November contain repeated payments to several individuals which are specified as
"office" (number 5 in the Secretary of State's report form). These
payments are, we assume, for salaries for office personnel hired on
a more or less "permanent" basis, and probably working in the
Boston headquarters, since the addresses of most of them are in
Boston or in the vicinity of Boston. We recognize several names
of office employees that appear in Kennedy reports. According to
these reports, most Kennedy employees received $70 to $90 a week.
Kennedy's press secretary, the highest-salaried employee at the
Boston headquarters according to Kennedy reports, was paid
$389.43 semi-monthly. Approximately sixteen persons are listed
in the reports as receiving regular payments throughout the campaign. We became familiar with four who occupied important
full-time positions in the Kennedy organization for whom no
salaries were reported. These men said that they were unpaid volunteers. The treasurer of the Edward M. Kennedy Committee for
United States Senator reported the following payments, as "office," which we believe were for salaries:

Prior to July 31, 1962	$20,463.50
August 1–August 15	4,492.30
August 15–August 30	4,023.72
September 1–September 15	4,128.40
September 15–September 30	3,645.48
October 1–October 15	4,061.16
October 15–October 30	8,126.27
November 1–November 15	2,949.10
November 15–November 30	4,045.15
December 1–December 15	160.01
December 15–December 30	151.74

January 1–January 15 (1963)   130.09
January 15–January 30   68.21
                                _____
                               $56,445.13

Kennedy's treasurer also reported payment of $3,324.72 for withholding taxes and payments of $14,547.77 to his depository bank, as bank charges.

We turn now to the cost of the Kennedy campaign for the convention endorsement, which was one of Kennedy's major efforts. We have, of course, already analyzed some of the goods and services — printed materials, for example — a number of which were purchased for the June convention. We noted previously when analyzing McCormack's reported payments for the convention that our knowledge of convention costs is fragmentary because the law permits candidates to pay for goods and services purchased prior to July 31 by cash rather than campaign check. However, the Kennedy operation in preparation for and at the convention was impressive. Kennedy, for example, visited almost all the delegates, held numerous meetings, breakfasts, brunches, and dinners with delegates during April, May, and June, and rented many hotel and motel rooms in the Springfield area during the convention. He also rented two, two-place telephone switchboards at Springfield with trunk lines to neighboring hotels and motels. His agents on the floor were equipped with walkie-talkies. No candidate in modern Massachusetts politics had available to him the kind of communications network that was set up for Kennedy. Kennedy novelties — banners, signs, pins, buttons, streamers, lapel tabs, and hats — were much in evidence. The main Kennedy headquarters in Boston was operating at full capacity by May, and substantial amounts of printed material were mailed and distributed during May and June. The Kennedy effort at the convention, according to literally every newspaperman and professional politician, was the most extensive, best equipped, and well organized in memory. One Kennedy aide — a university professor, referring to the 1960 national nominating convention — described the Kennedy effort in Springfield as "a little Los Angeles." McCormack men, however, who were bitter, compared the Kennedy machine to the Wehrmacht.

McCormack committees, as we noted, reported expenditures of $31,505.37 to July 31. Various Kennedy committees reported expenditures of $50,224.48 and zero liabilities to July 31. Lodge committees reported expenditures of $70,788.54 to July 31. Expenses to this date cover about two months of campaigning prior to the convention, activities at the convention, and about seven weeks of campaigning for the primary. Included in the Kennedy reports were payments of $3,412.13 for hotels and motels, most of which were in the Springfield area, $1,742.50 for signs and displays, $422.74 for meetings, $1,703.46 for travel, zero for catering, and $30,069.64 for "office" of which $20,463.50 was for salaries. In other words, exclusive of salaries, Kennedy's treasurers reported payments of about $30,000 for all goods and services for approximately two months of campaigning for delegate support and two months of campaigning for the support of registered Democrats who might vote in the primary.

For the amount Kennedy's treasurers reported for "signs and displays" ($1,742.50) a candidate could purchase two billboards for one month, and not in the best location. For the amount Kennedy's treasurers reported for "meetings" ($422.74) a candidate could rent one meeting room in a good hotel in Boston for one afternoon and serve lunch to perhaps 100 ladies. The Kennedy organization sponsored, during the first seven weeks of primary campaigning, several such meetings in many cities throughout the state.

Kennedy, as noted, personally visited more than 1,000 delegates all over the state prior to the convention, and from June 8 (the date of the convention) to July 31 (the termination of the period for which we are analyzing Kennedy payments at this point) the candidate again traveled, several times, across the state — most of the time by car, on occasion by rented airplane. Kennedy aides also traveled throughout the Commonwealth during this time. Kennedy's treasurer reported payments of $1,703.46 for "travel" through July 31, or about $120 per week for travel expenses for fourteen weeks.

During this period the Kennedy organization held several meetings throughout the state at which food was served. Kennedy's treasurers reported no payments to firms we could identify as caterers, although some of the Kennedy reported payments to hotels and motels ($3,412.13) may have included payment for catering. However, since almost all payments reported to hotels and motels through July 31 were to payees in the Springfield area, it seems unlikely that they included payment for catering in other cities.

Before analyzing briefly Kennedy reported payments for novelties, we should note that novelties of various kinds — sashes, ribbons, buttons, streamers, tie clasps, hats, ribbon badges, plastic badges, and promotional pens — although not a major cost of campaigning may well consume several thousand dollars. Kennedy, in our opinion, was a major purchaser of novelties, yet whereas Lodge's treasurer reported approximately $10,000 for novelties, we were able to identify Kennedy payments of only about $750 to firms that produce or wholesale novelties. If Kennedy spent only 25 per cent more than Lodge for similar items, they would have cost him approximately $12,500.

Throughout this chapter we have not even attempted to deal with many additional goods and services that are customarily purchased for major candidates in Massachusetts: printing of 24-sheets in three colors for billboards, painted billboards, transit advertising (space and printing), placards, palm cards, cards to distribute at the polls, photographs, photograph blowups for headquarters, airplane rentals, automobile rentals, sound equipment for rallies, sound recordings, searchlights for rallies, newsclip services, and music, to name a few. We observed all of these during the campaign and we know that the cost of some of them is not insubstantial.

*   *   *

We have attempted to suggest something about the actual costs of this campaign and the way the amended reporting statute was complied with by the representatives of the McCormack and Kennedy organizations. Those who favored revision of the law hoped that, if this information were made public during the campaign and if it were widely publicized in the press, the electorate would become aware not only of the high cost of campaigning but also of the true sources of campaign contributions.[22] Advocates of the bill assumed that candidates would respond to a more sophisticated and informed public by spending less money or by fully disclosing contributions and expenditures. They also assumed that candidates would become more wary of accepting substantial contributions made solely for the purpose of influencing future public policy. The reformers hoped, moreover, that if the cost of campaigning were lowered, qualified men of modest means, who are now unable to run for public office, might successfully compete. In their opinion, an effective law which limited the amounts that any individual could contribute would force candidates to finance campaigns with a large number of small contributions rather than a small number of large contributions — as is now the case in most campaigns. This, in turn, would lessen the influence of a few large contributors and thus help democratize the financing of campaigns and the purchasing of political influence.

There is no reason to believe that their assumptions were realistic or their hopes fulfilled.

[22] In 1962 the Secretary of State made copies available to the press room in the State House, and several newspapers in the Commonwealth gave prominent coverage to the reports although none of them, to our knowledge, made a serious effort, while the campaign was in progress, to investigate the accuracy of the reports. During the later stages of the campaign the reports were, in most cases, relegated to the back pages.

CHAPTER 6 ☒ *The Political Campaign as Pseudo Event*

My that's a beautiful baby you have there! Oh, that's nothing — you should see his photograph.

— from Daniel Boorstin's *Image*

THE PARTY CAUCUS, the nominating convention, and the political campaign have fascinated journalists in this country since Federalists and Jeffersonians first contested for public place. In terms of human interest and intrigue, few events in American history equal the struggle of brilliant and tempestuous men, of fools, knaves, and nonentities competing for the favor of party leaders, delegates, and voters. The cabal of the caucus, the quid pro quo of the power brokers of the convention, the hoopla, the vulgarity, the appeal to idealism and civic virtue, to callous self-interest and blind prejudice, and the sublimated and symbolic violence of the campaign — all this is high drama occasionally tragic, frequently comic, but certainly the stuff of great journalism.

Political conventions and campaigns have also been a prime concern of historians. True insight into our national history depends, in part, on understanding how political power is achieved and who can achieve it. Who wins and who loses elections, and how, profoundly affects the direction of public policy and the quality of national life. Our major parties frequently advocate similar doctrine, but during much of our history they have proposed somewhat different versions of what constitutes the good society and different means for achieving it. Rhetoric of left- and right-wing critics of American politics notwithstanding, the candidates nominated by the parties always differ — in intelligence, in integrity, and in imagination. With some exceptions, what one did another would not have done.

Although our journalists and historians have given us a sizable body of reportage and history dealing with candidates, issues, and strategies, most of their writing is more descriptive than analytic. Our understanding of the process by which political power is achieved, however, has been enriched in recent years by the application of several new and exacting research techniques to the study of the political process. The development of reliable methods for sampling and probing public opinion and advances in computer technology, game theory, systems analysis, and statistics, have made it possible for scholars to analyze voting behavior and political campaigning with a precision and refinement not available to journalists and historians of the past.

A substantial amount of information has now been collected by pollsters and by political scientists, who have analyzed the financing of campaigns, the power structure of nominating conventions, the impact of televised debates between candidates, and the formulation and execution of political strategy. In many instances the data are so extensive and detailed that the pollster, for example, can predict more accurately how an undecided or cross-pressured citizen will vote than can the citizen himself. The astute game theorist can frequently predict the utility of alternate strategies more accurately than can the professional politician, who traditionally relies on arcane rules of thumb. These developments are reflected in the use of the professional pollster and communications expert by the more affluent and sophisticated candidate.

Some students of political behavior, however, are disturbed by much of the data. Some now have serious doubts about the political sophistication, competence, and activism of the American voter and his ability to make rational choices. Some are concerned about the low level of campaign discussion — the mud-slinging, the slander, the libel — and the failure of most candidates to educate the public during campaigns. Few candidates will discuss issues when they and their managers decide that such discussion might lose votes. The public, in consequence, is usually poorly informed by the election process. Moreover, on the advice of pollsters, candidates may take public positions on issues that they privately disagree with and perhaps even believe to be harmful to the commonweal. The successful candidate is frequently the one who seeks to become a mirror image of the electorate, a hollow shell who stifles his own views, a chameleon whose coloration changes with each new public opinion poll, a moral weasel who passively follows rather than actively leads.

Some scholars have commented that most candidates "talk past" each other rather than engage in meaningful debate and dialectic. Other students of campaigning have noted the subtle and not so subtle appeals to race and religious prejudice and to ethnicity that characterize many American campaigns. Pollsters now agree that John Kennedy's Catholicism was among the most significant variables in the 1960 campaign. Millions of anti-Catholic and scurrilous pieces of literature were distributed during that election. The findings of various committees concerned with fair campaign practices indicate that such distribution is not at all uncommon, particularly in state and local elections.

Some of those who have studied the problem of campaign finance are troubled by the fact that the bulk of the funds raised to wage most campaigns is contributed by a relatively small number of donors, many of whom have a direct and personal stake in the outcome of the campaign, a fact particularly well documented in municipal and state elections where contractors, real estate operators, and others who do business with city and state governments traditionally give large sums. Alexander Heard, the leading authority in the field of campaign finance, has estimated that approximately 15 per cent of all monies contributed to candidates come from members of the underworld. A big campaign fund does not always guarantee election, but the absence of support from party "fat cats" almost always guarantees defeat. Seats in Congress are, in this respect, up for sale. Is it surprising that very wealthy men can establish residences in congressional districts or states, raise and spend very substantial amounts of family and friends' money, and get elected?

Numerous professional politicians and political scientists know that men of modest means, regardless of their qualifications, frequently can no longer compete for major office in this country. The nation is therefore denied the services of first-rate men who simply cannot afford to run, while it is offered the services of wealthy candidates who may or may not be second-rate.

Pollsters, both professional and academic, have now concluded that often the personality, physical characteristics, style, ethnic background, social position, and accent of the candidate are far more significant to many voters than his experience, intelligence, or position on issues. Some of the collected evidence indicates that since the advent of television American political campaigns have become more personality and less issue oriented, which is perhaps, another way of suggesting that less meaningful and relevant criteria of selection may be superseding more relevant and meaningful criteria of selection. However, according to journalistic accounts of American campaigns in the eighteenth and nineteenth centuries, and innumerable historical studies, issues have frequently played a minor role and many elections have been little more than personality and beauty contests or demonstrations of blind party loyalty. The elevation to the Presidency of several ex-generals and military heroes had little or nothing to do with their stands on issues. McKinley, of course, was advised to sit at home on his front porch during the campaign.

These are a few aspects of our system of nomination and election which have disturbed some students of political campaigning. Much of the data gathered by scholars, however, suggests that at times the system works and works fairly well. Men of extraordinary competence and integrity have been elected and reelected to high office — which after all is the ultimate test — and an occasional candidate has raised and discussed critical issues even when he suspected that such discussion might lose votes or be misunderstood. The electorate has periodically rejected incompetents and fools and sometimes for the right reason. The better-financed candidate has not always been elected. Crude appeals to racial and religious bias have probably diminished in this century. In recent years the parties have even made more serious efforts to broaden the base of campaign contributions and to recruit capable candidates.

One might even argue persuasively that a substantial majority of American voters since the thirties have acted rationally — if one considers voting in terms of one's pocketbook rational behavior — at least in many presidential and congressional elections, since most lower-middle- and lower-class voters now identify with the Democratic party, which has favored the less affluent, while most middle- and upper-middle-class voters identify with the Republican party, which has favored the well-to-do. Socioeconomic status sharply differentiates Democrats and Republicans. This suggests that millions of voters perceive a causal relation between their self-interest, their definition of the "goodness" or "badness" of the times, and the particular party in or out of office. The commonly held stereotypes of the Democratic party as the party of the working man and the Republican party as the party of the businessman may be gross and crude clichés but they are not without merit.

Honest critics of our electoral process are aware of these facts and realize that a balanced and reasonable evaluation of the behavior of American voters and candidates must take them into account. The optimism warranted by much of the data, however, does not negate the relevance of their concern.

Despite every bit of evidence that can be marshaled to "prove" that the system works well, a handful of scholars and journalists who are of neither the doctrinaire Left nor Right continue to argue that something fundamentally unsound and ominous characterizes the manner in which some candidates have won nomination and election to high office. It is not easy to articulate that something with precision, but it has to do with the possibility that men skilled in the arts of communication and persuasion can successfully merchandise a vacuous and hollow shell, or a dim-witted fool, or, what is really more to the point, a very average fellow, by creating for him a public image that bears little or no resemblance to his private reality but is so astutely constructed and sold that it is accepted as the real thing. The fool or the fellow must, of course, be affluent or supported by the affluent, because image making is an expensive business. It is helpful if he is physically attractive, photogenic, telegenic, able to read a teleprompter, able to shake hands well, and able to smile. Put in different and more concrete terms, the concern of these scholars is whether or not it is now possible for the image makers to substitute and sell sham for reality, non-being for being, shadow for substance.

The "distance" which now separates the candidate from the

voter is frequently so great that the voter neither sees nor hears the "real" candidate. The candidate, at least if he is affluent, is thus "separated" from the electorate by pollsters, makeup men, television consultants, speech writers, account executives, public relations counsel, advance men, fund raisers, documentary film makers, and a host of minor noisemakers. His words flow from their pens. His strategy is based on their findings. His answers to the inevitable League of Women Voters questionnaire are written by them. His profile on television is affected by their lighting and makeup. The candidate and his entourage become fused.

In the intelligently managed and adequately financed political campaign a synthetic, fictitious reality almost always displaces reality and pseudo or manufacturd events displace spontaneous events. A truly ugly man probably cannot be made beautiful, nor can a complete idiot be transformed into a knowledgeable and profound savant. But we are not concerned with the truly ugly and stupid because they seldom run for the highest offices. We are concerned with the ex-movie star, the space hero, the rich oil man, the prominent socialite, the famous football coach, the ex-general, or the member of a famous family who seeks high office, or is sought, and who can pay the bills or find someone to pay them, hires shrewd counsel, and has a patina of education, a smattering of rote knowledge, a pretty wife, and the aura of celebrity.

The problem is, of course, critical since democracy is based on the dual assumption that the average man can distinguish the spurious from the genuine and that he will prefer the latter. If it is now possible to manufacture a synthetic or pseudo reality, more attractive and vibrant than reality and neither completely false nor true, through a series of carefully staged, picturesque events which appear to be spontaneous, the distinction between sham and reality disappears. The public then can neither tell sham from reality nor prefer the latter. The creator of the counterfeit events which we call the political campaign then becomes the king maker — the producer and director. The campaign becomes a contest between two sets of professional pseudo-event makers who attempt to stage an attractive scenario. Politics becomes a spectator sport. The candidate, of course, is the leading onstage actor. He may be just a marionette. Each actor attempts to un-mask the other before the audience, which in democratic societies is the electorate.

The concept of the pseudo event was first articulated by Daniel J. Boorstin in his fascinating and disturbing volume *The Image or What Happened to the American Dream*.[1] The burden of Boorstin's book is that American experience is now flooded with illusions rather than reality, with images rather than ideals, and with celebrities who are manufactured rather than true heroes. The pseudo, counterfeit, and manufactured event, he contends, has all but replaced the spontaneous event and our ex-perience, therefore, has become characterized by an increasing secondhandness. Much in American life, in other words, is phony, illusionary, and contrived.

Boorstin contends that unreality dominates American life be-cause Americans are ruled by extravagant expectations. They expect the world to hold more than it does in fact and they exag-gerate their ability to shape the world. They expect and demand more novelty and news than occurs, more heroes than exist, more masterpieces than can be created. The demand for illusions is supplied by advertising agencies, public relations men, ghost writers, movie makers, journalists, radio and television commen-tators, makeup men, speech writers, and campaign managers. It is they who produce, stage, and direct salable illusions, counter-feit happenings, and pseudo events. Their clients may be poli-ticians, movie stars or business institutions, but these illusions could not be sold unless the public wanted and expected them.

The pseudo event is not spontaneous. It is planned, or planted, or incited by someone for the immediate purpose of being reported or reproduced. As Boorstin points out, "Typ-ically, it is not a train wreck or an earthquake, but an inter-view."[2] Staged for the convenience of the reporting or repro-ducing media, the pseudo event's success is measured by how widely it is reported and believed. The success of a documentary

---

[1] Daniel J. Boorstin, *The Image or What Happened to the American Dream* (New York: Atheneum Publishers, 1962).

[2] *Ibid.*, p. 11.

film produced for a candidate is measured, in part, by the number of times it is televised.

Time relations in it are commonly fictitious or factitious; the announcement is given out in advance "for future release" and written as if the event had occurred in the past; the question "Is it real?" is less important than "Is it newsworthy?" Its relationship to the underlying reality of the situation is ambiguous. Concerning a pseudo event the question, "What does it mean?" has a new dimension. While the news interest in a train wreck is in what happened and in the real consequences, the interest in an interview is always, in a sense, in whether it really happened and in what might have been the motives. Did the statement really mean what it said? Without some of this ambiguity a pseudo event cannot be very interesting.[3]

The pseudo event is usually intended to be a self-fulfilling prophecy. The documentary film produced for the candidate and staged to portray him as a wise and distinguished public servant tends to make one of him. We believe that the Kennedy-McCormack campaign (and many other political campaigns) can best be understood by interpreting them as a combination of real and pseudo events. Frequently it is difficult to distinguish one from the other.

We may illustrate what we mean by describing one of the most extreme examples of pseudo happenings of our time — the career of Senator Joseph McCarthy of Wisconsin, which was built almost entirely of pseudo events. McCarthy's career was based primarily on his ability to manufacture reportable happenings that bore an ambiguous relation to reality. Boorstin quotes Richard Rovere, who perceptively described how McCarthy's career prospered through his ability to create pseudo events.

He knew how to get into the news even on those rare occasions when invention failed him and he had no un-facts to give out. For example, he invented the morning press conference called for the purpose of announcing an afternoon press conference. The reporters would come in — they were beginning, in this period to respond to his summonses like Pavlov's dogs at the clang of a bell — and McCarthy would say that he just wanted to give them the word that he expected to be ready with a shattering announcement later in the day, for use in the papers the following morning. This would gain him a headline in the afternoon papers: "New McCarthy Revelations Awaited in Capital." Afternoon would come, and if McCarthy had something, he would give it out, but often enough he had nothing, he wasn't quite ready, that he was having difficulty in getting some of the "documents" he needed or that a "witness" was proving elusive. Morning headlines: "Delay Seen in McCarthy Case — Mystery Witness Being Sought."[4]

McCarthy's career was promoted by newspapermen, many of whom despised him. Without the active participation of newspapermen, he could not have created the pseudo events based on non-facts which made him notorious and powerful. Their need to create a more or less continuous stream of news, even when none exists, forces them to report non-news, non-fact, or to create news — frequently through the interview technique.

We suggest that Edward Kennedy's rise to power and subsequent political stardom, and that of many other candidates, was based partly on the public's extravagant expectations — their need for heroes and illusions, albeit illusions of a particular kind — and on Kennedy's ability to pay for the services of men expert in the business of creating and selling pseudo events. His success was also based on the fact that he possesses some attributes, some substance, and some presence which makes it not difficult for him and his employees to create and sell an attractive public profile.

Pseudo events could not have replaced spontaneous events in America until "the graphic revolution" had taken place, i.e., the invention and development of the telegraph, the rotary press, the high-speed press, the telephone, dry-plate photography, the radio, motion pictures, television, and mass circulation magazines and newspapers. These techniques and means of communication make it possible to report an event widely and almost instantaneously, and to report it in terms that are so vivid that the orig-

4 Quoted in *ibid.*, p. 21.

inal often seems pale by comparison with the touched-up photograph or the Vistavision, wide-screen, Cinemascope moving picture.

The contrived and counterfeit happening is rapidly driving the spontaneous event out of circulation. Describing the advantages of pseudo events, Boorstin says:

> Pseudo-events are more dramatic. A television debate between candidates can be planned to be more suspenseful (for example, by reserving questions which are then popped suddenly) than a casual encounter or consecutive formal speeches planned by each separately.
>
> Pseudo-events, being planned for dissemination, are easier to disseminate and to make vivid. Participants are selected for their newsworthy and dramatic interest.
>
> Pseudo-events can be repeated at will, and thus their impression can be re-inforced.
>
> Pseudo-events cost money to create; hence somebody has an interest in disseminating, magnifying, advertising, and extolling them as events worth watching or worth believing. They are therefore advertised in advance, and rerun in order to get money's worth.
>
> Pseudo-events, being planned for intelligibility, are more intelligible and hence more reassuring. Even if we cannot discuss intelligently the qualifications of the candidates or the complicated issues, we can at least judge the effectiveness of a television performance. How comforting to have some political matter we can grasp!
>
> Pseudo-events are more sociable, more conversable, and more convenient to witness. Their occurrence is planned for our convenience. The Sunday newspaper appears when we have a lazy morning for it. Television programs appear when we are ready with our glass of beer. . . .[5]

This discussion illuminates the intense struggle concerning the format of the Kennedy-McCormack debate. The basic question was whether the debate should be a managed or pseudo event. To everyone's surprise, including McCormack's, the Attorney

[5] *Ibid.*, p. 39.

General vigorously attacked Kennedy. He "broke through" the formal structure of the panel — made several unprepared, unexpected, and spontaneous statements — and turned the debate into a not completely contrived event. The results were disastrous for him. However, both camps wrongly predicted the impact of his spontaneity, and the Kennedys were pained by the fact that a non-pseudo event had occurred, at least until they could accurately determine the public's response.

* * *

Campaign managers are concerned with both pseudo events and propaganda. They are distinguishable although they have some common characteristics. Propaganda, in the traditional sense, is information intentionally biased. As Boorstin points out:

> Its effect depends primarily on its emotional appeal. While a pseudo-event is an ambiguous truth, propaganda is an appealing falsehood. Pseudo-events thrive on our honest desire to be informed, "to have all the facts," and even to have more facts than there really are. But propaganda feeds on our willingness to be inflamed. Pseudo-events appeal to our duty to be educated, propaganda appeals to our desire to be aroused. While propaganda substitutes opinion for facts, pseudo-events are synthetic facts which move people indirectly, by providing the "factual" basis on which they are supposed to make up their minds. Propaganda moves them directly by explicitly making judgments for them.[6]

Edward Kennedy's campaign brochure can be analyzed to illustrate these differences. The brochure did not substitute opinion for fact. It did not contain information that was intentionally biased. It did not contain appealing falsehoods. It is not a classic bit of propaganda although it did make judgments for readers. The brochure showed photographs of Kennedy with General Norstad, Prime Minister David Ben Gurion, and President Gronchi of Italy. Kennedy was, in fact, photographed with these men. The brochure also presented a photograph of the candidate with his wife and children. The caption under the

[6] *Ibid.*, p. 34.

first three photographs read: "Familiarity with World Problems."
The caption under the family picture read: "Edward M. Kennedy, Devoted Husband and Father." The photographs and
captions appeared with a list of "Kennedy's Community Service":
"Named as one of the ten outstanding men of the year by the
Boston Junior Chamber of Commerce," "Member of the Board
of Trustees of Boston University," "Judge Advocate of the
Polish American Veterans Post of Boston." Are these ambiguous
truths or synthetic facts? Certainly they are "contrived" achievements since Kennedy had none of the customary political or professional achievements to his credit as the term is traditionally
used. This list of "achievements" and the photographs were designed to move people indirectly, by providing the "factual" basis
upon which voters could decide to favor Kennedy. The photographs of Kennedy with General Norstad and Prime Minister
Ben Gurion are supposed to lead to the conclusion that Kennedy
is "familiar with world problems." The photograph is the "proof."
In this sense it is also a self-fulfilling prophecy.

McCormack, without using Boorstin's terminology, frequently implied and occasionally stated boldly that Kennedy's
achievements were synthetic, that the Kennedy campaign was a
pseudo-event carefully created by Kennedy and his staff at great
expense, and that Kennedy, whom he saw as a hollow shell, was
made to look like an intelligent and dedicated statesman. As
the Attorney General said during the first debate, "If his name
was Edward Moore . . . your candidacy would be a joke. . . ." The
McCormack brochure, entitled "The Qualified Candidate," listed
twenty-six "qualifications" for McCormack and under "His Opponent" only "Brother of the President." The brochure was obviously designed to suggest that Kennedy's achievements were nonexistent, made up — in short, pseudo.

During the pre-election weeks numerous statements were
made by McCormack supporters to the effect that Kennedy was
spending a fortune on the campaign. Their purpose was, in part,
to heighten the impression that Kennedy employed a substantial
number of image-makers. Sometimes the public senses that big
money implies a good deal of image making. The suggestion that

the opponent is spending a fortune is meant to communicate this latent message.

The more clever men who manufacture political campaigns and other pseudo events have now discovered the techniques by which fame can be manufactured. Fame, in fact, is the product they purvey. It is enormously costly to manufacture fame and it is probably impossible to manufacture a true hero in the classical sense, a man who has shown greatness in some achievement, but it *is* possible to make a celebrity and perhaps out of whole cloth. C. Wright Mills defines celebrities as

. . . the Names that need no further identification. . . . Those who know them so far exceed those of whom they know as to require no exact computation. Wherever the celebrities go, they are recognized, and moreover, recognized with some excitement and awe. Whatever they do has publicity value. More or less continuously, over a period of time, they are the material for the media of communication and entertainment. And when that time ends — as it must — and the celebrity still lives — as he may — from time to time it may be asked, "Remember him?" That is what celebrity means.[7]

Would it be incorrect to suggest that Edward Kennedy, Robert Kennedy, and Lyndon Johnson are the only national celebrities now holding public office? Does any other American family evoke the kind of excitement and awe comparable to that evoked by the Kennedys? We think not. Elizabeth Taylor might attract a more excited and awestruck crowd, particularly if she appeared with Richard Burton, but we doubt that Hubert Humphrey, Richard Nixon, George Romney, William Scranton, or any other American politician would. People do not gape at these men the way they do at the Kennedys.

Edward and Robert Kennedy are newsworthy because of their relationship to John F. Kennedy, their social and political positions, and the decisions and money they command and because of the qualities they have. Mills has written that "Heavy publicity, the technique of the buildup and the avaricious de-

[7] C. Wright Mills, *The Power Elite* (New York: Oxford University Press, 1957), p. 71.

mand of the media for continuous copy have placed a spotlight on those people [celebrities] such as no higher circles of any nation in world history has ever had upon them."[8] The national magazines, the press, and the television networks remind the American public, almost daily, of the prestige of the Kennedys. The media need them because they are newsworthy but the media also make them newsworthy. The Kennedys aid this buildup by holding press conferences, climbing mountains, attending the opera, sometimes taking controversial stands on issues or personalities, walking fifty miles, skiing in Aspen, throwing large parties for the famous and near famous, making large contributions to charity, and frequently making very good sense on national and international problems. The buildup is partly instigated by the media, partly manufactured by the Kennedys, who have always been much concerned with their "image."[9] As is the case with every celebrity, the living, breathing person — the "real" Edward Kennedy — is known to the public only as a photograph in a magazine, an item in a newspaper, or an image on a television tube.

The celebrity has prestige, which is perhaps the most powerful of all vote getters. Prestige originally meant "dazzling the eye with conjuring tricks." Prestige reinforces power and often converts it into authority. Authority, in turn, protects the prestigious and powerful from criticism. Most people are afraid to criticize the prestigious and the powerful. The umbrella of immunity that covers them is a vital part of their armamentarium and their mystique.

The person who is well-known for his well-knownness is often a human pseudo event; the phrase is Boorstin's:

He is neither good nor bad, great nor petty. He is the human pseudo-event. He has been fabricated on purpose to satisfy

---

8 *Ibid.*, p. 84.

9 Robert Kintner, President of NBC, wrote in *Harper's* (May, 1965) that President Kennedy had telephoned him after Jacqueline Kennedy had been on television several times. He wanted to know if Kintner thought she was "overexposed." Kintner thought she was, and the President canceled some of her future appearances.

our exaggerated expectations of human greatness. He is morally neutral. The product of no conspiracy, of no group promoting vice or emptiness, he is made by honest, industrious men of high professional ethics doing their job, "informing" and educating us. He is made by all of us who willingly read about him, who like to see him on television, who buy recordings of his voice, and talk about him to our friends. His relation to morality and even to reality is highly ambiguous. He is like the woman in an Elinor Glyn novel who describes another by saying, "She is like a figure in an Elinor Glyn novel."[10]

The candidate for public office is frequently a human pseudo event, "made" by a series of carefully staged pseudo events known as the political campaign. The political campaign makes him a star by calling him a star — on radio, on television, in documentary films, in billboards, in press releases, in ghost-written speeches, in brochures, in handouts, and in one-sheets. Of course, he can be "made" only if he can afford the money required by competent human pseudo-event manufacturers. With their help, he must be able to break through the curtain of indifference and apathy that shrouds so much of the electorate. He must get his face and name before that mass of voters who have little interest in politics and who tend not to expose themselves to campaign propaganda. These people are open to persuasion because they are disinterested and therefore uncommitted, but they are among the most difficult people to contact. To reach them the candidate must purchase prime time and purchase it frequently. This costs vast sums but it is "worth" the expenditure since the outcome of many elections depends on their response.

In addition to his money, the candidate as human pseudo event is frequently distinguished by what is called his image or trademark, rather than by his achievements. As Boorstin notes:

National politics (with the full paraphernalia of make-up, rehearsals, and kleig lights) has adopted the star system which dominates it more with every election. Yet anyone — or almost anyone — can be transformed into a star. Originally a

10 Boorstin, *op. cit.*, p. 57.

person destined for stardom is chosen less for his intrinsic value than for his capacity to be "built up." How good a receptacle is he for what the public wants to see in him? A star, then, must allow his personality to dominate his work; he is judged by his personality in place of his achievement.[11]

Although many argue, perhaps correctly, that Kennedy is a man of much substance, was he not originally nominated for the United States Senate because of his capacity to be built up rather than his intrinsic value as a future senator? Was not this also true of a host of other successful candidates? Some of these men had or have something that can realistically be called "intrinsic value" as national leaders, but many do not or did not. The point is that they possess or possessed some qualities other than political experience, high intelligence, integrity, or a first-class education which made it possible to build them up. Their appropriateness had little to do with things intrinsic, real, and political and much to do with things contrived, with shadows and images.

In American political campaigns, and many other kinds of sales campaigns, the campaign or sales managers are more concerned with the image of the candidates and the products they purvey than with the actuality. Each candidate strives not so much to improve what the electorate thinks of him as to improve, as they say, his public image. Boorstin suggests that "Our age betrays its deference to images. Each of us hopes for a pleasing 'personality' and our personality is the attention-getting image of ourselves, our image of our behavior."[12] The personality of the candidate is his attention-getting image and that is probably what most people vote for or against.

Ideals may have been now more or less displaced by images in this country. American dictionaries define "ideal" as a conception of something in its most excellent or perfect form. "The image," Boorstin writes, "is a pseudo ideal. . . . it is synthetic, believable, passive, vivid, simplified, and ambiguous."[13]

11 *Ibid.*, p. 168.
12 *Ibid.*, p. 202.
13 *Ibid.*, p. 185.

Although the image is synthetic, it must not "outrage the ordinary rules of common sense."[14] The image maker is not entirely free to craft whatever he may desire. Some fact, some substance, must underlie the image for it to be believable. The campaign manager, the advertising agency, and the motivational research savant are limited by reality, to some degree, in their efforts to cut, edit, and create a synthetic reality. The simple-minded view, often tinged with conspiratorial foreboding, that hidden persuaders can make a believable "reality" out of nothing — that they are magicians or prestidigitators of inordinate power, who can turn "yes" into a "no" and "no" into "yes" — is just what we have termed it: simple minded.

Reality sets bounds to image making. One critical problem of democratic theory — whether or not you can fool all the people all the time — can be resolved only if we can determine the degree to which reality can be tampered with and the conditions that make tampering more or less possible. We have merely suggested that the graphic revolution coupled with the extravagant expectations of Americans now permit tampering with reality to a degree hitherto not imagined.

The student of political campaigning would be less concerned about the image maker's manipulative prowess if it were possible to debunk and unmask images. Their very characteristics, however, make them more attractive, vivid, and believable than reality. They are easier to grasp than reality because they are less anxiety provoking. They are also more convenient to perceive than reality since they are designed and presented at the appropriate time for perceiving them. Thinking in terms of images, or stereotypes, as Walter Lippmann noted in his classic *Public Opinion*, is more characteristic of and satisfying to the perceiver than thinking in terms of reality.

Democratic theorists take heart in the thought that the "opposition" party or the "opposition" candidate or the "independent and free" press or the underdog has a stake in exposing or debunking images. The democrat periodically reminds himself of

14 *Ibid.*, p. 188.

the Holmesian doctrine that truth, i.e., reality, will emerge from the free play of ideas. This assumes of course that one's commitment can be changed by exposure to "contradictory" ideas. Was the Kennedy-McCormack televised debate a case in point? McCormack's "criticism" of Kennedy in part was clearly realistic. The overwhelming majority of viewers, however, reacted to the debate not according to the validity of McCormack's critique, but according to their emotional commitment to Kennedy. McCormack's statements upset them, intensified their anxiety. They reduced their anxiety by denying what McCormack said and they used it as another reason to dislike McCormack and like Kennedy.

Boorstin suggests that

> Strictly speaking, there is no way to unmask an image. An image, like any other pseudo-event, becomes all the more interesting with every effort to debunk it. For this reason, some of the most effective advertising nowadays consists of circumstantial descriptions of how the advertising images are contrived: how tests were devised, how trademarks were designed. . . . The stage machinery, the process of fabricating and projecting the image fascinates us.[15]

This may well be one of the major reasons why books on political campaigning — particularly Theodore White's books which are titled significantly *The Making of The President* — become best sellers. People are enthralled by how Presidents are "made." They surmise that the public and the private are quite different and assume that the private and the spontaneous are more intriguing and real.

We suspect that part of the Kennedy appeal stems from the fact that people come to know — through books, articles, newspapers, and personal observation — that the Kennedys and their confreres spend in a highly efficient fashion substantial amounts of money and energy in creating their image. The elaborateness of the Kennedy campaigns — the tremendous expenditure, the hundreds of headquarters, thousands of workers, millions of bits

---

[15] *Ibid.*, p. 194.

of literature, the trouble the Kennedys go to to get elected — becomes proof to Kennedy supporters that their enthusiasm for the Kennedys is justified. The efficiency, grandiosity, and opulence of the campaign are taken as indications of the candidate's competence. This may or may not be true. Campaigning for major office is big business. It requires considerable intelligence and much money. An efficiently run campaign may well demonstrate that the candidate is efficient and thoughtful, assuming that the candidate runs the campaign.

In the middle of the twentieth century, politics has become excedingly complicated and technical. The major domestic and foreign issues are not such as can be mastered by a man with a good, untrained mind or a man dedicated to the ideals of the small town or working-class urban life. Economics, foreign affairs, etc., demand knowledge, intellectual sophistication, and a familiarity with the complexities of bureaucratic-technological civilization. At the same time, American society has become culturally stratified to an increasing extent, with the middle-class, college-educated segment sharply marked off from the working-class high-school-educated segment. It is now more difficult to enter the professions without a college degree and more difficult to rise in the social and economic hierarchy without the early start which sets the cultured apart from the uncultured.

At the same time, there has emerged, thanks to national television, national newsmagazines, high geographic mobility in the top executive ranks, and the rise of "national" rather than regional colleges (even Harvard was, until quite recently, essentially a regional college) a nation-wide upper-middle-class culture which is the common property of the elite elements of American society. The portrait of America as a landscape of local pyramids, of local elites semi-disconnected from one another, of distinct racial, religious, ethnic, and geographical elites, is decreasingly valid.

Perhaps the objective demands placed upon modern politicians, coupled with the sociological developments we have noted, have greatly lessened the opportunity for a self-made man to rise in politics. The new men of American politics are therefore more likely to come from the elite segments of the population. Necessarily, then, they will appeal to the electorate not as men of the people — this may no longer be the best image — but as being Senate born. However, in a society with egalitarian values, a somewhat populist past, and an anti-aristocratic bias, it will take much skill for image makers and pseudo-event creators to fabricate images and human pseudo events that are not so aristocratic as to offend populist sentiment but aristocratic enough to attract the man predisposed to vote for his betters.

The techniques developed during the graphic revolution, the skill that is now devoted to fusing sham with reality, and the fact that millions seek illusion may well mean that the distinction beween the true and the false, the real and the unreal, and the image and the ideal no longer can be made. As Boorstin suggests: "In this new world, where almost anything can be true, the socially rewarded art is that of making things seem true." [16]

The Kennedy brothers and the men who help manage their careers and campaigns have mastered the art of creating shadows and taking advantage of substance.

[16] *Ibid.*, p. 212.

Aaron, E. Norman Fund, Inc.: viii
Academic community: 146, 150, 172,
    173; McCormack supporters: 55,
    144, 146, 147, 171, 173; J. F. Ken-
    nedy support: 144
Adams family: 23
AFL-CIO: 206
Aid to education: 141–142
Alexander, Hunter: 156
Amalgamated Union: 28
American Bar Association: 129
Americans for Democratic Action
    (ADA): 39, 55, 61
Arnold, Thurman: 129
Association of the Bar of the City of
    New York: 129
Autobahn: 209
Azores air base: 154

Bank, depository: 238, 239, 240, 271
Barnett, Ross: xii
Beacon Hill: 78
Beatles: 121
Beer, Samuel: 55, 171
Bellotti family: 103
Berkshire Eagle: 26, 191, 197, 217,
    219, 258
Berlin: 201, 209, 229
Billboards: 163, 166, 235, 243, 255,
    266, 273
Boland, Edward M.: 66
Boorstin, Daniel J.: 291, 292, 296, 298,
    299, 300, 302, 304; advantages of
    pseudo events: 294; propaganda and
    pseudo events defined: 295
Borman, Bernard: vii, 246, 248
Boston Bar Association: 12, 128
Boston City Council: 16, 128, 195
Boston College: 39
Boston Globe: 54, 75, 154, 171, 222,
    226, 234, 244, 258, 272, 273
Boston Herald: 17, 74; sympathetic to
    Kennedy: 217–218
Boston Herald-Traveler: 258
Boston Irish: 16, 112, 190, 201; atti-
    tudes toward politicians: 24, 42;

disadvantages in state-wide elec-
    tion: 125
Boston Junior Chamber of Commerce
    ten outstanding men of the year
    award: 11, 296
Boston Politics: 17, 88, 89, 120, 126,
    136
Boston Record-American: 258
*Boston Record-American and Daily
    Advertiser:* 272
Boston Traveler: 165
Boston University: 11, 39
Boston University Law Review: 15,
    128
Boston University Law School: 15
Boston wards: 28, 174, 176, 252
Boston Young Democrats: 191
Brandeis University: 39
Brazil: 220
Buck Printing Company, Boston: 250
Buckley, Edmund: 74
Bunker Hill Day parade: 256
Burns, James McGregor: 55, 155, 171
Byrd, Harry, *Senator:* 131
Byrd family: 23

Café society: 152
Callahan, William: 42, 43, 44
Camelio, Salvatore: 66, 67
Campaign contributions: 131–133,
    241, 245, 247, 249, 284, 287; broad
    definition: 241
Campaign expenditures: 235–237, 242,
    244, 246, 248, 251, 252, 255, 256,
    259–267, 271–284, 299, 303; cost of
    major office in Massachusetts: 234;
    television costs in Boston, 235; law
    regulating: 238, 240, 241, 250; state-
    ment of purpose: 239; Massachusetts
    Crime Commission refused invoices:
    250; radio, television, newspaper
    advertising: 258; campaign novel-
    ties: 263, 266, 277; cost of Congres-
    sional seat: 287; *see also* entries un-
    der individual candidates
Campaign finance: sources: 130, 287;

difficulties in raising funds for senatorial campaigns: 130, 131; James S. Doyle's evaluation of problem: 244, 245; reform in methods: 284; Alexander Heard, leading authority in: 287

Campaign Full Reporting Act: 250

Campaign funds: deposit required in depository bank: 238; individual contributions limit: 239

Campaign issues: 153; see also entries under individual candidates

Campaign laws: 132, 133, 240, 250, 283

Campaign literature: 11, 164, 176, 236, 251, 260, 261, 266, 273, 295, 296

Campaign slogans: Kennedy use of: 220, 227; "He Can Do More for Massachusetts": 12, 98, 147, 157, 162, 166, 182, 188, 195, 204, 220, 274; "The Qualified Candidate": 87, 182, 261, 296; "A Voice That Will Be Heard": 204, 220; "Kennedy, the Man for Massachusetts": 269

Campaign techniques: xi, 37, 43, 45, 115, 146, 179, 278, 300

Candidates: selection by delegates: 34; evaluation by public: 84, 110, 116; use of resources: 114; tasks: 115; need for good merchandizer: 183

Canham, Erwin D.: 191–194, 209, 210, 212

Capitol Hill: 19, 20

Cardinal Richard Cushing Benefit: 54

Cater, Douglas: 71

Childs, Marquis: 20, 21

Christian Science Monitor: 218

Civil rights and civil liberties: 16, 91, 92, 196; appointment of assistant attorney general for: 129

Civil Rights Division established by McCormack: 129

Clark, Joseph: xii, 83, 142

Clurman, Richard: 7

Commentary: 68

Communism: 104, 105, 192, 202, 206, 208

Consumers' Council established by McCormack: 16, 205

Convention, State Democratic: see Democratic State Convention

Corruption in Massachusetts: 8, 42, 89, 105–109, 124

Curley, James Michael: 125, 126

Curtis, Laurence: 24, 244, 264, 270; campaign expenses reported: 237, 241, 248; asked for 1962 invoices; 243

Daily Record: 191, 198

Dalton, Cornelius: 165

Debate, Kennedy–McCormack on television: 181–217, 221–223, 226, 228, 294; interpretation and repercussions: 218, 302; second Holyoke debate: 184, 232

Debates, American political: 183, 220, 221

Delegates to state convention: 26, 28, 32–37, 47, 50; McCormack strategy for getting: 40, 42; Kennedy competition against McCormack for: 42, 44, 47, 50; distribution of: 55; claim of Newburyport switch: 62; heavy Kennedy majorities reported: 65; last-minute efforts to convert: 66; polling before television cameras: 69; influences on: 76; significance to City Hall, State House, and White House: 77; fear of retaliation: 132; see also Edward McCormack — Campaign Strategy

Democratic candidates: financial supporters in Massachusetts: 130

Democratic party: 24, 42, 57, 59, 80, 92, 102, 104, 105, 194, 288; COD reform group: 39; need for reform: 49, 171, 284; town committees: 49; disunity: 94; dominant factor in Massachusetts: 103

Democratic primary election: viii, xiv, 270; differences with state convention: 99, 100

Democratic Registration Committee: 176

Democratic State Committee: 65, 79, 98; control wrested from John McCormack by John F. Kennedy: 20

Democratic State Convention: viii, xiv, 5, 20, 61, 78, 96, 98, 99, 219, 262, 263; control of: 30, 47; scene:

61; press coverage: 61; "Little Los Angeles": 281

Democrats: 78, 102, 175, 176, 193; registered in Massachusetts: 252; socioeconomic differentiation from Republicans: 289

De Mott, Benjamin: 109, 110

Dickinson, John: 161

Dilworth, Richardson: xii, 83

Disarmament: unilateral: 24; McCormack position: 148, 201; Kennedy position: 201

Doherty, Gerard: vii

Doyle, James: 234, 244, 245

Dynastic politics: 22, 23, 24, 63, 141; *see also* Kennedy family

East Berlin: 192

East Germany: 205

Education, importance of: 303

Edward M. Kennedy Committee for United States Senator: 244, 265, 273; salaries reported: 280

The Edward M. Kennedy Story (documentary campaign film): 269

Egan, Leo: 191, 200, 206, 208

Egleston Square: 27

Eisenhower, Dwight D., *General:* 114

Elections, methods for winning: xii, 99, 233, 285–288; setting for Kennedy victory: 113

European Common Market: 199, 205

Fall River: 160, 192, 230

Federal aid for Massachusetts: 58

Federal Communications Commission: 270

Federal court system, appeal to: 10

Federalists: 285

Fitzgerald, John F. "Honey Fitz," *Mayor:* 26, 192

Fitzgerald, Rose: *see* Kennedy, Rose Fitzgerald (Mrs. Joseph P.)

Food and Drug Administration: fish flour approval sought: 154

Fourth Amendment: 10, 197

Fulbright, Newton H.: 236, 244

Full Disclosure Law: enforcement procedures lax: 243, 245

Fund raising: 233, 240, 262

Furculo, Foster, *Governor:* 3, 54

Gargan, Joseph: 168

General Electric Company: 166

Geneva talks: 200, 201

Germany: 209

Ghana, Upper Volta project: 204

Gloucester fishing problem: 204, 220

Gordon, Lincoln: xv

Great Society: 104

Greece: 207

Greenwald, Norman: 55

Hallstein, Walter, 199

Hartigan, William C.: 62

Harvard Law School: 127, 145

Harvard University: 39, 55, 171, 183, 303

Healey, Robert: 171

Heard, Alexander: 287

Hebrew Bakers' Union: 27

Hebrew Butchers' Union: 27

Hoffa, Jimmy: xii

Holland, C. Edward: 191, 198

Holmes, Oliver Wendell: 128, 209, 302

Holy Name Societies: 5, 25

Housing discrimination: 16

Howe, Mark DeWolfe: 21, 145, 260; endorsement of McCormack: 128

Hughes, Charles Evans, *Chief Justice:* 24

Hughes, H. Stuart, vii, viii, 24, 142, 201, 232, 235, 243, 245, 270; campaign expenditures: 163, 237, 241–243, 245, 252, 261, 272, 275

Humphrey, Hubert H., *Vice-President:* 297

Hungary: 201

ILGWU: 27

Illinois, cost of governorship: 233

Image making: 12, 115, 146, 287, 300–302

The Image or What Happened to the American Dream: 291

Independent Citizens Committee for McCormack for U.S. Senator: 258

Ingalls Associates: 256–260, 262

Internal Revenue Service: 133, 134

Irish Catholics: 24–26, 104, 105

Iron Curtain: 207

Jackson, Age of: 23

Jeffersonians: 285
Jerry Williams Show: 259
Jews, voting preferences: 103
John C. Dowd, Inc., Boston: 250, 265, 266, 271, 272, 276
Johnson, Carl: 273, 274
Johnson, Lyndon B., *President:* 5, 55, 297
Joseph Napolitan Associates, Springfield: 265, 277
Junior Chamber of Commerce, Boston, ten outstanding young men of the year award: 12
Junior Chamber of Commerce, Greater Boston: 238, 246; questioned accuracy, campaign financial reports: 244; contributions in kind, report on: 247

Katanga Province: 202
Kennedy family: xi, 6, 12, 25, 26, 75, 86, 87, 89, 95, 102, 103, 105, 111, 115, 147, 149, 211, 233, 297, 298; Kennedy brothers: xii, xiii, 304; appeal in Massachusetts: xii, 5, 24, 77, 111; wealth: xii, 17, 95, 152, 155, 165; image: 12, 17, 24, 86, 94, 111, 112, 145, 150, 155, 180, 181; Irish identification: 25; campaigns: 32, 302; Catholic Church identification: 112; Kennedy sisters: 170; *see also* Dynastic politics
Kennedy–McCormack contest: 19, 42, 43, 95, 100, 119, 155, 195, 219; as struggle between Kennedys and McCormacks: 19; between President and Speaker of House: 21, 22; contest not of issues but personalities: 196; seen as series of pseudo events: 292; *see also* Debate, Kennedy–McCormack on television
Kennedy, Edward Moore, *Senator:*
  Background: qualifications: xi, 8, 10, 56, 86, 93, 110, 122, 129, 296; appointment as assistant district attorney of Suffolk County: 4; record of community service: 11, 12; attendance at Harvard: 11, 13; cheating episode: 12, 13–18, 95, 145, 146, 187; as underdog: 44; political power: 48, 72, 75, 85; family relations: 58, 86, 115, 229; voting record: 63, 145; understanding of national and international affairs: 86; identification with Catholic Church: 112; Italian language knowledge: 154; South Boston settlement house work: 160; as U. S. Senator: 223, 298; named one of ten outstanding men by Boston Junior Chamber of Commerce: 296
  Campaign expenditures: analyzed: 163, 179, 235, 249, 264–283; campaign films: 163, 268, 269; television, radio, and newspaper advertising: 163, 248, 266; signs and displays: 163, 268, 272, 273; mailings: 167, 274, 275; workers' salaries: 170, 280; expenses reported: 237, 241, 242, 244, 282; payments to advertising agencies: 246; printing: 247, 252, 275, 276; telephone: 248; novelties: 266, 281, 283; bumper strips: 276; office equipment: 278; Western Union: 279; food charges: 283
  Campaign organization: 48, 52, 68, 163, 165, 166, 167, 170, 171, 173, 176, 178, 180; brain trust: 19, 25, 35, 43, 55, 56, 70, 98, 104, 125, 143, 153–155, 171, 225, 229; function of boss: 32; local level: 32, 175; at convention: 47, 61, 65, 68; campaign workers: 49, 99, 167, 168, 177–180; modeled after J. F. Kennedy campaign organization: 50; support from younger legislators: 50; command headquarters at convention: 68, 281; backstage room at headquarters: 68; campaign headquarters: 163, 168, 173, 174, 177, 253, 267, 277, 278, 279; ethnic groups: 164, 168; payroll: 164; function of campaign manager: 173, 174, 187
  Campaign strategy: xi, 37, 43, 116, 149, 157, 164, 173, 179, 219, 227, 228, 229, 232, 293; announcement for candidacy: 7; office-holding relatives: 37; techniques with delegates: 46; use of campaign data: 52; control of key committees: 65; predictions of victory: 65;

transportation to polls: 163, 178; attack on McCormack: 180; public appearances: xi, 4, 53, 54, 65, 111, 112, 150, 152, 155–157, 179, 231, 268, 281; telephone tactics: 58, 59, 164, 168, 175, 176, 177; primary election: 98, 101, 232; *see also* Debate, Kennedy–McCormack on television

Personal traits: 10, 18, 19, 42, 96, 111–113, 116, 121, 126, 151, 152, 155, 223; speech mannerisms: 18, 211, 222, 223; vigor: 19, 54, 223, 232; vote getting ability: 26, 54, 55, 58, 59, 96, 150, 165, 190; speech similar to John F. Kennedy: 53, 54; conduct: 85, 86, 224

Pre-campaign tactics: pre-primary exposure: 157–160; pre-convention operation: 5, 44, 45, 47, 57, 149; preliminary planning: 116, 167

Public opinion polls: 116, 117, 149, 150, 156, 266, 277; indicated early victory: 149; classification of voters: 149

Stand on issues: federal aid to private schools: 7; bypass convention proceedings: 37; party reform: 49, 55; international, national, and state issues: 153; local issues: 154; Walter-McCarran Immigration Act, criticism of: 154; national higher education: 161; tax cut: 198

Travels: Africa: 4, 6, 205; Latin America: 6, 166, 205; Iron Curtain: 161; Caracas, Venezuela: 166; Italy: 167, 269; time spent: 205; Europe: 205; Ireland: 206

Kennedy, Jacqueline Bouvier (Mrs. John F.): 211

Kennedy, John Fitzgerald "Jack," *President:* 7, 8, 10, 12, 16, 19, 25, 36, 39, 45, 54, 57, 58, 75, 83, 87, 93, 104, 129, 131, 132, 145, 155, 168, 195, 197, 200, 203, 206, 211, 219, 220, 230, 232, 236, 261, 297; assassination, xiii; campaign techniques: xiv; as President-elect, 3; knowledge gained from campaigns: 14; federal patronage: 20; relationship to Edward Kennedy: 21, 64, 72, 75; likeable qualities: 26; pre-convention campaign: 44; attitude toward by Boston politicians: 5; aloofness from Massachusetts Democratic politics: 45; concentration on national and international politics; Edward Kennedy campaign strategy inherited from: 45; political machinery inherited: 47; instituted no state party reforms: 48; Burns' biography: 55; dominant pre-convention figure: 57; effect of Edward Kennedy's candidacy: 66; machine developed at Los Angeles convention: 52, 68; as President limiting to John McCormack's influence: 72; reverence for: 78; relationship to Edward Kennedy: 89, 149; identification with Boston Irish: 112; appeal in Massachusetts 120; on federal aid to education: 142; supported by academic community: 144; compared to Edward Kennedy as campaigner: 150; "house parties": 156; frequent mention of: 157; size of campaign comparable to Edward Kennedy's: 165; area secretaries: 167; Presidential prestige at stake: 181; advocated debates: 186; campaign slogan used by Edward Kennedy: 209; Kennedy-Nixon debates: 220; Catholicism: 287

Kennedy, John Francis: 6

Kennedy, Joan (Mrs. Edward Moore): 4, 54, 155, 156, 168

Kennedy, Joseph P., *Ambassador:* xii, 86, 149

Kennedy, Robert F., *Senator:* xii, xiv, 8, 9, 10, 36, 57, 72, 75, 83, 145, 170, 211, 297; ambitions for Presidency: xi; relationship to Edward Kennedy: 89

Kennedy, Rose Fitzgerald (Mrs. Joseph P.): 26, 157, 168, 274; speeches to Catholic Holy Name Societies: 5

"Kennedy Secretaries": 45, 46, 99

Kennedyisms: 221

Key, V. O., Jr.: vii, 100

Labor, organized: 151

Labor Day: 144
The Last Hurrah: 15, 36, 190
League of Women Voters question-
naires: 290
Leather industry: 199
Legislative Research Bureau: 128
Lerner, Max: 22
Letters of a Pennsylvania Farmer: 162
"Letters to the Editor": 148
Lindsay, John, *Mayor:* xii, xiii, 234
Lippmann, Walter: 301
Little League: 52
Lodge, George Cabot: vii, viii, 23, 56,
111, 227, 228, 235, 262, 270, 277;
campaign expenditures: 163, 232,
237, 241, 242, 247, 249, 252, 253,
261–264, 272, 273, 276, 282, 283;
campaign checks, 243
Lodge, Henry Cabot, *Ambassador:*
xii, 23, 83, 165
Long family: 23
Long, Huey, *Senator:* 131
Lowell: shoes, leather: 204, 220; tex-
tiles: 230
Lubell, Samuel: 220, 221
Lynch, John M. "Pat": 65

McCarthy family: 93, 103
McCarthy, Joseph, *Senator:* 16, 104,
117, 200, 292; ability to create
pseudo events: 292; promoted by
newspapermen: 293
McCormack, Edward J. "Knocko":
36, 67, 69, 88, 125; description of
son's position: 69
McCormack, Edward J. "Eddie", *Attorney General of the Commonwealth of Massachusetts:* 8, 9, 16,
89, 110; assistant attorneys general
help on campaign: 38
   Background: 15, 38, 40, 49, 85, 87,
88, 91, 92, 110, 120, 137, 210, 223;
family: 87, 89, 125, 133; Irish Catholic background forgotten: 112; academic credentials: 128; chairman
of Committee on Conflict of Interest, National Association of Attorneys General: 128; service on Boston City Council: 128; colonel in
Army Reserves: 138; graduate of
U.S. Naval Academy: 203

   Campaign expenditures: lack of
campaign funds: 99, 133–135, 149,
182; television and radio time: 163,
259; estimate of: 235; payments
classified: 250–263; payments reported: 237, 241, 242, 251, 282;
"office": 252, 253; telephone: 255;
"other": 256, 257; Professor Howe
letter mailed: 260; brochure: 261;
when costs incurred: 262; campaign novelties: 263; printing: 276
   Campaign organization: 129, 130,
136, 139, 148; office-holding relatives: 37; campaign workers: 38–40,
135, 136, 139; brain trust: 39, 64,
139, 140, 142–144, 147, 148; pre-
convention support promised: 44;
campaign example of mismanage-
ment: 116; campaign headquarters:
117, 253, 254; lack of telephones
and manpower: 135; campaign
manager: 137; personal secretary:
137; backers wanted no new people: 138; convention headquarters:
264
   Campaign strategy: 18, 37, 41–43,
62, 75, 119, 120, 123, 126–128, 140,
148, 184, 190, 211, 228; attacks on
Kennedy weaknesses: 12, 17, 62, 64,
90, 119–121, 127, 184, 186, 189,
224, 296; relations with delegates:
16, 38, 39, 42, 44, 62, 70–72, 90;
attitudes of supporters: 26, 37,
61, 72, 91, 93, 94, 117, 136, 147,
229; public appearances: 41, 120;
campaign charges: 64, 74; convention activities: 65–68; party approval: 92; defeat in primary after
convention: 98, 101, 232; *see also*
Debate, Kennedy–McCormack on
television
   Personal traits: 18, 19, 22, 43, 56,
90, 93, 96, 97, 116, 123, 140, 189,
221–223; artificial smile: 91; South
Boston accent: 91, 125, 127, 140;
projected poorly on television: 126
   Public opinion polls: 118, 119,
216
   Stand on issues: federal aid to
private schools: 9; on foreign policy: 9; invasion of privacy: 10; capi-

tal punishment: 39; wire tapping: 39; civil rights and liberties: 39, 147; party reforms: 56; nuclear testing: 142; federal aid to education: 142; campaign issues: 147, 148; invasion of privacy: 197; tax cut: 197; unemployment: 197

Weaknesses in campaign: 56, 65, 96, 111, 123, 131, 144, 227, 231; no use of voter sampling: 116, 117; need to counteract "Boston pol" image: 119; in office when corruption alleged to be prevalent: 124; lack of enthusiasm: 135; unpopularity: 137; not suited for debate: 187; attack on Kennedy, 224

McCormack, John, *Speaker of the House of Representatives:* viii, 8, 15, 19, 20, 40, 72, 88, 139, 200, 219, 232, 236; grudge against John F. Kennedy: 20; personal feelings vs. obligations as party leader: 21; influence on Edward J. McCormack: 36; dispenser of patronage under Roosevelt administration: 40

McDonough, "Sonny": 36

McGrath, "Mucker": 36

McGrory, Mary: 99, 222

McKinley, William, *President:* 288

McNeil, David: 191, 201, 205

The Making of the President: 302

Massachusetts: 124, 193, 199, 204, 205, 209, 253, 277; politics: 15, 20, 102, 113, 195, 224; patronage: 57; corruption: 71; conservatism: 104; investigations of public officials: 105; religious division of parties: 105; taxpayers: 204; law enforcement: 208

Massachusetts Attorney General: 128, 208; Division of Civil Rights: 16; assistants: 38; appointments: 93; *see also* Edward McCormack — *Attorney General of the Commonwealth of Massachusetts*

Massachusetts Crime Commission: 250; report for 1956: 106

Massachusetts General Laws Chapter 55 (requiring reporting of campaign expenses): 238

Massachusetts Great and General Court: 103, 128

Massachusetts Institute of Technology: 55, 171, 183

Massachusetts Irish: identification with Kennedys: 25

Massachusetts Parking Authority: 9

Massachusetts Secretary of State: 132

Massachusetts State Labor Council, AFL-CIO: 66

Mayoralty campaigns, cost of: 234

Medicare Bill: 193, 220

"Meet the Press": 6, 8, 9, 124, 140, 141; McCormack's preparation for: 140

Metropolitan District Commission: 9

Michelson, A. A.: 26, 191, 197, 198, 204, 205, 208, 219

Middle East: 202, 207

Middlesex Registry of Deeds, alleged firing of clerk: 74

Mills, C. Wright: 297

Money factor in elections: 100, 233, 244

Morrissey, Francis Xavier, *Judge:* 5, 47

NAACP, Boston Branch: 39

National Defense Act: 7

NATO: 207

Negroes in the South: 10

New Deal: 34, 104

New Frontier: 34, 104

New Republic: 57

New York: 129, 163

New York Herald Tribune: 236, 244

New York Times: xiv, 13, 140, 258, 259

Newspapers, New York and Massachusetts: McCormack advertising costs: 259

Nixon, Richard M., *Vice-President:* 19, 105, 127, 297; Checkers speech: 223

Nuclear stockpiling: 220

"The Open Mind": 145

Opinion Research Corporation, Princeton: 277

Ostreicher, Bernard: 256–260, 262

Owens, C. R.: 226, 273

Panama: 205
Patronage: 29, 34, 59, 72, 73
Peabody, Endicott "Chub," *Governor:* 30, 83, 269; campaign expenditures: 234, 237, 247, 261, 262
Pell, Claiborne: xii, 83
Pennsylvania governship, cost of: 233
Phillips, John: 68
Plank, John: 55
Poland: 201, 207, 208
Politics and professional politicians: xiii, 31, 32, 36, 102, 110, 111, 114, 116, 141, 182, 190, 225, 226, 233, 285, 286, 301, 303
Politics, apolitical: 110
Polls, public opinion: 114, 116, 262, 277; *see also* Edward Kennedy — *Public opinion polls* and Edward McCormack — *Public opinion polls*
Population, explosion: 206
Portugal: 154
Portuguese-Americans: 154
Portuguese Daily News: 272
Postmastership appointments: 62, 69, 73, 170
Pratt, J. D.: 256, 257, 260, 262
Primary elections: 6, 100, 101, 165
Protestants, 103, 105
Pseudo event: 290–294, 299
Pseudo event, defined: 295
Pseudo events and propaganda, differences: 295
Public Defenders Committee: 16
Public Opinion: 301
Purcell, Joseph: 256–258, 260, 262

Questionnaire from author to delegates after convention: 79–83

Radio, cost in campaign: 236, 259
Radio stations: English-language: 270; foreign-language: 271
Radio-television campaign expenditures: *see* Television and radio campaign expenditures
The Reporter: 71
Republican party: 59, 102, 104, 105, 289
Republicanism, Eisenhower brand: 102
Republicans: 175, 176, 180, 181, 193;

election of Kennedy, attitude toward: 63
Republican State Committee: 262; public opinion polls, 277
Rhode Island: 163
Ritz-Carlton Hotel, Boston: 46
Rockefeller, Nelson, *Governor:* xii, 83
Romney, George, *Governor:* 297
Roosevelt family: 23
Roosevelt, Franklin Delano, *President:* 20, 83; Burns' biography: 55
Rostow, Walt W.: xv
Rovere, Richard: 292
Russia: race to moon: 192; Soviet foreign policy: 201, 206

Saltonstall, Leverett, *Senator:* xii, 83
Scranton, William, *Governor:* xii, 83, 297
Secretary of State report: *see* Campaign expenditures
"Shanty Irish" speech differences, urban suburban: 125
Sheraton-Kimball Hotel: 65
Smith, Benjamin II: 3, 71, 94
Smith, Stephen: 46, 50, 52, 68, 168, 189
South America, problems: 192
South Boston: 192–194, 209
South Boston accent: 127
South Boston High School: 196, 210, 226; McCormack alma mater: 191
South Boston Irish: 88, 190
South Boston politicians: 15, 17, 18, 97, 196, 214
Southeast Asia: 141
South Viet Nam: 192
Spellman, Francis Cardinal: aid to parochial schools: 142
Spivak, Lawrence: 6
Springfield: 264
Springfield convention: *see* Democratic State Convention
Springfield Daily News and Union: 258
State Convention, Democratic: *see* Democratic State Convention
Stevenson, Adlai, *Ambassador:* xii, 105
Stolley, Richard B.: 233

Suffolk County, assistant district attorney: 4, 11
Suffolk County Democrats: 85
Sunday Independent, Dublin: 205, 206
Symington, Stuart, *Senator:* xii

Taft family: 23
Tax cut question: 231
Taxes wasted: 107
"The Ted Kennedy Story": 164, 267, 275
Television strategy: 114; Kennedy panel discussions: 155; impact of: 157–163, 221, 222
Television and radio campaign expenditures: 259, 264, 270, 271
Thompson, John: 43, 44
Touré, Sekou: 204
Truman, Harry S, *President:* 20

Unemployment: 206
United Nations: 142, 202, 203, 220
United States: 201, 208, 226
United States Attorney General, power of: 198
United States Department of Housing and Urban Affairs: 55, 220
United States Department of Justice: 145
United States House of Representatives, cost of seat: 234
United States Naval Academy: 15
United States Senate: vacancy: 3; actions pointing toward: 4, 192–194, 198, 300; types of bills: 155; legislation pending: 231; seat, cost of: 233; defeated Republican candidate: 244
University of Virginia: 196
University of Virginia Law School: 11, 13, 195, 197
Upper Volta project, Ghana: 204, 220, 230
U Thant: 202

Vision Associates, New York City: 269
Vogue: xii

Volpe family: 103
Volpe, John: 3, 30; campaign expenditures: 237, 246, 247, 249
Vote, Protestant-Jewish: 141
Voters: concept of: 17; control of: 27, 33, 102; apathy of: 28; "deference vote": 83; abstention: 84, 102, 110, 111, 113; evaluation of candidates: 84, 88, 98, 102, 108, 109, 127; manipulation of: 96, 102, 294–297; classification: 100, 103, 111, 144, 148, 200; independent, usually balance of power: 102; reached by television, rally: 114; fears of minority; 115

Wagner family: 23
Ward politics: 27–31, 33; spoils system: 88
Warren, Earl, *Chief Justice:* xiii
WBZ-TV, Boston: 259, 268
Wehrmacht, Kennedy machine compared to: 282
West Germany: 199
West Virginia coal miners: 204, 220
WHDH-TV, Boston: 270
White House involvement in campaign: 5, 21, 58, 64, 72, 78, 89, 145, 149
White, Kevin: viii, 257
White, Theodore: 78, 106, 302
Williams College: 55, 155, 171
Wilson, Woodrow, *President:* 23
Wiretapping: 10, 16, 197, 198
Wisconsin dairy problems: 204, 220
Withholding tax: 281
WJAR-TV, Providence: 270
WMEX, Boston: 259
Wood, Robert: 55, 155, 171
Worcester Telegram: 185
WPRO-TV, Providence: 270
Wrentham State School: 5
WROB-TV, Albany: 270
WTEN-TV, Albany: 270
WWLP-TV, Springfield: 259
Wyzanski, Stefan Cardinal: 207–209, 229

Yugoslavia: 207